THE POLITICS OF GREEN TRANSFORMATIONS

Multiple 'green transformations' are required if humanity is to live sustainably on planet Earth. Recalling past transformations, this book examines what makes the current challenge different, and especially urgent. It examines how green transformations must take place in the context of the particular moments of capitalist development, and in relation to particular alliances. The role of the state is emphasised, both in terms of the type of incentives required to make green transformations politically feasible and the way states must take a developmental role in financing innovation and technology for green transformations. The book also highlights the role of citizens, as innovators, entrepreneurs, green consumers and members of social movements. Green transformations must be both 'top-down', involving elite alliances between states and business, but also 'bottom up', pushed by grassroots innovators and entrepreneurs, and part of wider mobilisations among civil society. The chapters in the book draw on international examples to emphasise how contexts matter in shaping pathways to sustainability

Written by experts in the field, *The Politics of Green Transformations* will be of great interest to researchers and students in environmental studies, international relations, political science, development studies, geography and anthropology, as well as policymakers and practitioners concerned with sustainability.

Ian Scoones is a Professorial Fellow at the Institute of Development Studies (IDS), Sussex, UK and Director of the ESRC STEPS Centre.

Melissa Leach is Director of the Institute of Development Studies (IDS), Sussex, UK.

Peter Newell is Professor of International Relations at the University of Sussex, UK.

Pathways to Sustainability Series

This book series addresses core challenges around linking science and technology and environmental sustainability with poverty reduction and social justice. It is based on the work of the Social, Technological and Environmental Pathways to Sustainability (STEPS) Centre, a major investment of the UK Economic and Social Research Council (ESRC). The STEPS Centre brings together researchers at the Institute of Development Studies (IDS) and SPRU (Science and Technology Policy Research) at the University of Sussex with a set of partner institutions in Africa, Asia and Latin America.

Series Editors:
Ian Scoones and Andy Stirling
STEPS Centre at the University of Sussex

Editorial Advisory Board:
Steve Bass, Wiebe E. Bijker, Victor Galaz, Wenzel Geissler, Katherine Homewood, Sheila Jasanoff, Melissa Leach, Colin McInnes, Suman Sahai, Andrew Scott

Titles in this series include:

Dynamic Sustainabilities
Technology, environment, social justice
Melissa Leach, Ian Scoones and Andy Stirling

Avian Influenza
Science, policy and politics
Edited by Ian Scoones

Rice Biofortification
Lessons for global science and development
Sally Brooks

Epidemics
Science, governance and social justice
Edited by Sarah Dry and Melissa Leach

Regulating Technology
International harmonization and local realities
Patrick van Zwanenberg, Adrian Ely, Adrian Smith

The Politics of Asbestos
Understandings of risk, disease and protest
Linda Waldman

Contested Agronomy
Agricultural research in a changing world
Edited by James Sumberg and John Thompson

Transforming Health Markets in Asia and Africa
Improving quality and access for the poor
Edited by Gerald Bloom, Barun Kanjilal, Henry Lucas and David H. Peters

Pastoralism and Development in Africa
Dynamic change at the margins
Edited by Ian Scoones, Andy Catley and Jeremy Lind

The Politics of Green Transformations
Ian Scoones, Melissa Leach and Peter Newell

An all-star team provides a clear, critical and fascinating discussion of the concept and practice of green transformations for a more sustainable and just world. Drawing on critical social theory they show us who has the power to define and implement transformations – comparing technocentric, marketized, state-led and citizen-led movements for sustainability – and the politics of knowledge and science that defines environmental crisis and responses. What adds depth to their arguments is that these authors are not isolated academics – they have been out there in the world of international relations, government policy, and NGOs with a thoughtful and engaged approach to change.

Diana Liverman, Institute of the Environment, University of Arizona, USA

In the twenty-first century environmental imperatives will increasingly define economic policy and societal choices. Key questions such as who will make these choices, who could be the winners and losers and how will our political and governance systems mediate this process of transition are key to understanding the political economy of green transformation. The dynamics of innovation and policy discourse on the green economy have been remarkably fast and diverse. The questions and interpretations put forward by the authors in *The Politics of Green Transformations* are timely and provide important context and focus for a rapidly evolving paradigm of sustainable development.

Achim Steiner, United Nations Under-Secretary-General, Executive Director,
United Nations Environment Programme (UNEP), Kenya

The world has moved from why to what? No longer is the question why we should act. Instead the question is what should we do, at the scale that can make a real transformation? The problem is that current solutions are small because they are at best transitional. The world needs real solutions that can be scaled up at speed to meet the needs of all – transformational solutions. What then can we do? What is working and where? This is what the 'politics of green transformations' is about. This is what we must understand so that we can move beyond the fluff of green verbiage to real pathways that can bring us real change. I would encourage you to read this book because we must relearn the message of sustainability for a world that is increasingly warmer, riskier and unjust.

Sunita Narain, Director General, Centre for Science and Environment, India

This book is a thoughtful and robust exploration of the concept of green transformation. It will make a significant contribution to better understanding this complex and sometimes contested issue. The authors offer an essential reading for anyone who wants to invest in making development more sustainable.

Youba Sokona, Co-Chair IPCC WGIII and Special Advisor,
South Centre, Switzerland

If you have ever wondered why there is so much talk about green transformations and so little action, this is the book to read. It is a fascinating and enlightening tour of the green political map in all its complexity. It won't give you all the answers, but it will enable you to ask the right questions.

Carlota Perez, London School of Economics, UK and Nurkse Institute,
Estonia, author of Technological Revolutions and
Financial Capital: the Dynamics of Bubbles and Golden Ages.

THE POLITICS
OF GREEN
TRANSFORMATIONS

Edited by
Ian Scoones, Melissa Leach and
Peter Newell

LONDON AND NEW YORK

from Routledge

First published 2015
by Routledge
2 Park Square, Milton Park, Abingdon, Oxon OX14 4RN

and by Routledge
711 Third Avenue, New York, NY 10017

Routledge is an imprint of the Taylor & Francis Group, an informa business

British Library Cataloguing-in-Publication Data
A catalogue record for this book is available from the British Library

Library of Congress Cataloging-in-Publication Data
A catalog record for this book has been requested

ISBN: 978-1-138-79289-0 (hbk)
ISBN: 978-1-138-79290-6 (pbk)
ISBN: 978-1-315-74737-8 (ebk)

Typeset in Bembo
by Florence Production Ltd, Stoodleigh, Devon, UK

CONTENTS

ILLUSTRATIONS

Figures

Tables

CONTRIBUTORS

Adrian Ely is a Senior Lecturer at SPRU (Science Policy Research Unit) at the University of Sussex and Deputy Director/Head of Impact and Engagement at the ESRC STEPS Centre. His research interests are broad but focus in particular on international, transdisciplinary studies of the regulation and governance of emerging biotechnologies, for example co-authoring the book *Regulating Technology: International Harmonisation and Local Realities* in 2011. Adrian is involved in ongoing research projects focusing on grassroots innovation for sustainability (Argentina, India), low-carbon innovation (China) and collaborative research in the life sciences (Europe–Asia).

Melissa Leach is Director of the Institute of Development Studies (IDS) at the University of Sussex. She founded and directed the STEPS Centre from 2006 to 2014 and is co-Chair of the Science Committee of Future Earth. A social anthropologist and geographer, her research in Africa and beyond has integrated social science with science-policy and natural sciences across environmental, agricultural, health, technology and gender issues. Recent books include *Dynamic Sustainabilities: Technology, Environment, Social Justice* (2010); *Epidemics: Science, Governance and Social Justice* (2010); and *Green Grabbing: A New Appropriation of Nature?* (2013).

Matthew Lockwood is a Senior Research Fellow in the Energy Policy Group at the University of Exeter and a Visiting Research Fellow at the School of Global Studies at the University of Sussex. He was previously Head of the Climate Change Team at the Institute of Development Studies at Sussex. His main interest is in the politics of energy and climate policies, in both developed and developing countries. He has recently published work on the political sustainability of the UK Climate Change Act, and on the political economy of fossil-fuel subsidy reform in emerging economies.

Mariana Mazzucato holds the R.M. Phillips chair in the Economics of Innovation at SPRU in the University of Sussex. Her work looks at the relationship between innovation and economic growth at the firm, industry and national level. Her new book *The Entrepreneurial State: Debunking Private vs. Public Sector Myths* (2013) – on the *2013 Books of the Year* list of the *Financial Times, Forbes* and *Huffington Post* – focuses on the need to develop new frameworks to understand the role of the state in economic growth – and how to enable rewards from innovation to be just as 'social' as the risks taken. In 2013 the *New Republic* called her one of the 'three most important thinkers about innovation'. She advises governments around the world and the European Commission on innovation-led growth.

Erik Millstone is a Professor of Science Policy at the University of Sussex, and co-convenor of the STEPS Centre's Food & Agriculture work. Much of his research has focused on the ways in which public policy-makers reach decisions concerning the protection of environmental and public health, and particularly on the impact and interpretations of uncertainties and the interactions between scientific and non-scientific considerations. His publications include: *BSE: Risk, Science and Governance,* (Oxford University Press, 2005), co-authored with Patrick van Zwanenberg.

Peter Newell is Professor of International Relations at the University of Sussex and Director of the Centre for Global Political Economy. His research focuses on the (global) political economy of climate change and energy transitions, including a current project on the role of rising powers in low-carbon transformations. He is author most recently of *Globalization and the Environment: Capitalism, Ecology and Power* (2012), co-author of *Climate Capitalism* (2010) and *Governing Climate Change* (2010), and co-editor of *The New Carbon Economy: Constitution, Governance and Contestation* (2012).

Hubert Schmitz is Professor of Economic Development at the Institute of Development Studies and leader of its Green Transformations Group. His current research investigates: How does the global power shift from West to East affect the transformation from high to low carbon economy? Who drives climate-relevant policies in the rising powers? What are the critical success factors for green industrial policy? Key to his research is a political economy approach which centres on the role of transformative alliances. He has a long track record of publishing in development journals, managing international research teams and integrating competences across disciplines.

Ian Scoones is a Professorial Fellow at the Institute of Development Studies at the University of Sussex, and is Director of the STEPS Centre. He works on the intersections of science and policy, particularly around environment, land and agriculture in Africa. Recent books include *Dynamic Sustainabilities: Technology, Environment, Social Justice*; *Green Grabbing: A New Appropriation of Nature?* and *Science and Citizens: Globalization and the Challenge of Engagement.*

Adrian Smith is a Researcher at the STEPS Centre and SPRU (Science Policy Research Unit). His work covers grassroots innovation, sustainable development, and the political and social aspects of technology. Past projects have looked at a variety of sectors, including energy, food, housing and water, and in Europe, Latin America and India. He is currently researching grassroots digital fabrication.

Stephen Spratt is a Research Fellow at the Institute for Development Studies, University of Sussex. Stephen's research focuses on development finance, financial regulation, low-carbon development and environmental taxation. Professionally, he has been Head of the Sustainable Markets Group at IIED, Chief Economist at the New Economics Foundation and a Lecturer in international finance at the University of Reading. He has also worked in the private sector in the City of London. Stephen holds a BA from the University of East Anglia, an M.Sc. from the School of Oriental and African Studies (SOAS) and a Ph.D. from the University of Sussex.

Andy Stirling is a Professor at SPRU (Science Policy Research Unit) and a co-Director of the STEPS Centre at Sussex University. He is an Interdisciplinary Researcher, with a background in astronomy, social anthropology, and the green and peace movements. Focusing on challenges around 'opening up' more democratic governance of science, technology and innovation, his work addresses issues such as uncertainty, precaution, scepticism, sustainability, resilience, diversity, transformation, participation and power. He is especially interested in why progress proceeds in some directions rather than others, and making these social choices more accountable. He has served on many advisory bodies in the EU and UK, on issues around energy, the environment, GM foods, and science and technology policy.

PREFACE AND ACKNOWLEDGEMENTS

This book asks what it takes to create the multiple 'green transformations' required if humanity is to live sustainably on planet earth. It focuses on the politics of transformations and the diverse directions of pathways that can be taken.

Different chapters examine what we mean by 'green' and the discursive contests about limits, boundaries and what this implies for clarifying what transformations are required. It examines the role of science in this debate and the way that science frames what is most effective and suitable according to different perspectives. It also debates the contrasts between a more technical focus on transitions and the more political emphasis of transformations.

Recalling past transformations, the book examines what makes the current challenge different, especially around questions of urgency and time-frames. It examines how green transformations must take place in the context of particular moments of capitalist development and driven by particular alliances. The role of the state is emphasized, both in terms of the type of incentives required to make green transformations politically feasible and the way states must take a developmental role in financing innovations and technologies for green transformations. The book also highlights the role of citizens, as innovators, entrepreneurs, green consumers and members of social movements.

Green transformations must be both 'top-down', involving elite alliances between states and business, but also 'bottom-up', pushed by grassroots innovators and entrepreneurs, and part of wider mobilizations among civil society. Each of these forms, styles and sites of politics combine and play out in different ways in different places. The chapters draw on examples from across the globe, emphasizing how contexts matter in shaping pathways to sustainability.

The book emerged during 2013–2014 from discussions at the University of Sussex, convened by the ESRC STEPS Centre (Social, Technological and Environmental Pathways to Sustainability). These brought together researchers working in different places and from different disciplinary angles on broad questions of the politics of green transformations. In many ways this project builds on and is shaped by long-standing work at the intersection of the natural and social sciences taking place at the Science Policy Research Unit (SPRU), the Institute of Development Studies (IDS), and more recently through the ESRC STEPS Centre and the Centre for Global Political Economy (CGPE) at Sussex.

We hope the eclecticism afforded by this collaboration across disciplines, theoretical perspectives, regional and sectoral foci, linking macro and micro across different contexts North and South, that characterizes Sussex research on development and environment, enriches the insights the book provides.

Finally, we would like to acknowledge the support of the ESRC STEPS Centre in supporting the process of production and publication of this book, three anonymous reviewers, and Naomi Vernon at IDS for her help with editing the book.

Ian Scoones, Peter Newell and Melissa Leach
Falmer, Brighton
July 2014

ACRONYMS AND ABBREVIATIONS

AARP	American Association of Retired Persons
AD	accelerated depreciation
ADIs	acceptable daily intakes
AEIC	American Energy Innovation Council
BNDES	Brazilian Development Bank
BNEF	Bloomberg New Energy Finance
CDB	China Development Bank
CDM	Clean Development Mechanism
CDP	Carbon Disclosure Project
CFC	chlorofluorocarbon
CFS	UN Food and Agricultural Organization's Committee on Food Security
CGPE	Centre for Global Political Economy
CIGS	copper indium gallium (di)selenide solar panels
COP	UNFCCC conferences of parties
DDT	dichlorodiphenyltrichloroethane
DEFRA	Department for the Environment, Food and Rural Affairs
DOE	Department of Energy (of the United States)
EC	European Commission
EEA	European Environment Agency
ENSSR	European Network of Scientists for Social and Environmental Responsibility
EPA	US Environmental Protection Agency
EU	European Union
FAO	Food and Agriculture Organization of the United Nations
FDA	US Food and Drug Administration
FIT	feed-in tariff

FSD	financial sector development
GDP	gross domestic product
GE	General Electric
GHG	greenhouse gas
GIS	Geographic Information Systems
GM	genetically modified
GMO	genetically modified organism
GWEC	Global Wind Energy Council
HFT	high frequency trader
IAASTD	International Assessment for Agricultural Science and Technology for Development
IDS	Institute of Development Studies
IEA	International Energy Agency
IGBP	International Geosphere-Biosphere Programme
IHDP	International Human Dimensions Programme
IPCC	Intergovernmental Panel on Climate Change
IUCN	International Union for Conservation of Nature
JTA	Just Transition Alliance
MDG	Millennium Development Goal
MTD	maximum tolerated dose
NGO	non-governmental organization
OECD	Organisation for Economic Co-operation and Development
OSHA	US Occupational Safety and Health Administration
OTC	over-the-counter
PES	payments for ecosystem services
PV	photovoltaics
R&D	research and development
RO	Renewables Obligation
RSL	Royal Society of London
SDGs	Sustainable Development Goals
SDSN	Sustainable Development Solutions Network
SME	Small and medium enterprise
SPRU	Science Policy Research Unit
SRIs	Socially Responsible Investors
STEPS Centre	Social, Technological and Environmental Pathways to Sustainability
STI	science, technology and innovation
STN	Social Technologies Network
SWFs	Sovereign Wealth Funds
TEEB	The Economics of Ecosystems and Biodiversity
UNEP	United Nations Environment Programme
UNFCCC	UN Framework Convention on Climate Change
UN-REDD	United Nations collaborative initiative on Reducing Emissions from Deforestation and forest Degradation

US NAS	US National Academy of Sciences
VC	venture capitalist
WBCSD	World Business Council for Sustainable Development
WBGU	German Advisory Council on Global Change
WHO	World Health Organization
WTO	World Trade Organization

1

THE POLITICS OF GREEN TRANSFORMATIONS

Ian Scoones, Peter Newell and Melissa Leach

The green transformation imperative – and its politics

Talk of transformation is back in vogue. This time the call is for a green transformation,[1] but what would one look like and who will bring it into being? While such a discussion implies a key role for technology and markets, it is also deeply political. What makes it political, and which and whose politics will shape the sorts of transformations that are desirable and possible?

A confluence of financial and ecological crises, in particular, have once again raised issues about the ecological, social and economic sustainability of the global economy, and the extent to which we have the sorts of political institutions able to contain crises and steer positive and progressive change. This has prompted calls for a new green industrial revolution, transitions to a low-carbon economy, or for more radical restructuring for degrowth or the pursuit of prosperity without growth (cf. OECD, 2011; Jackson, 2011).

While calls for radical transformations are often made but mostly ignored, this one has captured attention at the highest levels, whether through the launching of the Sustainable Development Goals, heightened mobilization around a 'make-or-break' climate agreement for Paris 2015, or renewed calls for a World Environment Organisation at the time of the Rio+20 summit in 2012. Emphasis is often placed on the need for massive public and private investment in new technological revolutions (Stern and Rydge, 2012) or on greening capitalism through pricing nature (Costanza *et al.*, 2014). What is often missing, however, is attention to the politics that are inevitably implied by disruptive change of this nature: questions of institutional change and policy, as well as more profound shifts in political power. This is the starting point for this book.

Why politics? What is it that makes green transformations political? The chapters in this book provide a number of answers. Questions surrounding what counts as green, what is to be transformed, who is to do the transforming, and whether transformation, as opposed to more incremental change, is required are all deeply political. For many, the green transformation is like no other we have witnessed so far. While history has witnessed numerous waves of disruptive economic and social change, brought about by technology, war and shifts of cultural values – from the Industrial Revolution, to the end of slavery to the rise of feminism – none has been primarily driven by the goal of rendering the economy and existing model of development more sustainable. That is not to say that key shifts have not had positive environmental consequences. Think of the effect of the 1970s oil crisis on rising investments in renewable energy and energy efficiency, or the argument that the ecological unsustainability of previous civilizations have been key factors in their demise (Ponting, 2007). In most cases, however, the principal drivers and goals were not the pursuit of a 'green' transformation.

The political nature of the green transformation is heightened because speed of change is seen as essential. There is a sense of urgency that pervades current debates about sustainability amid talk of tipping points, thresholds and planetary boundaries (Rockström et al., 2009; Lenton, 2013). Furthermore, the threats of the Anthropocene era have prompted calls for truly global responses (Crutzen and Steffen, 2003; Steffen et al., 2007) that must take place in today's thoroughly multi-polar world. The governance challenges of redirecting so many types of human activity across so many levels are staggering and quite possibly unprecedented, prompting calls to strengthen 'earth system governance' (Biermann, 2007; Biermann et al., 2012a) and the social science of transformation (Leggewie and Messner, 2012a; Brown et al., 2013).

The aim of the book is to engage with these debates, from a variety of different perspectives and settings, and lay out some of the core challenges, trade-offs and directions for a new politics of green transformation. Intellectually, getting a handle on these challenges requires a fusion of insights from disciplines such as anthropology, development studies, ecology, economics, geography, history, international relations, political science, science and technology studies and sociology, among others. We cover a range of sectors and issues from energy, food, natural resources, transport, urban infrastructure and finance in a diversity of settings from Denmark to China.

This interdisciplinary and multisited approach allows us to conceive of more multidimensional understandings of politics. These include political economy and political ecology (with an accent on material and structural forms of power and their implications for questions of access and justice), to institutional politics (focusing on national and global organizational forms) to discursive expressions of power (through knowledge and values). The aim, collectively, is to offer a deeper and more rounded understanding of and engagement with the politics of green transformations, beyond a more narrow focus on institutions and policy, or the perspectives of mainstream political science.

Our emphasis on transformations also moves beyond, while engaging with, the substantial body of literature on sociotechnical transitions that cover some aspects of these debates. Indeed, our focus on politics and broader questions of structural change suggests 'transformation' rather than 'transition', as the key term (Stirling, this book; see also Brand, 2012b). Within the 'transitions' literature there has been a recent move to address questions of power and politics more explicitly (e.g. Geels, 2014), suggesting a move from a narrow sociotechnical understanding of transitions to one more aligned with a wider debate about transformative change. Yet the conceptualizations of power and politics, and their relationship with questions of knowledge and social justice, require further elaboration. Our focus on transformations assists this. Transformations are inevitably multiple and contested, as pathways interconnect and compete (Leach *et al.*, 2010). Politics and power are important to how pathways are shaped, which pathways win out and why, and who benefits from them.

By prefacing the transformations with the word 'green' our intention is to focus on the environmental dimensions of change, but these almost inevitably raise questions of social as well as environmental justice. The constitution of 'green' transformations varies depending on the setting in which they are occurring. In many, perhaps especially developing country contexts, there is unlikely to be any green transformations if questions of social justice are not part of the debate. This is captured in calls for a 'just transition' (Swilling and Annecke, 2012; Newell and Mulvaney, 2013), which requires attention to both distribution and direction as part of any assessment (STEPS, 2010).

Respecting differences of context and perspective, the book does not follow a single definition of 'green transformations'. Instead, there is a variety of approaches, ranging from those focusing on environment (e.g. Schmitz, this book, for whom 'green transformation is the process of structural change which brings the economy within the planetary boundaries') to those focusing also on social justice and distribution, either as intrinsic to the definition (e.g. Stirling, this book) or in talking of 'green and just transformations' (e.g. Leach, this book). In contrast with definitions focusing on the need to respect environmental limits, others link 'greening' intimately with the multiple dimensions of sustainability – social and economic as well as environmental. A common normative view unites the chapters: all authors share a concern both for environment, and for people's inclusion and well-being. Yet differences lie in conceptualization and analytical implications, with implications too for which dimensions of politics are highlighted.

We understand 'greening', therefore, as a process rather than a measurable end-state. Just as it is impossible to conceive of the end-point of the unfolding low-carbon transition, so previous transformations did not start out with clear blueprints and plans that were then rolled out. Rather, they were the product of competition and interaction between a number of pathways, supported by diverse social actors with highly uneven political power.

In this book, the notion of 'green' is therefore not just reduced to 'green' technology or business, but to more radical shifts to sustainable practices. There are, of course, various shades of green implied by weaker and stronger versions of sustainability (Spratt, this book), and throughout the book, we are interested in how different versions of green are represented in politics – in other words, asking 'what does green mean?' and 'whose green counts?' (Leach, this book). Politics are often about reconciling tensions between different versions of 'green', and here links with social justice and equity concerns are vital.

Contests over pathways are thus not just about end-points, or the role of technology, markets or the state, but also about the knowledge underpinning them. In this sense, the science that is invoked to legitimate calls for green transformations is also a site of political contestation. It does not provide neutral value-free guidance as to what is to be done and by whom (Millstone, this book), even though it may be represented as doing just that. Dig a little deeper and we find the assumptions embodied in understandings of complex processes of (global) environmental change to be subject to scrutiny and dissent. There is a politics around knowledge production in debates about green transformations, turning both on what we think we know (consensus and uncertainties) and on who knows it (whose knowledge counts). We must ask which scientists or other stakeholders, which forms of expertise, from the official to the informal, which disciplines and which regions have most voice in the construction of knowledge about the predicaments that underpin calls for green transformations. Put another way, a 'reflexive turn' is needed that treats the governance of expertise about global environmental and green issues as a matter of political contestation (Beck et al., 2014). Who sets the terms of debate about green transformations is crucial because organized knowledge, explicitly or implicitly, demarcates ways forward. Such knowledge in turn suggests who can use which resources in order to live within environmental limits and planetary boundaries, and gives an indication of which causal processes should be addressed. The impacts of these decisions affect everyone, but perhaps most those whose livelihoods are tied up with day-to-day interactions with ecologies and natural resources: the majority of the world's poor.

We are therefore concerned in this book with a very material politics, but also a politics of knowledge. These are deeply intertwined. While drawing attention to the sometimes problematic ways in which knowledge gets produced might play into the hands of sceptics and distract from the hard politics that must address the political–economic structures that are leading us towards planetary disaster, there are dangers too associated with an uncritical embrace of dominant knowledge production for green transformations. Instead, we argue that so-called soft and hard politics are deeply connected. Knowledge politics matter because they are so closely entwined with material political economy (Leach, this book), and making them explicit can lead to more open, robust and grounded knowledge for green transformations (Stirling, this book).

At the same time, discourses of catastrophe and imminent ecological collapse raise unsettling questions about the ability of democratic institutions to deliver fast and effective solutions, or whether the scale and urgency of ecological crises warrants some suspension of normal democratic procedures. There are undoubtedly trade-offs around the efficiency of decision-making and inclusion, and around negotiation versus coercion, but this book cautions against deriving political action from 'ecological imperatives' without attention to the principles of democracy (Stirling, this book). Similarly, others have highlighted the dangers of 'post-political' discourses (Swyngedouw, 2010) around environmental threats such as climate change that restrict the contours of legitimate political debate precisely on grounds of the need to suspend social conflict. Instead, clear urgencies and imperatives may call for a 'slow race' – making haste slowly – in a way that is respectful of inclusion, deliberation, democracy and justice (Leach and Scoones, 2006).

What is to be transformed and how?

There is widespread acknowledgement of the multiple environmental stresses the world faces – from climate change, air and water pollution, and biodiversity loss to land use change, for example. There is growing consensus that these will prove deeply damaging to human well-being and futures unless they are addressed. There is a robust debate, but a lesser consensus, about the drivers that exacerbate them – including overconsumption, urban expansion, population pressures, unequal economic relations and globalization. But how these are to be tackled remains much disputed, and a clear vision of what green transformations are required, for what and for whom remains elusive.

This is, of course, due to political contention. There is intense competition around framings of how to read and react to the observed trends: what diagnoses they allegedly provide of the origins of the crisis and the sources of the remedies. There is much at stake in the construction of what drives unsustainability (who is to blame for what) and of what forces can be aligned to rebalance socionatures. Whether wholesale transformations, as opposed to more discrete sociotechnical transitions, are required, and what it is that is to be transformed, has major implications for actors and interests – which are supported and which challenged. Whether transformations should be technology-led, marketized, state-led or citizen-led has huge implications for the processes, institutions and instruments deployed. Should the entry point be individual behaviour change, pricing of environmental externalities and ecosystem services, state restructuring and support for 'green' industrial sectors, or green technological innovation? All have different implications for who should be involved on what terms and who wins and who loses. Such choices about 'green' directions therefore inevitably have implications for social justice and social inequality.

In recent years, debates about economic growth have taken centre stage – both its desirability as an end in itself (Jackson, 2011; Dale, 2012), and the extent to which it improves broad well-being in highly unequal, richer societies (Wilkinson and Pickett, 2010). Measures of growth, and appropriate metrics and accounting systems, have also been widely debated, with calls for 'green accounting', 'ecological footprint' assessments and 'circular economy' measures (Vincent, 2000; Mathews and Tan, 2011; Wackernagel and Rees, 2013). Debates about growth have also prompted deeper reflections about the scope for the greening of capitalism, or whether the idea of green(er) capitalism constitutes an oxymoron (O'Connor, 1994; Foster, 2002; Newell and Paterson, 2010; Newell, 2012). All of these debates identify fundamental conflicts and trade-offs, centring again on questions about what is to be sustained and what we mean by green.

Glib policy statements of win–win green economies often obscure the many hard trade-offs implied by attempts to square environmental aims with social justice, or to pursue a just transition (Agyeman *et al.*, 2003; Swilling and Annecke, 2012; Newell and Mulvaney, 2013). While some focus only on green limits and planetary boundaries, others argue that attending to distributional issues first is essential – creating a 'safe and just operating space for humanity', with a basic floor of welfare, human rights and dignity (Raworth, 2012; Leach *et al.*, 2012, 2013). These perspectives are reflected in attempts to protect 'development rights in a carbon constrained world' (Baer *et al.*, 2008) or to specify 'contraction' on the part of richer countries and 'convergence' on the part of poorer ones towards agreed per capita entitlements to what remains of available carbon budgets (GCI, 2014).

Rather than divide up the existing cake (albeit an ever smaller one) in more equitable ways, one alternative invokes what some term 'green sufficiency'. Thus the claim that continuous exponential economic growth can ever be compatible with long-run environmental sustainability is contested (Trainer, 1996). Prosperity, not growth, is seen as the appropriate goal for green economies and societies, to be built through emphases on well-being, social sustainability, services and care (Jackson, 2011). Such perspectives are promoted by Green political parties in some countries, with a focus on public provision of sustainable energy and water, and support for community-based economies (Douthwaite, 1996; Levidow, 2014).

A related set of alternatives emphasize green well-being and justice. Some argue that mainstream versions of the 'green economy' and 'green growth' function primarily as a means to maintain existing patterns of capitalist development and the inequalities associated with them, just now under a green veneer (Lyon and Maxwell, 2011). While some reject the concept of the green economy entirely (Wanner, 2014), others seek to elaborate it to incorporate questions of justice, promoting ideas of a 'green and fair economy' (Green Economy Coalition, 2014).

Understanding the politics of green transformations

All transformations are replete with governance challenges, and this book asks: whose rules rule, which institutions define visions of change and the terms of change, and which relations of power shape different pathways?

Given the variety of perspectives on green transformations, it is not surprising to find a diversity of literatures that offer interpretations and frameworks for understanding them. One important area is the growing literature on sociotechnical transitions. This has generated many important insights into how, when and why sociotechnical change is possible: how niche technologies emerge and displace incumbent regimes and how a series of landscape factors can frustrate or enable this change (Geels, 2005a; Scarse and Smith, 2009; Geels and Schot, 2007; Loorbach, 2007; Grin *et al.*, 2010).

One area where this literature has fallen short is in its understanding of power and political economy (Smith *et al.*, 2005, 2010; Meadowcroft, 2011; Baker *et al.*, 2014). An understanding of politics is important in explaining which pathways get supported and legitimized, and which are ignored and so fail to gain traction. This is starting to be recognized in recent contributions around the 'multi-level perspective' of the sociotechnical transition literature (e.g. Geels, 2014). A deeper understanding of the processes of knowledge politics, political conflict and accommodation, bargaining and disciplining, as niche experiments challenge existing regimes is clearly highly pertinent (Smith and Raven, 2012).

The politics of green transformations implicate multiple levels of governance and decision-making, and the challenges of coordinating these to pull in the same directions. A plethora of approaches labelled multilevel, polycentric, global and earth systems governance has been suggested (Galaz *et al.*, 2012). However, each raise the key questions of who steers, and which actors and institutions govern transformations, through which institutional mechanisms operate. This in turn raises questions about how far transformations can, in fact, be managed and directed, as often assumed in earth systems governance and transition management debates, as opposed to emerging from below in unanticipated ways that are difficult to anticipate and direct. Questions are also raised about roles and actors. Should transformations be overseen by nation states or global institutions, and in what relation? Given the track-record of national environmental policies and global governance of the environment, what can realistically be expected? Assumptions about capacity, commitment and willingness are built into many green economy policy proclamations, but will the key players be prepared to intervene, and if so, what type of green transformation will be backed (Allen, 2012; Fouquet and Pearson, 2012)?

The politics of green transformations are also about the politics of accountability and participation – whether at global, national or local levels. These become especially pertinent as global institutions and governments seek to extend their reach in efforts to create – or under the guise of building – a green economy. Will these interventions be inclusive or exclusive, top-down or bottom-up, and who gets the rent from 'managing' such transformations? As Lockwood (this book) describes, depending on the political–economic setting, the incentives for policy elites to back a green transformation and for states to intervene will vary dramatically. The role of elite politics, and alliances of states, businesses and finance, becomes important, as different groups seek to capture the benefits of any transformative shift. Power and political authority in alliance-building, influenced by particular political economic context, is central to any understanding of what is likely to happen, and what is not (Schmitz, this book).

The political dimensions of long-term change are also important. History offers highly relevant lessons about the circumstances in which 'technological revolutions' come about – whether the move to coal under the Industrial Revolution or the shift to mass mobility under Fordism – are also relevant. Perez (2002, 2013), building on Schumpeter, highlights the critical role of finance capital in unleashing 'waves of creative destruction' that unsettle incumbent regimes – a theme picked up by Mazzucato, Spratt and Newell in this book.

Histories often involve the co-evolution of policies, institutions, infrastructures and even whole political systems with technologies and material resources. As Mitchell (2011) argues in relation to coal and then oil, for example, forms of democracy are deeply entwined with particular material energy resources. In this sense, politics is co-constructed with sociotechnical systems and particular resources, whether coal or oil, water or land. Some types of transformation are thus affected by the biophysical, material qualities of those resources, with water, for example, being described as the 'un-cooperative commodity' – its fluidity making it difficult to govern (Bakker, 2010). The materiality of resources can also provoke an unravelling of political systems, technologies and infrastructures built around them, as is claimed for peak oil and its ability to destabilize incumbent power (Leggett, 2014). Unravelling such co-constructed complexes of technology, infrastructure, institutions and politics and creating alternative pathways is therefore a central challenge of the politics of green transformation. Opportunities may emerge during periods of crisis (or interregnum) in which a new politics of transformation becomes possible.

The politics of transformation also involve the politics of knowledge and culture. Building more sustainable pathways involves transformations in behaviour at personal and collective levels, underpinned by convictions that change is necessary and desirable. Green transformation thus requires transformative knowledge (Hackmann and St Clair, 2012). Yet as longstanding experiences and literatures from the sociology and anthropology of science and policy tell us, such knowledge cannot just be imposed from above by expert science; to have traction, it must make sense to people in diverse settings (Jamison, 2001; Jasanoff and Martello, 2004). There is a politics to the ways that different people and groups, with different cultural backgrounds, invoke particular forms of knowledge to define and contest the nature of environmental problems, why they matter and to whom, and what should be done about them. The intensity of these knowledge politics is picked up in different ways in Chapter 2 by Leach, Chapter 3 by Millstone, Chapter 4 by Stirling and Chapter 7 by Smith and Ely. They underscore the potential of grassroots and citizen-based knowledge to contribute to green transformations, and the need for transformations in the ways different knowledge producers and holders interact in order to enable this.

Underpinning these different conceptualizations of transformation, and how and when they occur, different emphasis is placed on the desirability and possibility of incremental institutional change and transitions within capitalism as against the need for more radical transformations of capitalist structures and relations (Kovel, 2002). This raises a series of entrenched and contentious questions about strategy: how much change is 'good enough'; whether reform or more radical revolution is the appropriate strategy, and whether the urgency of delivering green transformations necessarily prioritizes immediate incrementalism over longer term, more radical restructuring. It underscores the very different visions of sustainability which run through all debates about green transformations, reflected in the diversity of perspectives of contributors to this book. Much depends on the framing of competing visions of sustainability, a theme to which we now turn.

Framing green transformations

At the broadest level, therefore, many agree that the world is on an unsustainable path and that business-as-usual is not an option. 'Hard' disagreements exist, for sure, with those fundamentally opposed to change in sustainable directions – such as institutions and businesses whose profits and power are fundamentally interlocked with the status quo. Yet even among those sharing a broad 'green' consensus lie a range of hotly contested visions of sustainability that define the framing of and approach to green transformations. These 'soft' disagreements are also important, and they too implicate material questions of economy, interest and resource allocation. Visions of what is to be done reflect starkly conflicting diagnoses of what the problem is and who is best placed to act on it.

Such visions partly reflect longstanding debates about how to reconcile environment and development, or growth and sustainability. Current discussions about green transformations bear the legacy of debates about sustainable development in particular. 'Sustainable development', of course, has been a rallying call for those concerned with the relationships between environment and development over several decades (Adams, 2003). Brundtland's original formulation was 'development that meets the needs of the present without compromising the ability of future generations to meet their own needs' (Brundtland, 1987). This inspired the Rio Earth Summit discussions in 1992, and the plans that emerged around Agenda 21, and many conferences, summits, conventions and policy statements since.

Mobilized by this idea, the early 1990s saw strong momentum in the form of environmental legislation, policy, business and community action, locally, nationally and internationally. However, this had slowed by the early 2000s (Vogler and Jordan, 2003; Redclift, 2005), and attempts to resuscitate the sustainable development vision at the Rio+20 conference in 2012 largely failed (Bulkeley *et al.*, 2013). Progress on the major 1992 targets was disappointing, and many national sustainability action plans became forms of managerialism that failed to challenge the economic and institutional interests and practices that supported unsustainability (Berkhout *et al.*, 2003; Scoones, 2007; Jordan and Adger, 2009). Sustainability and sustainable development could easily be used as empty rhetoric, masking a variety of decidedly environmentally unfriendly actions through 'greenwash' (Rowell, 1996).

One response to this disappointing history would be to recommit to the idea of sustainable development with renewed vigour, recasting this as a concept to drive a new round of political and policy change. Indeed, the Rio+20 outcomes document, *The Future We Want* (UN, 2012), is framed in these terms and commits countries to defining and implementing a set of Sustainable Development Goals (SDGs). Yet, as the SDG process unfolds, many are questioning whether, again, this will prove to be an ineffective discourse that drives only more rhetoric, bureaucracy and managerialism. Meanwhile, though, others have picked up and run with alternative 'green' framings – especially around the green economy and ideas of green limits or 'planetary boundaries', seeing these as more potent in galvanizing politicians, businesses, policy-makers and publics for real change.

For example, Jacobs (2012a) elaborates on the politics surrounding the rise of the green economy concept. These have included the perceived need to replace, for Rio+20, the managerial, statist concept of sustainable development. Many also recognized that discourses focused on costs and green limits – including the two-degree safety barrier in climate change and planetary boundaries, as well as climate discourses focused on the costs of mitigation – would struggle to gain political support in a post-financial crisis world where economic growth and employment remained the core priority of voters, businesses and governments. In this context, ideas of 'green growth' offer a positive spin, claiming 'that protecting the environment can actually yield *better* growth' (Jacobs, 2013, p6).

However, 'sustainable development' and 'green economy', while the most visible and mainstream, are not the only ways of framing green transformations. Our focus on politics reveals others and differences and contrasts within these. In the sections below we identify four broad narratives of green transformation, each reflecting different framings of problem and solution, and different versions of sustainability. Others have proposed similar typologies of environmental world views on the question of 'pathways to a green world' (Clapp and Dauvergne, 2011; see also Szerszynski, 1997; Dobson, 1998, 2000; Jamison, 2001; Hopwood *et al.*, 2005) that correspond in some ways to those we outline here. Each narrative embodies a different perspective on what it is (if anything) that needs to be transformed; and each reflects different understandings, prejudices and theories of change, informing how, when and why transformation is possible. In other words, each narrative suggests a pathway (or set of pathways) to green transformations, and so a particular politics of transformation.

The chapters that follow take different positions with respect to these narratives, often advocating a combination of pathways, and so a diversity of political strategies, demonstrating that there is no one-size-fits-all approach to green transformations and their politics.

Technocentric transformations

First, we identify a 'technocentric' view of sustainability and transformation. Here the challenge essentially lies in finding the right combination of technologies to meet rising demands in greener ways. For example, lower carbon energy, fewer agricultural inputs but higher yields, less water-intensive systems, and so on. The aim is to reduce ecological footprints through technological innovation without altering systems fundamentally. Reorganizing economies or institutions and unsettling prevailing power relations is less of a priority. The emphasis is much more on creating incentives and enabling the 'right' kinds of technologies to compete with incumbent ones: through picking winners, appropriately designed R&D and intellectual property policies, supportive industrial and tax policy, and heroic entrepreneurs – what Elkington (2012) calls the 'zeronauts'. This is a reformist perspective on green transformations, which offers a relatively limited account of politics. Politics is essentially understood as policy, providing policy fixes in support of sustainable technologies. Such proposals are in many ways radical in terms of the ambition and are, of course, deeply political, as in calls for decoupling and some arguments for a 'green industrial revolution' noted above. Likewise, for some, an advocacy of geoengineering, as a technical solution to climate mitigation, is informed by an assessment that other options are unlikely any time soon due to the power of vested interests (Lomborg, 2013).

In some versions of a 'green economy' position, a dominant emphasis is on technological innovation and investment – mostly by the private sector – in low-carbon and other environmental technologies. In this narrative, ideas of green and new technology are firmly interlocked, and often coupled with assumptions of business-led growth. For some, green technoscience is on the brink of creating a 'new industrial revolution' (Stern and Rydge, 2012) set to transform economies. Such techno-optimistic visions are echoed in applications to developing countries, where groups such as the Sustainable Development Solutions Network (SDSN, 2014), as well as a host of private companies, suggest that a combination of bio-, info-, nano- and engineering technologies, and markets to enable their spread, will transform economies in green directions. Both the Organisation for Economic Co-operation and Development (OECD) and the United Nations Environment Programme (UNEP) also emphasize technoscientific innovation, highlighting the need for international cooperation in facilitating trade and technology transfer, to allow for 'leapfrogging', if developing countries are to go green (Levidow, 2014).

In such discourses, 'greenness' is often presented as if it were an attribute of a technology itself, and as if the technology had agency in economic transformation. Yet this is, of course, to ignore the vast array of political–economic and social arrangements associated with both technological innovation and application in particular settings that shape whether and how technologies work, and towards what ends (Bryne *et al.* 2011). While there are exceptions, such as the more recent emphases of the SDSN, the focus on technological solutions generally downplays the governance contexts of technologies and the ways they become part of diverse pathways. Arguments about imminent technological revolutions similarly downplay the embedded political and institutional regimes that have shaped such 'long waves' of technology-related growth in the past (Perez, 2013).

Technocentric narratives often imply that innovation originates in the hi-tech laboratories of firms and technology start-ups, largely in the global North, or in the emerging economies of China, India or Brazil. Notions of green technology transfer, leapfrogging and catch-up reinforce this view. Yet such versions of green technology marginalize or devalue technoscientific innovation that emerges from the global South (Ely *et al.*, 2013), while also concealing the North–South inequalities of access and capacity that shape innovation capabilities (Levidow, 2014).

Likewise, the focus on hi-tech innovation obscures and marginalizes innovation from the grassroots (Smith and Ely, this book) and through wider mobilizations of citizens (Leach and Scoones, this book). Such local innovation processes are frequently motivated by a mesh of sociocultural and livelihood concerns, and understandings of ecology and sustainability, which diverge from the narrow notions of 'green' and 'economic benefit' encompassed in most technocentric green economy discourses.

Marketized transformations

A second narrative centres on calls for marketized transformations to sustainability. Here, the market is the agent of transformation, which through pricing, creating markets and property rights regimes, unleashes new rounds of 'green accumulation'. Hence the diagnosis of the problem is market failure, lack of green entrepreneurialism and failure to allocate and sufficiently protect private property rights. For example, the World Bank's 2003 World Development Report on 'Sustainable Development in a Dynamic Economy' advances the idea that the spectacular failure to tackle poverty and environmental degradation over the last decades is due to a failure of governance, 'poor implementation and not poor vision' (World Bank, 2003). The report notes, 'Those [poverty and environmental problems] that can be coordinated through markets have typically done well; those that have not fared well include many for which the market could be made to work as a coordinator'. The challenge for governments is therefore to be more welcoming of private actors through, among other things, 'a smooth evolution of property rights from communal to private' (World Bank, 2003, p133). Markets are thus emphasized as the key drivers of sustainable development, while recognizing that markets can only work in this way once states have intervened in particular ways.

The emergence of ideas about the marketization of nature and the green economy has been dramatic. As Jacobs (2012a) documents, rarely heard before 2008, market-oriented green economy concepts are now prominent in policy discourses across governments and international economic and development institutions alike. Thus, the World Bank and other multilateral development banks have ostensibly embraced green growth as a core goal, while the OECD has committed itself to a green growth strategy (OECD, 2011). Similarly, the UNEP has strongly promoted a green economy agenda (UNEP, 2011). These international institutions have jointly established a 'Green Growth Knowledge Platform' to build knowledge about the field. Green growth and/or a green economy have been adopted as explicit policy objectives in a number of countries, including some of the world's largest economies, and many NGOs and alliances have also bought into the concept.

Those now promoting green growth and the green economy claim that it is not a substitute for sustainable development, but a way of achieving it. However, this elision overlooks the extent to which the framing of a green economy represents a distinct set of meanings, politics and imperatives. As Jacobs (2012a) argues, the emphasis is on a level of environmental protection that is not being met by current or 'business-as-usual' patterns of growth. This gives the concept both its political traction and its discursive power to justify transformations. Proponents of a marketized green economy perspective argue that this could be a driver of higher output and rising living standards, and in the relatively short term. This positive framing has united diverse public and private organizations, whether in energy, transport or natural resources. It has also co-developed with the number and power of environmentally oriented businesses for whom 'green' and 'commercial success' are deeply intertwined.

These perspectives emphasize the need to recognize and value economically the natural capital on which growth depends. 'Putting a price on nature' as a way to overcome so-called market failures has a long history in green economic thought and policy, with environmental economists during the 1980s and 1990s putting much effort into the development of methods, measures and metrics (Pearce and Warford, 1993). Today, discourses centring on valuing natural capital are extending ever more widely into previously unpriced and non-marketized dimensions of nature and ecosystems. This is associated with new forms of financialization and commoditization, deeply embedded in and thus furthering capitalist networks of control and appropriation (McAfee, 2012; Sullivan, 2013).

A number of governments have embraced these concepts and are translating them into policy. For instance, the UK has established a Natural Capital Committee (DEFRA, 2014), has positioned itself at the centre of the 'new carbon economy' (Newell et al., 2012) and embraced controversial practices of biodiversity off-setting. Internationally, UNEP (2011) has been among the key proponents of this marketized version of green economy discourse and its application to developing country contexts. The UNEP-hosted Economics of Ecosystems and Biodiversity (TEEB) initiative advocates strongly for the concept of natural capital in 'making nature's values visible' (TEEB, 2014). An array of schemes is now unfolding to value and trade aspects of ecosystems now (re)defined as financialized commodities. They include schemes for trading carbon credits and offsetting emissions, such as those associated with clean energy, forests and agriculture under the Clean Development Mechanism (CDM), the United Nations collaborative initiative on Reducing Emissions from Deforestation and forest Degradation (UN-REDD), and a host of voluntary schemes. They include emerging markets for 'offsetting' species and biodiversity loss. They also include an array of 'payments for ecosystem services' (PES) schemes. They are in turn linked to new forms of venture capital and speculation, as derivatives circulate as fictitious and liquid capital (Büscher et al., 2012). Yet whether the claimed benefits are realized in practice, amid imperatives for project developers to realize profits in often uncertain markets, and in the context histories of weak local resource tenure and control, is highly variable (Newell and Bumpus, 2012; Leach and Scoones, forthcoming, 2015). Interventions promoted in the name of green marketized approaches can easily become forms of 'green grabbing' that dispossess local resource users of rights and livelihoods (Fairhead et al., 2012). Meanwhile, narrow forms of financial valuation of ecosystems and landscapes overlook alternative social and cultural values, including those that have emerged from the long co-existence of people and ecologies in diverse settings (Martin *et al.*, 2013).

Markets always depend to some extent on state action, on the ways that states enable the emergence of particular markets, and through providing incentives and regulation, shape how they operate. Pathways of green transformation therefore often involve combinations of market and state action, even while narratives of marketized transformations portray markets as if they acted alone. In contrast, other narratives focus on the role of the state.

State-led transformations

A third narrative focuses on state-led transformations to sustainability. The starting point is often the need to re-embed markets in stronger frameworks of social control, combined with a recognition of states' historically central role in previous waves of innovation and financing of technology and growth. Arguments for a 'green entrepreneurial state' (Mazzucato, 2013b, this book), or green industrial policy (Schmitz, this book), or earlier work on the 'green state' (Eckersley, 2004), all emphasize the central role of state action.

Unsurprisingly, the state also features highly in accounts of transition management and its critical stabilizing, backstopping and stimulus roles have been underscored by recent crises. Jacobs (2013) documents how the recent case for greening economies emerged in the wake of the 2008 financial crisis. Amid neo-Keynesian policies to rebuild economies by replacing lost private-sector demand with public expenditure and thus create multiplier effects, public initiatives aimed at protecting the environment were highlighted. Thus, areas such as energy efficiency, renewable energy, water quality improvement, agricultural and landscape management, public transport and pollution control were seen to offer ways to get people into work and to increase demand for goods and services. Many of the countries that introduced fiscal stimulus packages in 2008–2009 included 'green' programmes of these kinds. In 2009, UNEP proposed a Global Green New Deal, including an agenda to expand public services, regulate private-sector activities and promote less resource-intensive patterns.

What has attracted particular interest in recent years is the role for developmental entrepreneurial states with the growth of 'rising powers' such as China, Brazil and India, willing and able to use proactive industrial policy to spur marketized and technological transformations. In a new multipolar global context, it is these countries that are often leading in green transformations, and they are countries where the state is playing an active role. Investments in renewable energy – wind and solar – provide key examples. These efforts are often financed by powerful and well-resourced development banks able to support ambitious investment strategies, as Spratt (this book) shows for Brazil and Mazzucato (this book) describes for Chinese investment in solar power. States are thus not just providing counter-cyclical lending, but are even 'directing' that lending towards key, innovative parts of the 'green' economy.

Emphasis on the role of the state in steering green investment can also be seen as a response to a sense of crisis in states' more conventional environmental governance roles. Failures of institutional arrangements and architectures nationally and globally to tackle climate change, biodiversity loss and key areas of pollution successfully have led some to revise expectations that such agreements are possible, in the face of overwhelming national and interest-group political–economic interests. Other views, such as perspectives in the Earth system governance literature, are more optimistic, stressing the scope to accelerate green transformations by strengthening global architectures and institutions, and if necessary creating new ones, such as the World Environment Organisation much discussed around Rio 2012.

Citizen-led transformations

A fourth narrative suggests that transformations will have to come from below. This represents a more populist version of sustainability, centred on taking control over resources from state-capital elites who have shown little serious interest in more profound green transformations and whose ability to deliver them is highly compromised by their commitments to growth at any cost. There is a strong emphasis on degrowth and bottom-up transitions to alternative solidarity-based economies (Dobson, 2009; Utting, forthcoming, 2015), including examples of transition towns and alternative agri-food movements (Leach and Scoones, this book). Civil society groups have also proposed alternative ways of 'living well'. Among the most celebrated are plans for *buen vivir*, now endorsed by government ministries in Ecuador, that combine environmental justice, common goods, agroecology and food sovereignty. *Buen vivir* (the Quechua term is *sumak kawsay*) also emphasizes indigenous, non-Western concepts, such as *miriachina* – the idea that people and groups contribute to the realization of goods collaboratively and with nature, rather than producing things as individuals (Martínez Novo, 2012). These proposals imply quite different routes to achieving green transformations that involve challenging the social and political–economic structures that sustain individualist, capitalist development paths.

Mobilizations for alternative pathways in which rights to food, water or energy often have a central role are combined with resistance to existing forms of extractivism and business-as-usual developmentalism (Bond, 2012; Gottlieb and Joshi, 2010). As well as 'weapons of the weak' (Scott, 2008) and transnational mobilizations (Tarrow, 2005), as Leach and Scoones (this book) illustrate, they combine with initiatives around 'citizen science' and grassroots innovation (Smith and Ely, this book). From projecting alternatives to current unsustainabilities, to demonstrations and experiments within 'niches', the emphasis is often on diversifying and democratizing knowledge for transformations, and so 'culturing' sustainability (cf. Stirling, this book), through an emphasis on everyday and lifestyle politics.

Table 1.1 offers a schematic summary of the diagnoses and associated solutions proposed under these four narratives of green transformations. As the chapters that

TABLE 1.1 Narratives of green transformations: diagnoses and solutions

Narratives of green transformations/ diagnoses	Solutions
Technocentric	
Either about to or already exceed many planetary limits; urgency and crisis	Technologies as global public goods to tackle environmental crisis
Emphasis on population; Malthusian models of scarcity and conflict	Low-carbon transitions: new energy technologies
Highlighting the role of technology as magic bullets . . .	Including 'technical fixes', from geoengineering to genetically modified crops, but also bottom–up, grassroots innovation
. . . but also potentials of alternative technologies	Top-down governance arrangements in favour of 'the planet'
Marketized	
Crisis results from market failures, externalities	Technological entrepreneurs, green capitalists and consumers to lead
Primacy of (green) growth	Prices will reflect scarcity of resources and demand to protect them, and reward ecosystem service providers
Corporations as agents of change	Need to allocate and enforce property rights and use institutions to this end
	Economic investments and market incentives to achieve green growth and a green economy
State–led	
Need for state involvement in steering transformation and re-embedding markets	At the national level, need for a green state, adopting green Keynesian industrial policies of stimulus, infrastructural projects, creating green jobs
State-backed R&D and wider finance central to a 'developmental state'	At the international level, modifying and reforming existing institutions or creating new ones (World Environment Organisation)
Crisis of governance at national and global levels; importance of institutions, agreements, international architectures	Strengthening global architectures (Earth System Governance)
Citizen–led	
Change comes from below, cumulative actions of multiple, networked initiatives	Power from below, involving connected social movements (e.g. green consumers, green living/transition towns; food, water, energy-sovereignty movements)
Linking niches, experiments and demonstrations through movements	Radical system change required (e.g. arguments for eco-socialism, eco-feminism, Third World environmentalism, post-developmentalism)
Behaviour change, advocacy and demonstrating alternatives central: 'another world is possible'	Bio-communities; self-sufficiency; dematerialization; degrowth

follow show, these are not mutually exclusive categories, and many instances exist where narratives are strategically combined to suit particular circumstances. As we go on to argue, the important point is that each suggests different frames, different politics, different alliances between actors, and so different routes to achieving green transformations.

One thing that is notable from these narratives is the neglect, explicitly at least, of questions of justice. Across each of these narratives, justice is implicitly assumed to be delivered. In the technocentric version, this occurs through supposedly benign elites stewarding global public goods. In the marketized version, just transformations will only be effective, efficient and tenable if consumers support them through their purchasing power, and the market will deliver the best technologies and goods at the best price. For those emphasizing state-led transformations, only the state has the authority and legitimacy to protect rights, oversee redistribution and ensure that the interests of the majority are served by particular green transformations. By contrast, in narratives that place the accent on citizen-led action, neither states nor markets nor technocratic elites have proven their ability to defend their citizens from the impacts of previous transformations, and there are few grounds for thinking they will do so in relation to green transformations. Conceptions of justice thus must derive from popular understandings about what is fair and socially acceptable.

This is not to suggest there are not hard trade-offs between justice and sustainability (Dobson, 1998; Agyeman et al., 2003; Leach et al., 2010; Martin, 2013; Sikor, 2013; Sikor and Newell, 2014). Indeed, work on political ecology has long drawn attention to the intimate connection between social relations of race, class and gender, for example, and the likelihood that social groups will either benefit from or be further excluded from access to natural resources and projects aimed at their protection (Martínez-Alier, 2002; Newell, 2005; Robbins and Watts, 2011; Wichterich, 2012). In relation to green transformation debates, North–South non-governmental organization (NGO) networks have attacked the dominant agenda of the 'green economy'. Tensions between agendas have pervaded official texts and debates, with arguments for human well-being and social equity existing cheek by jowl with contradictory statements that promote dependence on an unregulated private sector. These tensions often remain hidden in narratives about green transformations, yet making them explicit is crucial if justice concerns are to be given due consideration. Again, this requires focusing attention on the politics of green transformations.

The politics of green transformations

Each narrative thus employs, explicitly or implicitly, very different theories of power, politics and governance, and so implications for justice and distribution. They also embody distinct understandings of 'the market', of 'states' and 'citizens', in terms of their transformative potential, whose interests they serve and the forms of power they exercise and are subject to.

In some renditions we can see traces of 'technocratic global control', either through centralization of authority globally or via polycentric or multilevel governance or through faith in technological magic bullets that bypass the need for political change and compromise. A fallacy of control is often demonstrated, and such calls for planetary management have provoked powerful critiques (Sachs, 1993), particularly in relation to the growing role of corporations in framing and financing global responses to environmental threats (Hildyard, 1993). By enrolling ever more areas of the global commons in circuits of global economic and political power, and subject to global institutional oversight, such a technocratic turn can undermine democratic responses.

In the case of technocratic governance, power lies with benign elites who seek to globalize the benefits of technologies, act upon the insights of planetary science, marshal a 'global consensus' and then allocate resources for the protection of global public goods. The Green Climate Fund of the World Bank is perhaps a good example. This perspective draws on an essentially liberal view of power where trust in (global) institutions, and states/policy elites derives from their assumed autonomy from particular interests and classes, and their respect for the rule of law. They are able to align the comparative advantages of public and private (and philanthropic) interests though a variety of public private partnerships (Bäckstrand, 2006). Citizens, in this view, benefit from protection by such elites acting on their behalf, without much requirement for their direct input. Rather, public participation comes through interest-group representation in national democratic processes.

Likewise, accounts of marketized transformations present themselves as apolitical, devolving power to the market to seek out optimally efficient outcomes by setting the right prices and creating new markets with minimal institutional oversight. Market-based mechanisms such as emissions trading, tradable fishing quotas and carbon-offset projects are all examples. States oversee exchanges in the market and provide appropriate regulation and, most importantly, allocate and enforce property rights. Citizens are relevant as passive consumers of products and services produced through the market, but not as shapers of markets or the rules by which they are governed. Such accounts also overlook the deeply politicized nature of market creation, the scope for capture by capital and the lack of attention to social justice issues in such projects (Brand, 2012a). In their favour, such approaches reflect the new global distribution of power – including the rise of political–economic power in countries like China, India and Brazil – and a realpolitik of who owns the technology, production and finance that, for many, will be critical to the prospects of most green transformations. In this reading, green transformations will inevitably be market led, and markets, corporations and finance capital need to be enlisted, including from other parts of the world.

For those who place more faith in state-led transformations, as Mazzucato argues (this book), many things that get attributed to entrepreneurs and markets are, in fact, shaped and financed by states. Markets have to be made and brought into being (Çalışkan and Callon, 2009); nowhere are there markets independent of the societies that create and shape them; they are always socially embedded (de Alcántara, 1993). Rather than wishing away the state or denying its relevance, these accounts point to the potential of state-led Keynesian, or developmental states (Chang, 2002; Fine *et al.*, 2013) as an important corrective to some of the naivety, as well as ideological tone, apparent in some market-based versions of green transformations. In more paternalist versions, states are assumed to have the interests of citizens at heart and a sincere commitment to the advancement of development. Yet such models need to be nuanced with an appreciation of the uneven capacity and resources that most states have, especially those in the majority of the world. Only some states have the policy autonomy and developmental space (Evans, 1995) to pursue ambitious and autonomous strategies for green developmental transformation.

Contexts matter, and as the chapters in this book show there are a whole variety of states, with different financial, bureaucratic and technological capacities, and different possibilities of state-led or guided transformations follow from this. Other critiques coming from marketized narratives would take issue with the idea that the state knows best, and equally those emphasizing social justice issues would question whether states are willing and able to act in benign ways rather than serve as vehicles for the expression of the particular interests that capture them. State-led perspectives thus still require an explanation of who sets the direction of change and how the overall goals of green transformations are set. They also require reflection on how issues of distribution, accountability and chronic power imbalances will be addressed.

Those advocating more citizen-led transformations take as their point of departure that neither state nor market can deliver. Either captured by or with interests aligned to capital, state or marketized transformations inevitably serve the interests of the minority, not the majority. Issues of ownership and control over the process and the tools of change (production, technology, finance and institutions) are key. In this narrative, greater faith is placed in the role of mobilized citizens to democratize technology, production and the institutions that oversee them. This assumes a much more active and inclusive view of citizenship (Leach and Scoones, this book). In this rendition, citizens are creative, knowledgeable actors exercising active agency, individually and through networks across scales. The cumulative and diverse unruly politics of movements offer diverse possibilities for transformations, and perhaps reflect more accurately where the momentum for change has come from historically (Stirling, this book). This requires thinking about transformations in terms of cultures, practices and mobilizations that create the pressure for change, acting both to disrupt incumbent pathways, but also construct alternatives (Smith and Ely, this book), connecting across scales and between movements.

Yet, given the nature of the contemporary political landscape and prevailing distributions of power, as well as the scale of change required, there are doubts as to whether citizen-led action alone is up to the challenge. This is either because of the urgency of the situation or because of the inevitable need to enrol powerful actors in transformative projects, given their control over many of the very things that need to be transformed: production, technology and finance. There is also a danger of romanticizing and exaggerating the potential for citizen action in terms of people's time and capacity to engage in constant mobilization, or because of the high personal and political risks of doing so in many parts of the world where mobilizing citizens quickly run up against elite control over resources.

These four narratives, while conflicting in many respects, contain elements of critique and propose solutions that cut across one another. For example, some might share the view that a more whole-scale reordering of society–nature relationships is ultimately required, but would see a role for pricing mechanisms, technological innovation and institutional reforms in the meantime. It is partly a question of time-frames of change, partly an assessment of how the world is now and the practicalities of meaningful shifts, and partly a function of ideal futures and ideological leanings. Ultimately, it is about the messy politics of day-to-day negotiations and alliance-building amid shifting circumstances, opportunity structures and prevalent uncertainties, and the pragmatic politics of tactics and strategy that any green transformation requires (Schmitz, this book).

Overall, then, some types of transformation politics are more likely around some issues in some parts of the world than others. This depends, among other things, on the degree of democratic space that exists, available technological capacity, the development and functioning of markets, the power and commitment of the state, and the influence of citizen mobilization and action. Some environmental challenges are perhaps more amenable to technological fixes, while others are more characterized by murky political economy and more challenging struggles, though none, we would suggest, is devoid of politics, despite implicit assumptions to the contrary. Unsurprisingly, therefore, there are no standard solutions, and no singular roadmap or blueprint, for realizing green transformations.

Multiple transformations: strategies for change

What, then, do the chapters say about theories of change, the building of alliances and the practical politics of green transformations? Clearly, contributors to this book come at these issues from different angles, conceptually, politically and practically, drawing on different theories of power and change, reflected in different visions of sustainability and narratives of green transformations outlined above. Some emphasize the politics of knowledge (Leach, Stirling, Millstone); others state policy (Mazzucato, Spratt); others change through networks (Smith and Ely, Leach and Scoones), others the incentives required to form interest-based coalitions (Schmitz, Lockwood) and others the historical role of broader social forces (Newell). And indeed many chapters combine perspectives, as power and politics take many forms and these are inevitably co-constituted and context-specific.

Likewise, and emerging from these perspectives on power and politics, each of the chapters suggests different pathways of change. Each provides different accounts of what alliances could be constructed, what accommodations might be reached, what practical tactics and strategies could be deployed, and how these combine different narratives, and respond to different imperatives of green transformation. What this all suggests is that, rather than there being one big green transformation, it is more likely that there will be multiple transformations that will intersect, overlap and conflict in unpredictable ways. Many indeed may already be underway, competing with one another for the political attention, support and financial resources of states, businesses and publics. There will be failures, setbacks and unintended consequences, as with any project of reorganizing society.

Change will therefore come about in a multitude of different arenas and sites, and through diverse alliances and movements. We are likely to see a series of competing – at times divergent, other times convergent – green transformations. How might these come about? Drawing from the chapters, four broad, and overlapping, strategies for change are seen.

Shaping and resisting structures

As already alluded to, one key fissure in debates about green transformations is around the scope for change within capitalism. Most chapters here emphasize the diversity and unevenness of capitalist development in relation to varieties of capitalism (Lockwood, this book) and fractions of capital (Newell, this book) as a way of getting a more differentiated handle on the possibilities of transformations within capitalism(s). Newell (this book) shows how activists have sought to mobilize the power of finance capital given its heightened power to drive decarbonization, while Spratt (this book) shows, in turn, how important it is to disaggregate different types of finance in order to appreciate what transformative potential (if any) they might have.

Due to prevailing structures of capital and finance, some strategies of green transformation might gain traction in the neoliberal heartlands of the US and Europe, but are far less likely to work elsewhere. In neoliberal settings, the power of transnational corporations reshapes democratic possibilities, due to their market power, lobbying influence and control of states and claims to be in the vanguard of social and environmental responsibility (Crane et al., 2008; Crouch, 2011). This suggests new challenges for the 'post-democratic' era, where organized civil society becomes crucial to challenge the power of the corporation (Crouch, 2004; Crouch and Streeck, 2006).

As well as appreciating the macro context, what this points to is the need for more nuanced, and regionally and nationally specific theories of change (Lockwood, this book), given that common structures of power express themselves in distinct forms around the world. This requires the building of national strategies and locating transformations within understandings of national political dynamics.

Reframing knowledge

Structures of power are not just economic, of course. Many contributors place emphasis on discursive structures that limit how we see and imagine problems and solutions, and how we come to define, know and frame futures. Closing down debates and the capture of terms and styles of discussion are common features. We must ask whose knowledge counts in the development and articulation of authoritative and legitimate knowledge about transformations. Many of the book's contributions argue for the need to 'open up' discussions, allowing for discursive reframing, and deliberation and dialogue as part of a process of knowledge production for and within transformations. These structures of knowledge production have concrete, material and distributional implications, as the contributions from Leach, Stirling and Millstone make clear. This raises important challenges about the robustness of institutions to deal with the plurality and diversity of knowledge, as Millstone suggests. Previous experience of global assessments (Scoones, 2009), or attempts to manage public engagement though global institutions charged with governing technology (Newell, 2010) offer important lessons (Beck *et al.*, 2014).

Realigning institutions and incentives

Several chapters point to the potentially key role of strong (entrepreneurial or developmental) states in pushing (rather than just nudging) change (Mazzucato, this book), and the importance of different institutional configurations to the prospects of green transformations (Lockwood, this book). They also raise questions about the capacity of states to fulfil what is imagined or expected of them. The potential for state capture is also highlighted when so much is at stake and powerful actors feel threatened by the direction of change and seek to control the pace and direction of it.

This is not just about differences between states in the global North and South, since while resources are critical, corporate capture of states is a worldwide phenomenon. This is just one aspect of the changing global context, including the rise of the BRICS, which is rendering old North–South distinctions obsolete, and highlighting both global commonalities and new axes of political–economic power and privilege. There are issues everywhere, then, of whether states can or should 'pick winners', and their willingness and ability to challenge incumbent power – to discontinue sunk investments and avoid technological and infrastructural lock-in, for example. The nimbleness of the state to reflect, challenge and change direction is often questionable (Lockwood, this book), although there are also positive examples (Mazzucato, Schmitz, this book).

Mobilizing and networking

Civic action to disrupt, discontinue and challenge incumbent power has always been a central part of historical transformations and will continue to be part of future ones. Smith and Ely (this book) emphasize the potential of bottom-up innovation and grassroots practice. Movements play a key role in challenging the legitimacy of dominant framings, resource distributions, technological priorities and distributional consequences (Leach and Scoones, this book). This occasionally takes the form of proactive efforts to claim control over processes, priorities and resources, as in the case of the movements for food, water and energy justice/sovereignty. These illustrate the potential of place-based struggles to resonate and 'globalize' through transnational advocacy networks (Leach and Scoones, 2007; Sikor and Newell, 2014), while also inviting questions about the scalability and replicability of experiments and successful campaigns, given the contingent and context-specific nature of transformation politics.

Across these four strategies for transformation, there is a diverse, always messy (and often murky) politics at play. This highlights a profound mismatch between how transformations are currently and historically practised – always complex, over-lapping and contested – and how they are talked about and imagined in policy – often as a plan, specified in terms of goals and targets, implying hubristic illusions of control through management (Stirling, this book). Although with hindsight the temptation is to ascribe unidirectionality, linearity and clearly defined purpose to transformations in previous historical periods, when living through such periods of change, they appear open-ended, where goals and pathways to change are often unclear and contested (Newell, this book). Moreover, despite the best intentions and aspirations of planners and entrepreneurs, muddling through, constant adapta-tion and coping are the norm, and act to subvert and resist any plans that seek to predict and manage change (Folke *et al.*, 2002). Added to the importance of political–economic contexts, this should strike a note of caution about 'blueprints', 'models' and 'transfers' from 'success' stories such as Germany or China (see Schmitz, Lockwood, this book).

Across the book, the different contributions incline towards a stance of politically informed, yet pragmatic realism, drawing on combinations of the different strategies outlined above to map out ways forward. A scepticism towards simplistic win–win technocratic or market solutions comes across clearly. However, there is also an acknowledgement that the likelihood of radical change in the short term is small, while maintaining a commitment to longer term, more radical shifts, and to ensuring that decisions now do not constrain the possibility of such longer term changes. Collectively, there is a shared appreciation that current economic and political structures around markets, technology, finance and existing allocations of power are not delivering green transformations that are either just or sustainable. So a searching analysis of wider political economy and the structures of power is necessary. Yet the sense in which a radical and revolutionary overhaul is unlikely soon, even if ultimately desirable, suggests the inevitability of the messy politics of deal-brokering, compromise and alliance-building for green transformations.

Conclusion

So what does this all mean for the politics of green transformations? First, the chapters strike a note of caution about the idea that there will be one great, guided (normally assumed from above or through the market) green transformation. Neither a global Green New Deal, a World Environment Organisation or global pricing of 'natural capital' will do away with the need to engage with multiple, contested changes that may (or may not) add up to a broader politics of green transformations. Given the diversity of accumulation strategies being pursued by states and corporations in different parts of the world and the ways in which they enrol and collide with so many other social actors, we can expect a diversity of pathways. The contribution of a more political analysis of green transformations that this book offers helps clarify some of the trade-offs, highlighting the distributional implications and therefore enabling engagement and support for transformations that seem to be more 'just', 'equitable', 'inclusive' and 'democratic' – and consequently sustainable.

Second, recognizing, celebrating and encouraging diversity in transformative pathways is not the same as saying 'let all flowers bloom'. Power relations do need to change and transformations that are narrowly based – whether around technology or markets or bottom-up politics, for example – are unlikely to gain much traction, despite the illusions of order and clarity that they may afford. Likewise, scepticism about knowledge claims does not amount to critiques of the value of science, but highlight the politics of knowledge around such claims. As many of the chapters argue, there is therefore a need for more inclusive knowledge (co-)production in order to increase the robustness and credibility of knowledge for transformation.

Third, the emphasis on questions of equity and justice that run through many of the chapters underscore the imperative of ensuring transformations are 'just': that they pay due attention to those whose livelihoods are dependent upon the existing way of doing things and who stand to lose out under many proposals for green transformations, and that benefits and risks from change are fairly distributed. Democratic politics are vital to this, despite some calls that they are a luxury we cannot afford given the urgency of change. Political analysis is again required to understand how modes of governing, deliberating and participating can be adapted to help address the challenges thrown up by green transformations.

The chapters in this book therefore offer different perspectives on the politics of green transformations; there is no standard answer, and much depends on context, sector, political economy, timing, and so on. These politics will continue to play out on a terrain of competing discourses, institutions and material interests in diverse contexts. The challenge for all of us is to engage on that terrain in defining and realizing pathways that are both green and just. A political analysis, as outlined in the chapters in this book in different ways and from diverse perspectives, is central to this very practical and urgent aim.

Note

1   See, for example, *The Great Transformation* (Heinrich Böll Foundation, 2013), echoing the title of the earlier classic work by Polanyi (1980 [1944]).

2

WHAT IS GREEN?

Transformation imperatives and knowledge politics

Melissa Leach

Introduction

The idea that our societies and economies are in urgent need of green transformation is beginning to take hold – albeit to varying extents – across political, policy and public debate. Quite what sort of transformation is required, and how to achieve it, is a matter of high contention. But what does the other part of the term, 'green', mean? The 'green' terminology that now attaches to everything from policy concepts, political parties, campaigning organizations, movements and even consumer products can imply that this is a settled idea, connoting a clear set of shared values. At its bluntest, it suggests that the environment, and nature, matter, but dig beneath the surface and we find 'green' to be as contested a term as transformation. Its unthinking use begs important questions about the directions of societal and economic change, and where it is leading – what are 'green' goals and outcomes – and about the processes that might get us there, and who is involved. Embedded in both are questions about values, power and knowledge: who gets to define green with what consequences, and who and what are included and excluded. Such discursive politics (Burchell *et al.*, 1991; Hajer, 1995; Fairhead and Leach, 2003) are the focus of this chapter.

'Green' has carried many meanings in political and policy debates. Amid large, diverse literatures extending back many decades, one can broadly distinguish ecocentric and biocentric positions in which green is associated with the conservation of 'nature' for its own sake, including the rights of non-human species (Eckersley, 1992). In contrast, anthropocentric positions – our focus – emphasize the value of nature and ecosystems to human purposes. Here, multiple versions (see also Spratt, this book) include 'light green' positions, which see the environment as relatively robust, and green goals achievable by relatively modest economic shifts to price nature correctly, substitute for non-renewable resources, or redirect personal consumption and lifestyle choices. Much contemporary 'green growth' thinking fits this view (Jacobs, 2012a). In contrast, 'dark' or deep-green positions see ecosystems as much more vulnerable, interconnected and prone to damage, thus emphasizing a more conservationist, preservationist or precautionary approach that may require fundamental structural change (Sessions, 1995). Recently, the term 'bright' green has been deployed to distinguish optimistic approaches relying on technology and social innovation (Steffen, 2009).

Interplaying with these distinctions, versions of green also differ in how far they prioritize social and justice concerns. Thus, green socialist and Marxist positions associate green with fundamental restructuring of (capitalist) social relations (Benton, 1996). Green is also linked with social equity – as well as democracy and participation – in the political positioning of many Green political parties (Wall, 2010), as well as in various approaches to 'green development' (Adams, 2009). Overlapping with these are positions valuing community resources and institutions, and ways of life that have co-developed in interdependence with ecologies and nature (Guha and Martinez-Alier, 1997). Indigenous people's movements, and some versions of ecofeminism, emphasizing the interdependence of gender equality and ecological sustainability (MacGregor, 2006), broadly follow such meanings of green.

Yet cross-cutting such distinctions are questions of knowledge and power. Whose knowledge counts in defining 'green' goals and values? Who defines what a 'good' future might be and how to get there? Here again we can identify distinctions in types of knowledge, across spectra from expert science to citizen science; official to experiential expertise; formal to informal; global to local; and the many disciplines and subfields that contribute to each of these (see Leach *et al.*, 2005). Different ways of knowing are often associated with different ways of being, including different ways of living with and valuing 'nature'. People, institutions and knowledges often interact and combine in actor-networks (Latour, 2005) or discourse coalitions (Hajer, 1995) that can serve to represent or promote particular views, values or interests. There is no necessary affinity between any particular meaning of green and particular type of knowledge. Yet in practice, powerful actor-networks and discourse coalitions often converge strongly around certain green meanings and goals, while marginalizing or crowding out others.

How are these discursive dynamics playing out today? What versions of green are coming to dominate? A particular constellation of meanings has acquired growing power in the last few years and are the focus of this chapter: those around 'green limits', in particular ideas of 'planetary boundaries' and 'safety barriers' in climate change, linked with notions of 'the green economy'. The chapter traces how these provide novel, compelling justifications for the urgency of transformation to meet green goals, offering powerful arguments against planet-threatening 'business as usual'. Yet each has a history, produced by particular actors and institutions. In coming to be settled as powerful discourses, they risk marginalizing and crowding out other knowledges, as well as other meanings of green.

Centrally, the chapter argues that these discourses align all too neatly with top-down approaches that rely on regulatory, planning, technical or market 'fixes'.

In this they downplay the need for more fundamental social as well as economic transformations. They also downplay the significance of knowledge and values emerging from 'below', including from local people living with and experiencing social and ecological dynamics on a daily basis. As illustrated in examples of land use and tropical forests, discourses and interventions ensuing from them ignore such alternative knowledges at their peril. The result can be reduced robustness of policies and interventions, missed opportunities and injustices. The chapter concludes that a more inclusive and deliberative politics of knowledge is essential if green transformations are to be robust, effective and contribute to the social justice dimensions of 'green'.

Green limits

Green, today, is powerfully associated with respect for environmental limits: whether in relation to climate change, biodiversity, water, land, oceans or their 'nexus' interactions (see Stirling, this book). Growth and progress, it is argued, must keep within limits or else founder amid dangerous resource scarcities, crisis and turbulence.

Green limits have long been invoked in science, policy and popular debate to argue that human business-as-usual cannot continue. Their genealogy stretches back centuries, to the ideas of islands and their limited biogeography that inspired 'green imperialism' in early European encounters with the tropical world (Grove, 1996), to notions such as the 'carrying capacity' of local and regional environments co-constructed with colonial environmental and conservation science and policy, whether concerning forests or rangelands (Leach and Mearns, 1996). By the 1960s and 1970s scientists and social movements alike were pointing to the environmental costs of dominant industrial development paths, on a shared, constrained, small planet newly visible as such from the gaze of space. It was in this context that Meadows *et al.* (1972) articulated the supposed resource-based 'limits to growth' as demand looked set to outstrip supply. Throughout the 1980s and 1990s, policy analyses often purported to identify emerging imbalances between people's use of and demands on environments, and environmental capacities, resulting in resource scarcities and environmental degradation. Neo-Malthusian perspectives often dominated, highlighting the threat of rapidly growing, resource-consuming populations. This history of limits thinking has, notably, co-developed with vibrant critique around its assumptions and evidence, including the overlooked capacity of human innovation (e.g. Cole *et al.*, 1973).

Today, environmental limits are being invoked with renewed vigour and at planetary scales. This is underlain by a growing sophistication and authority of earth system science, and its understandings of thresholds, tipping points and the possible consequences of exceeding them (e.g. Lenton, 2013). The two most prominent contemporary concepts are the idea of a two- degree limit for global climate change and the more all-encompassing idea of 'planetary boundaries'. These have gone well beyond science to become settled as discourses linked with influential institutions and policies. How has this happened, and what meanings of green and forms of knowledge are included and excluded?

The two-degree safety barrier for climate change

In the last decade, the 'two-degree safety barrier' or 'two-degree target' has become a dominant guiding concept in climate change debate and policy, reinforced again in the latest Intergovernmental Panel on Climate Change (IPCC) report and associated policy and media commentary. The central idea is that any increase in average global temperature should be limited to two degrees above a baseline, the pre-industrial level in 1880. This is the maximum allowable warming before human interference in the climate is deemed 'dangerous'. Beyond it dire consequences are predicted, including potentially significant losses of food production, especially in Africa; high extinction risks for 20–30 per cent of species, more severe droughts and floods, and an unstoppable loss of the Greenland ice sheet, triggering escalating sea-level rises (Hansen *et al.*, 2007; IPCC, 2013).

This 'two-degree safety barrier' offers an important message about the need for green transformation:

> an indication, as simple as it is compelling, of the physical limits to the volume of greenhouse gases that can be dumped in the atmosphere [which] sets out the breathtaking message that the world's population must immediately begin to make significantly less use of fossil energy sources or leave them in the ground.
>
> (Leggewie and Messner, 2012b, p128)

Yet there is nothing natural or immutable about the existence of such a safety barrier, or that it should be set at two degrees. Rather, like previous green limits, this is socially and politically constructed, and has a history. As Randalls (2010) and Tol (2007) detail, it is rooted in the particular ways in which scientists and economists developed heuristics and models from the 1970s to guide understanding and decision-making about climate change. The two- degree figure was first pinpointed by the economist W. D. Nordhaus in 1979, assuming that this was the limit of the warming to have occurred naturally over the last 10,000 years. Through the 1980s, a series of integrated assessment modelling exercises, and the particular assumptions they incorporated, helped to support the idea of limits and thresholds to dangerous climate change, and two degrees in particular. It acquired growing weight in policy circles, with a link between limits and averted danger enshrined in Article 2 of the UN Framework Convention on Climate Change (UNFCCC, 1992). The proposition of two degrees as an actual policy target came in 1996 from the European Union (EU), backed by certain scientists and environmentalists. It gained in visibility and policy institutionalization through the 2000s – for instance, underpinning the UK's 2008 Climate Change Act and included in the 2009 Copenhagen Accord. In UNFCCC conferences of parties (COP) in Copenhagen (COP-15) and Cancun (COP-16) all parties to the UNFCCC (except Bolivia) agreed to pursue the aim of limiting global warming to two degrees above the pre-industrial level (Knopf *et al.*, 2012).

The two-degree target has come to function as an important anchoring device (Van der Sluijs *et al.*, 1998) or boundary object (Star and Griesemer, 1989) in climate science-policy analysis and public debate (Hulme, 2012): 'a socially constructed entity which is powerful and has endurance both because it has credibility in many different worlds and because it works to stabilize discourse across the boundaries of these worlds' (Leggewie and Messner, 2012b, p130). It is attractive as a target for international negotiations (albeit a recent and arguably not necessarily particularly successful one, given failures of global climate agreements); to governments wanting to claim commitments; and to media and public commentary aiming to raise the stakes of climate change mitigation. Economic justifications and interests were added when the Stern review (Stern, 2006) calculated and publicized the economic costs of going beyond two degrees. But in the particular ways this discourse has settled, what is excluded?

First, the portrayal of two degrees as a clear green goal overlooks significant uncertainties and ambiguities in the relationship between global temperature and the drivers and effects of human-induced climate change Hulme (2012). These range from uncertainties about the aggregate global effects of greenhouse gases, aerosols and black carbon, the sensitivity of climate to them, and the interaction with natural climate variability, to those around how particular energy systems, land and forest use and other human activities affect greenhouse gas emissions. Thus, 'as an "output index" the 2 degree safety barrier is compatible with many possible "input scenarios"' (Hulme, 2012, p124). Yet it may be precisely such 'input' processes and drivers – and the ways they connect with people's values, lifestyles and aspirations – that offer more meaningful versions of green in everyday terms, and can be more easily linked to policies and regulations towards behaviour change among people, governments and businesses.

Second, setting the safety barrier at two degrees is highly value laden. The establishment of any particular limit depends on the assumptions incorporated into models, and crucially, on the meanings, values and experiences likely to be associated with warming. Thus a two-degree target may be too high for areas of sub-Saharan Africa set to experience severe droughts, or small island states vulnerable to flooding from rising sea levels, at lower temperatures. The Association of Small Island States along with other developing nations has therefore argued for an upper limit 1.5 degrees of warming. Meanwhile, some people and places could tolerate, or even gain in productivity, from three or even four degrees of warming. Not surprisingly, geopolitical tensions have therefore opened up over precisely where the safety barrier should be placed. As Hulme (2012) points out, in attempting to avert such tensions politicians and campaigners frequently revert to arguments about expert 'sound science', declaring two degrees to be 'what the science demands' (cf. Millstone, this book). Yet most scientists – and indeed the IPCC – admit that identifying climate policy targets involves value-judgements that are well beyond the remit of scientific enquiry.

Third, the two-degree discourse defines 'green' in singular, climate-related terms. When applied to particular economies, societies or ecosystems, this can channel priority to climate over other possible green goals, with problematic consequences. For instance, large-scale investment in biofuels has been embraced by policy-makers as a means to reduce fossil-fuel dependence and contribute to meeting climate targets. Yet as many examples in African, Asian and Latin American settings show, tensions, trade-offs and conflicts have arisen where land use to grow biofuel feedstocks competes with food production or uses for local livelihoods (Borras et al., 2010). The latter may also be 'green', but defined in relation to alternative meanings, whether around sustainable national food security and food sovereignty, livelihoods, or community ways of life and rights.

Finally, a fixation on global climate targets – and the particular forms of scientific and modelling knowledge they rest on – can marginalize alternative meanings, values and forms of knowledge around climate-related phenomena. Social and cultural analyses, and attention to everyday and citizen expertise and experience, show how widely varying these are. Climate and weather may be understood and discussed in terms of practical struggles to 'get by' in uncertain, dynamic coastal, dryland, forest or Arctic settings, or to religious and moral codes, with weather events and the state of the climate in many societies interpreted as indicative of the good, or otherwise, state of social behaviour (e.g. Crate and Nuttall, 2009).

In the light of such critiques, some analysts suggest rejecting the two- degree safety barrier altogether, along with related, single global targets for climate change (Hulme, 2012). Others argue that it has value as an aspiration, until such time as more robust scientific and policy approaches 'improve' on it (Edenhofer et al., 2012). Rather than assess this particular green limit as a fixed end, though, it might be more appropriately treated as a means: appreciating its social contestation, the two-degree safety barrier might be reconsidered as a discursive concept to open up debates about legitimacy, values and uncertainty, thus creating space for and facilitating 'democratic discussion about what sort of world we want to live in' (Shaw, 2010).

Planetary boundaries

'Planetary boundaries' offers a more recent and also more all-encompassing 'green limits' discourse. From the mid-2000s, scientists started to propose that we have entered a new epoch, the Anthropocene, in which human activities have become the dominant driver of many earth system processes including climate, bio-geochemical cycles, ecosystems and biodiversity. The extent of human influence has grown rapidly since the Industrial Revolution, accelerating dramatically since the 1950s (Steffen et al., 2004, 2007). A series of nine planetary boundaries has been identified, referring to the biophysical processes in the Earth's system on which human life depends (Rockström et al., 2009). Together, these serve to keep the planet within Holocene-like conditions and thus define a 'safe operating space' for humanity. Human actions, it is claimed, are rapidly approaching (in the case of climate change) or have already transgressed (in the case of biodiversity and nitrogen pollution) key global thresholds, increasing the likelihood of unprecedented ecological turbulence. Potentially catastrophic thresholds are in prospect, which will dramatically compromise development both globally and locally (Folke *et al.*, 2011). The concept underpins an imperative for urgent green transformation to keep humanity within a 'safe operating space'.

Planetary boundaries concepts and their associated meanings of green have, like climate change limits, been constructed by particular actor-networks. Central have been global environmental change scientists, from climate and biodiversity science to oceanography and geochemistry. During interactions in the early 2000s around the major global environmental change science programmes – notably the International Geosphere-Biosphere Programme (IGBP) – the concept was first mooted as a way of integrating across programmes. The International Human Dimensions Programme (IHDP) drew in some social science perspectives, notably from geography. The widely cited *Nature* paper (Rockström *et al.*, 2009) drew from these scientific communities, led by Johan Rockström who rapidly became the high-profile ambassador for the concept on the global stage. Through the influence of his colleagues at the Stockholm Resilience Centre and in the wider Resilience Alliance, the planetary boundaries discourse has also drawn strongly on resilience thinking in its emphasis on thresholds, tipping points and whole-system transformation.

For many scientists, planetary boundaries ideas are ongoing work-in-progress. As argued in response to scientific critiques (e.g. Nordhaus *et al.*, 2012), they emphasize that boundaries are provisional, variable in character (e.g. some are 'fast', suggesting tipping points, while some, such as land degradation, accrete slowly) and that much further work is required to understand scale effects, boundary interactions and other matters (Rockström, 2012; Galaz *et al.*, 2012). Yet while the science is still developing, planetary boundaries has rapidly come to operate as a political and policy discourse embraced by many international and national actors and institutions. The High-Level Panel on Global Sustainability at the Rio+20 conference in 2012 drew on it to justify not just a renewed urgency to sustainable development, but a new paradigm in which environmental boundaries, at planetary scale, provide the framework for social and economic development. It is supported by major networks and initiatives playing key roles in the post-Rio, post-2015 process, including the Sustainable Development Solutions Network (SDSN, 2014, http://unsdsn.org/official) and the Planetary Boundaries Initiative (http://planetary boundariesinitiative.org/). The concept of planetary boundaries lends itself to evocative popular symbols and representations, from the inflatable ball earth in Johan Rockström's TED (Technology, Entertainment and Design) talk deflating as boundary after boundary is exceeded, to the website image of a precipitous waterfall with an African man, as an icon of humanity, standing just far enough away, within the boundary, to avoid tipping over the edge. Like two degrees, planetary boundaries is operating as a boundary object, uniting diverse actors and interests around a particular meaning of green.

Yet again, we must ask about the politics of this discourse: what it is enabling, and what meanings of green and associated knowledges it may be excluding. First, the planetary boundaries discourse can imply that the 'earth system' itself sets the limits and boundaries for human progress (Rockström, 2013). Yet the idea of an earth system is, to some degree, a social construction, associated with a particular set of 'earth system sciences', while questions of where limits should lie, and what is safe or dangerous, will always be open to human meanings and interpretations, and to cultural and personal beliefs (Hulme, 2013). Thus, dramatic loss of biodiversity in tropical forest landscapes might, in terms of planetary boundaries discourse, presage a contribution to a dangerous breakdown of interconnected ecological systems. Yet as West African examples show, some social groups believe that it is biodiverse forests that harbour danger in terms of wild animals, spirits, secretive cultural behaviour and disease; clear landscapes are culturally preferable, providing more 'open' social relationships and more productive agriculture and livelihoods (Fairhead and Leach, 1996). What is safe or dangerous depends on who, and where, one is.

Of course, one might counter that this is a question of gaze and scale; what is valued and seen as safe in diverse local places might add up, globally and over the long term, to planetary scale dangers. Indeed, this is precisely the argument of the planetary boundaries discourse, asserting the authority of science to know and predict these bigger dangers for humanity. Equally, it is important not to be over-relativistic; the bigger, longer term implications of human impacts on environmental processes do matter, and not all ways of life and beliefs are compatible with sustainability. The cultures of commercial logging firms driven by short-term profit, or of climate sceptics supportive of continued fossil-fuel burning, would be cases in point where values and beliefs underlie manifestly irresponsible environmental practices. These, and the economic and power relations associated with them, need to be challenged, for they threaten to breach even the broadest notion of green limits. Yet failing even to acknowledge alternative knowledges and perspectives, and to draw these into negotiation and debate when it comes to justifying policies and interventions, is a recipe for injustice and resistance.

This becomes clear when we address a second line of questioning. Even while ruling out some goals around profit and power as threatening planetary boundaries, the discourse can imply a singularity of green goals that stay within. The notion of a single, interconnected earth system aligns neatly with the idea of a single humanity in the Anthropocene, downplaying the real diversity of societies, contexts, identities and perspectives. Even within the broad 'green' of planetary boundaries lies a diversity of possible futures and pathways, shaped by much more precise, and varied, meanings of green, relating to particular ways of life, goals and priorities for ecosystem use.

Take a particular challenge, such as ensuring 'sustainable food futures' within global and regional boundaries of climate change, land use change, biodiversity loss and nitrogen use. Alternative green visions and futures could include prioritizing small-scale food production systems; participatory systems and their social benefits;

climate smart agriculture, or large-scale, input-intensive industrial agricultural investments. Each could be the basis of a green food future. However, they are very different futures; they incorporate different meanings of green, and small farmers, businesses, national policy-makers and others would value and prioritize them in very different ways. As controversies around genetically modified (GM) crops attest (see Leach and Scoones, this book), such contestation can be vibrant and highly political.

Alternatively, take an ecosystem in a place, such as a particular African tropical forest. Here, a plurality of possible goals could be associated with different people and groups, scales and particular boundaries. Thus, governments and international agencies might value the forest as a carbon stock to offset emissions in industrialized countries to help keep global humanity within climate boundaries, and businesses and public–private partnerships would value the profits to be made by trading carbon credits. Biodiversity scientists might value its endemic flora and fauna, seeking to protect forest habitat as a key contribution to steer development within biodiversity boundaries. The tourist industry might value the profits to be made from eco-tourism here. For nearby urban populations and water companies, the forest safe-guards hydrology and its protection is key to maintaining water supplies. For the timber industry and government production foresters, green goals would mean developing sustainable logging practices and timber supplies. For local residents, the same forest may be valued as a place of historical memories and ancestral spirits; a source of gathered foods, fibres and medicines; a source of bushmeat from hunting; a place to plant agroforestry trees under the shade of the forest canopy, or a set of potential fallows to sustain the fertility of household rice production. Indeed, a forest is all of these and more, but the point is that these diverse ecosystem properties, goods, services and cultural attributes are valued differently by different local, national and global populations. There is a wide diversity of green goals, but green in different ways. Some are compatible – gathering and biodiversity, for instance – but others imply tensions, trade-offs and potential contestation. Local people have often resisted biodiversity conservation and forest carbon schemes that have excluded them from forest access and jeopardized their livelihoods and ways of life (e.g. Fairhead and Leach, 1998; Corbera and Brown, 2010; Leach and Scoones, 2013).

Discursive appeals to broad planetary boundaries can often obscure such diversity, and contestation, around particular versions of green. This may create resistance that ultimately undoes even the best intentioned interventions, or suppress understandings and practices that offer valuable prospects for more sustainable futures. Taking diverse perspectives and goals seriously suggests not a single form of green transformation to steer within universal limits, but multiple transformative pathways, towards multiply-envisaged futures (Leach *et al.*, 2013) and a more negotiated approach that works through tensions with the diverse stakeholders involved.

A third set of questions, then, concerns the implications of planetary boundaries discourse for justice. At a global level, these surfaced in geopolitics around the Rio+20 conference. Many low-income and emerging economies contested the

concept, interpreting it as limiting their economic growth. The planetary boundaries term was excluded from the final Rio+20 Outcome document, and only
hesitantly used in formal intergovernmental processes post-Rio. Questions of
justice have also surfaced in debates about what might constitute a 'good' Anthropocene (Peterson, 2013). In this vein, Raworth (2012) has adapted the concept of
planetary boundaries, adding an inner circle to represent a 'social foundation'
incorporating well-being, gender equality and human rights. Between the circles
there lies a 'safe and just operating space'. Green transformations to remain within
it are thus helpfully reconceived as 'green and just', with meanings of green
more akin to socialist or green political versions, with social justice at their core.
Importantly, this framework also invites attention to the social inequalities and power
relations that leave many millions of people without the essential resources they
need, while allowing excessive resource use by others to push humanity across
multiple planetary boundaries. However, to be used effectively, it must also open
up consideration of the diversity of possible 'green and just' goals and pathways,
the social meanings attached to these, the possible tensions and contestations
between them, and who stands to gain or lose (Leach *et al.*, 2013).

Pathways of intervention and change: green limits and green economies

We have focused thus far on goals and futures – where humanity is going – and
the meanings of green and associated knowledges embodied in, but also excluded
by, contemporary green limits discourses in this respect. However, further key
questions turn on how to get there. What sorts of intervention and change – pathways for reaching green goals or steering within green limits – are envisaged? What
sorts of intervention, by whom, are suggested and supported by green limits
discourses – both of a two-degree climate safety barrier and of planetary boundaries
– and which are marginalized? Other chapters address transformation processes in
detail, so treatment here is brief. Nevertheless, it is important to highlight how
green limits discourses are justifying attempted 'fixes' of various kinds: whether
through regulation, planning, technologies or markets. In this respect, green limits
intersect with other powerful contemporary discourses such as around 'green
economies'. Notably, there is no necessary determinism of concept and approach
here, but several tendencies and alignments in practice have become so evident
as to be worth raising.

First, green limits discourses interlock with attempts at 'regulatory fixes'. The
two-degree climate target emerged, as already discussed, in the particular context
of international efforts to construct binding regulatory agreements to curb carbon
emissions. Lack of success over the last decade might suggest that the two-degree
target has not been particularly helpful, but more fundamentally, points to the
broader problems of regulatory fixes amid far more complex climate change politics. Despite – or perhaps because of – this experience with climate change, planetary
boundaries have been linked with arguments for a much strengthened power to

global institutions – for instance, in the notion that a 'global referee' should monitor national and local adherence to limits (Rockström *et al.*, 2009). Initiatives such as the Earth Condominium Project and Planetary Boundaries Initiative have taken this further, seeking the recognition of the 'earth system' and 'safe operating space' as legal entities that can legitimize supranational governance (Magalhães *et al.*, 2013). This is regulatory fixing and aspiration to global control at its extreme. Critics have alluded to the danger that planetary boundaries will justify a top-down power grab that will prove anti-democratic (Leach, 2013; Pielke, 2013; see also Stirling, this book).

Second, green limits align neatly with planning fixes: managerial approaches that attempt to rationalize spaces and places to meet a range of boundary-related goals. A recent example is the World Bank's landscape approach, in which areas for food, fuel, conservation and other uses are demarcated within multi-use landscapes (World Bank, 2014). We also see this in scientific and governance approaches to parcelling up, often literally from above through the use of satellite imagery and Geographic Information Systems (GIS), 'logical' places for food production, commercial cropping and biofuels. These approaches do appreciate the multiple uses of land in a world of intersecting challenges and simultaneous threats to multiple boundaries, but whose rationality prevails? Who is included and excluded from decisions and who suffers as a consequence? And what political–economic interests might apparent 'rationality' conceal? When governments and corporations arrange to put so-called 'unproductive wastelands' into large-scale cropping leases, rhetorically to maximize their sustainable use, the underlying profit motive is only barely hidden. Meanwhile, pastoralists and common property users can find themselves dispossessed in what amounts to 'green grabbing' (Fairhead *et al.*, 2012). As Stirling (this book) argues more generally, such aspirations to rational, top-down control fly in the face of the real, uncertain dynamics of social and ecological systems, and often founder where they meet diverse, contested perspectives and priorities.

Third, green limits discourses support attempted technical fixes. Large-scale technical solutions are seen as appropriate – indeed, sometimes as necessary – to meet planetary challenges at the speed and scale required. Here we see planetary boundaries discourses connecting with versions of contemporary 'green economy' advocacy focused on technoscientific green growth. In the climate change field, large-scale climate geoengineering is a classic example, with justifications for the large-scale use of carbon capture, cloud-seeding, albedo-reflecting and other technologies referring to their 'quick win' potential to keep the world within temperature limits. In the agricultural domain, green limits and technoscientific green growth discourses combine to prioritize modern agricultural biotechnologies, including genetically modified (GM), and their roll-out at scale. Such a focus on big, quick, technofixes often suits the government agencies and businesses involved in developing and promoting these. Yet their control-oriented focus may prove unrealistic in the face of the uncertain dynamics of sociotechnical and climate systems (Hulme, 2012; Stirling, this book). They may close out other technological options and pathways, perhaps more suited to diverse social and ecological contexts, and drawing on wider ranges of knowledge and innovation, including from citizens and grassroots users (see Smith and Ely, this book). Meanwhile, reliance on technofixes detracts attention from the underlying social, economic and political structures that support limits-breaching pathways, and the need to challenge and transform these.

Finally, green limits discourses increasingly support and justify market fixes. Planetary boundaries discourses are again aligning with those of the green economy to support the revaluation and trade of aspects of ecosystems now (re)defined as 'natural capital' and financialized commodities. They include schemes for trading carbon credits and offsetting emissions, associated with clean energy, forests and agriculture under the Clean Development Mechanism (CDM), United Nations collabotarive initiative on Reducing Emissions from Deforestation and forest Degradation (UN-REDD) and voluntary schemes, emerging markets for 'offsetting' species and biodiversity loss, and an array of payments for ecosystem services (PES) schemes. These are unfolding in many projects around the world, variously promoted by private, public and civil society actors, and linked with new forms of venture capital and speculation. UNEP (2011), The Economics of Ecosystems and Biodiversity (TEEB), the World Business Council for Sustainable Development (WBCSD), the International Union for Conservation of Nature (IUCN), World Wildlife Fund and The Natural Capital Project have all embraced such discourses and practices that link market-based instruments with green economies and green limits via natural capital. A financialization agenda was consolidated at the Rio+20 Summit, including several 'High Level Dialogues' hosted by the World Bank (Levidow, 2014).

While proponents often emphasize livelihood benefits (e.g. UNEP, 2011), whether these are realized in practice is highly variable. On the contrary, interventions promoted through these green discourses can often become forms of 'green grabbing' that dispossess local resource users of rights and livelihoods (Fairhead et al., 2012). Narrow financial valuation of ecosystems and landscapes overlooks alternative green meanings; look back to our tropical forest example, where carbon commodities are clearly only one among multiple ways of understanding and valuing this ecosystem. The discourse of natural capital, it can be argued, 'chops up' and individuates bits of nature, removing them from their social context (Unmüßig et al., 2012, p28). In the process, social arrangements in which people have held, valued and sustained resources, such as community-based commons arrangements, may be invisibilized and undermined (Levidow, 2014). As argued strongly by civil society actors at Rio, this green economy discourse proposes solutions to environmental crisis grounded in the same capitalist structures that produced the problems in the first place. The commoditization of nature reinforces the power of multinational corporations and financial institutions (ALAI and TNI, 2012, p11). By ignoring the structural social and political–economic conditions that shape planetary pressures, it is in a poor position to transform these towards genuinely greener futures.

Conclusions

These discursive alignments between green limits and regulatory, planning, techno-logical or market fixes are tendencies, not necessities. Others have argued, on the contrary, that planetary boundaries and other green limits ideas simply set the terms within which transformative interventions of many kinds might be pursued. Indeed, in some readings, planetary boundaries ideas – with their acknowledgement of complex system interconnectedness across scales – demand the very opposite of top-down fixes; connecting with resilience thinking, they can be mobilized to argue for polycentric, multiscale, adaptive approaches to governance that recognize and facilitate local institutions, experiences and responses (Galaz et al., 2012; Galaz, 2012). Yet the fact that the same concepts can be mobilized to argue for radically different approaches reinforces the point that there is a discursive politics in play; not just in how 'green' ideas are created, but also how they are used and by whom. Bottom-up adaptive approaches may be admissible within planetary boundaries discourses, but they are far from mainstream.

This chapter has asked a range of critical questions about how green transformations – their goals and pathways to achieve them – are defined and legitimized, locating these questions in a politics of knowledge. It has argued that powerful discourses around green limits have recently returned to prominence across science and policy, and are connecting in potent ways with discourses around green economies. These are important, highlighting and justifying the need for green transformations, and urgently and rapidly at that. Yet without denying this, on closer inspection these discourses present some serious problems. They rely on and support narrow mean-ings of 'green' that ignore large swathes of human understanding, culture, values and experience. They align too easily with top-down, control-oriented forms of inter-vention that attempt to substitute 'fixes' for required structural transformations, and can ride roughshod over people's rights and livelihoods. And by appearing as objective, necessary and universal, authorized by the best scientific and economic expertise, these discourses close out and stifle political debate – about the concepts themselves, about the goals and pathways they suggest, and about the validity of alternative forms of knowledge, experience and ways of life.

Why do these politics of knowledge matter? One could argue that they are a 'soft politics' distraction from the vital 'hard politics' that must tackle and transform the political–economic and corporate structures and interests that are leading us towards planetary disaster. Equally, it might be argued that an interest in diverse, alternative meanings of green and knowledges ushers in a dangerous relativism just when we can least afford it.

While these are dangers, however, they are not inevitable. As this chapter has argued, soft and hard are deeply connected – knowledge politics matter because they are so intimately entwined with material political economy. Appreciation of alternatives does not mean that 'anything goes' – on the contrary, some forms of knowledge and action are clearly incompatible with sustainable futures and need to be contested strongly. With these provisos, it is the discursive downplaying of alternatives that carries the greatest dangers. Seen in instrumental terms, if green approaches ignore the perspectives, values and interests of those involved, they will not be robust – they will fail to gain traction with stakeholders or be resisted. Seen in justice terms, approaches focused narrowly on singular green goals may prove undemocratic and unfair, ignoring people's rights to knowledge, identities, livelihoods and aspirations, thus denying the fundamental meanings of green that embed social justice within their definition (cf. Stirling, this book). Seen in terms of transformation, approaches that ignore alternatives may be most limited of all, either because they become fixated on 'fixes' that ignore the need for deeper transformative change, or because they presume a single green transformation where actually multiple transformations, respecting diverse identities and contexts, are required.

Fostering a plural, democratic politics of knowledge is therefore key to defining and achieving green transformations. Here, concepts like planetary boundaries and the two-degree climate change barrier, as well as particular concepts of green economy, need to be treated as means rather than ends. They should not be seen as closing down debate, but rather as boundary objects around which debate can open up: around questions such as whose boundaries and safety, whose goals, which pathways, who gains and loses, who bears costs and risks. This requires not just a polycentric and adaptive approach to politics and governance, but also a deliberative approach (e.g. Hajer and Wagenaar, 2003) that can recognize, and debate inclusively, diverse, contested goals, values and ideas of the future, and negotiate among these.

How and by whom such a deliberative politics might be fostered will vary according to scale and issue. Participation and representation of diverse social groups, including local people, in global fora around climate, biodiversity and sustainable food and energy offers one route, enabled by international agencies and often facilitated by civil society organizations. At regional and local scales – for instance, in deliberating over the futures of particular forests or food systems – collaborative approaches that bring communities, government, NGOs and sometimes business representatives together will be key. There are always dangers that 'invited' participation becomes tokenistic or co-opts participants into powerful pre-set framings of the issue. Yet awareness of the power relations that pervade deliberative exercises provides a basis to counter these in explicit design features (Leach et al., 2010). In other circumstances, it may be activism and mobilization that most effectively opens up debate and deliberation, as activist groups protest singular perspectives and highlight alternatives (see Leach and Scoones, this book).

Notions of green limits have value in this process, but we must see these concepts for what they are: as constructed by people, institutions and societies, as part of a contested politics of knowledge. Seen that way, they can become valuable foci for debate about societal and environmental futures. We should treat these meanings of green, along with alternatives, as ways to foster an inclusive, democratic and therefore transformative politics of knowledge that can and must be central to the politics of achieving green – and just – transformations.

3

INVOKING 'SCIENCE' IN DEBATES ABOUT GREEN TRANSFORMATIONS

A help or a hindrance?

Erik Millstone

The question

The question that this chapter will address is: when 'science' is invoked in debates about 'sustainability' and green transformations, is it a help or a hindrance to understanding the characteristics and consequences of unsustainable practices and transformational changes?

Introduction

Debates about the unsustainability of particular forms of resource extraction, processing, exchange, consumption and disposal arose as a consequence of scientific research into problematic changes in the conditions of our terrestrial environment. Evidence emerging from such research indicated that multiple kinds of harm were being inflicted on, for example, land, air and water, as well as on the flora and fauna (including people) that depend on those media. Without scientific research and the dissemination of its findings, we would never have known that chloro-fluorocarbons (CFCs) were damaging the earth's protective layer of ozone or that emissions of greenhouse gases are destabilizing our climates. The fact that environmental sciences are essential should not detract from a recognition that those sciences, like other forms of human enquiry, can also be profoundly problematic, epistemo-logically, culturally and politically.

The issue of the 'sustainability' and/or 'unsustainability' of prevailing practices gained traction on, and rose up, policy agendas due in part to publications like Rachael Carson's *Silent Spring* (Carson, 1962; Bouwman *et al.*, 2013). Carson's analysis was based on a careful integration of a very large number of fragments of evidence, focusing on the adverse environmental impacts of agricultural chemicals, and in particular on (what subsequently was termed) the eco-toxicity of dichlorodiphenyltrichloroethane (or DDT). Carson fully anticipated the ferocious response that came from the pesticides industry, and consequently was remarkably careful and thorough to ensure that her scholarship was of an exceptionally high standard (Anon., n.d.). According to the Natural Resources Defence Council (NRDC): 'she . . . compiled *Silent Spring* as one would a lawyer's brief, with no fewer than 55 pages of notes and a list of experts who had read and approved the manuscript' (NRDC, 2013). She propounded a powerful argument, which was explicitly based on scientific evidence in an acknowledged normative frame, for the assertion that industrialized agriculture, and especially its use of DDT and other pesticides, was causing serious harm to birdlife and other fauna.

An axis of contestation

From the start of policy debates about 'unsustainability', there have been cleavages between those who argued that achieving long-term sustainability will require radical socioeconomic transformations, as well as regulatory and technological changes, against others arguing that incremental regulatory and technological changes could be sufficient. A few have steadfastly asserted that all such problems are imaginary, but scientific evidence has repeatedly discredited such naive optimism.

Science as a (contested) tool in the contest

One of the means by which people have sought to impose their understandings of these complex debates on as wide a consensus as possible has, however, been by trying to control the agendas, conclusions and portrayals of the relevant sciences. One popular tactic among those who argue that incremental change would be sufficient to achieve 'sustainability' has been to suggest that technological changes on their own could provide adequate solutions so no major social or economic changes are required.

The publication in 1972 of *The Limits to Growth* by the Club of Rome intensified debates about the unsustainability of 'business as usual', and served to enrol wider ranges of actors and organizations into debates about (un)sustainability than had previously been the case (Meadows *et al.*, 1972). The impact of the analysis advanced by the Club of Rome was in part achieved because the report's conclusions were portrayed as if derived solely and rigorously from scientific evidence and analysis, and therefore as reliable and definitive.

The alleged rigour and reliability of the conclusions in *The Limits to Growth* were, however, contested. Freeman published an influential critique of the arguments advanced in *The Limits to Growth*, which he characterized and discounted as 'Malthus with a Computer' (Freeman, 1973). Freeman did not argue that environmental issues were unimportant, or that it was a mistake to try to develop models of the dynamics of the industrial economy in relation to global ecosystems, or to computerize them, but rather that the model produced by the Club of Rome was far too reliant on assumptions that were unacknowledged, ideologically driven and empirically unsubstantiated. Moreover, the data available as inputs to the model were a minute fraction of what the model required for reliability and precision. The authors of *Limits* subsequently acknowledged that they had only about '0.1 per cent of the data on the variables required to construct a satisfactory world model' (Freeman, 1973, p8), yet the modellers failed to explore the sensitivity of their forecasts to changes in the data or their assumptions or the equations and coefficients with which those assumptions were modelled. Instead of highlighting ranges of possibilities and uncertainties, they published relatively precise forecasts, and were shocked when their predictions were first contested and subsequently refuted.

Institutionalized policy responses

In the late 1960s and early 1970s, policy-makers responded to the growing recognition that some industrial practices were unsustainable by establishing regulatory institutions and regimes to control those practices, although there were often conflicts over whether regulations were necessary and what form they should take. A range of instruments were used such as technology standards (e.g. catalytic converters in vehicle exhaust systems and flue-gas desulphurization in coal-fired power stations) and quantitative emissions limits to, or concentrations in, for example, soil, air, water and food. More recently, economic 'market-based' instruments such as tradable emissions permits and 'carbon-pricing' have been favoured by corporations and governments. The selection of particular technologies, emissions or pollution levels has typically been justified by reference to expert scientific advice. Expert panels have often been willing to recommend, for example, maximum concentrations or doses, even in the absence of evidence of clear thresholds. A few toxicological and eco-toxicological thresholds have been measured, in respect of some identified effects, but more frequently thresholds have been presumed rather than discovered (Howard, 2003; US EPA, undated). This is important because concepts such as ecological 'boundaries' or environmental 'limits' presume that there are specific thresholds, and that they can be, and often have been, located, although they are often hard to locate and may be even be chimerical.

Policy-makers, powerful stakeholders and their chosen expert advisers developed a vocabulary of scientific-seeming concepts to refer to those standards (Gillespie *et al.*, 1979; Jasanoff, 1990; Majone, 1996). Concepts such as 'an acceptable daily intake', 'a recommended daily allowance', 'a maximum residue level', 'a maximum tolerated dose' and 'a threshold limit value' were coined and regularly invoked, initially in the USA, but subsequently in Europe and elsewhere. More recently, quantitative targets have been seen as not just attractive to, but essential for, managerialist and audit cultures.

Often particular standards were portrayed as justified by scientific evidence and analysis and as being sufficient to deliver sustainability, or at least significantly to diminish unsustainability. Leach (this book) explains in relation to the semi-official target of managing greenhouse gas concentrations to prevent average global temperatures from rising by more than two degrees Kelvin, compared to pre-industrial levels, that such targets are social constructs and political compromises, not facts of nature. Leach explains that if such numbers were recognized and acknowledged to be social constructs then:

> it might be more appropriately treated as a means: appreciating its social contestation, the two degree safety barrier might be reconsidered as a discursive concept to open up debates about legitimacy, values and uncertainty, thus creating space for and facilitating 'democratic discussion about what sort of world we want to live in'.

(Shaw, 2010)

An important feature of such concepts, which van der Sluijs has termed 'anchoring devices' is that they are often officially portrayed as if they reliably captured something like a natural constant, when they are in practice socially constructed hybrids, incorporating both scientific and policy considerations, but frequently masquerading as if purely scientific (van der Sluijs et al., 1998). As such, they can be understood as representatives of a broad category of devices that individuals and organizations use in an attempt to invoke science to exercise power, in large part by concealing the fact that they are doing so.

That normative considerations are involved can be revealed in part by scrutinizing the selection and deployment of the terminology. When quantitative figures are 'reported' as, for example, acceptable daily intakes (ADIs) or maximum tolerated dose (MTDs), judgements are invariably made about what is to be deemed 'acceptable' and 'tolerable' (JMPR, n.d.). However, what is deemed acceptable or tolerable by some individuals and organizations may well be judged intolerable and unacceptable by others. When organizations, such as the Joint Meeting on Pesticide Residues (of the World Health Organization (WHO) and Food and Agriculture Organization of the United Nations (FAO)), which are ostensibly scientific, assign quantitative ADIs or, for example, Maximum Residue Limits to particular active ingredients of pesticide formulations, they are providing hybrid science policy judgements that masquerade as if purely scientific. They are also assuming that the actions of each compound and products ingredient are independent of the actions of the others, despite empirical evidence to the contrary (Laetz et al., 2009).

A common tactic among incumbent institutions has been to invoke ostensibly authoritative narratives to try to legitimate policy decisions, and in a culture in which 'science' is widely supposed to deliver the requisite authority. While that tendency has been dominant, it has also been problematic. It is problematic for at least two reasons. First, the science relevant to many environmental issues is uncertain, equivocal and indecisive; consequently, scientific considerations on their own can never decide policies. Second, if the uncertainties could be diminished or even eradicated, scientific considerations alone could never settle policy issues. Scientific evidence and understanding will be necessary contributors to debates about enhancing sustainability, but they can never be sufficient.

The politics of uncertainty

While much of the relevant science is uncertain, it is not uniformly so; some things are known with far greater precision than others. Over the last 30 years the certainty and precision with which the toxicity of metallic lead and lead compounds has improved as a result of increasingly sensitive and thorough studies, has been remarkable (Millstone, 1997). On the other hand, estimates of the risks posed to human and environmental health from many other compounds, products and processes have become increasingly uncertain and imprecise, even though that has not been reflected in official statements or standards. The tactics used to try to control policy agendas concerning (un)sustainability include variously overstating or understating the uncertainties in ways that chime with particular interests; as Brian Wynne has pointed out, there is an important 'politics of uncertainty' (Wynne, 1992).

The persistence and contested nature of scientific uncertainties ensure that the role of expert advisers is both pivotal and problematic (Nelkin, 1984). If pertinent scientific knowledge was sufficient and reliably codified, then policy-makers and civil servants might need little more than a decent set of textbooks, but expert advisers are recruited and can be particularly influential when knowledge is incomplete; they are required not just to explain the content of the textbooks, but to provide seemingly authoritative judgements, because (supposedly) while their knowledge may be incomplete and uncertain, nobody knows better than they do.

The apparent authority of science is often invoked to portray a preferred narrative as either the only intelligible perspective or as the most reliable and authoritative perspective. Those tactics are intended to convey the impression either that 'there is no alternative' or 'we know best – trust us' (Stirling, 1998). The apparent authority of dominant perspectives can, however, often be challenged by questioning the truth, reliability or adequacy of dominant scientific narratives, and of the arguments and evidence on which they purport to rest.

Strategies and tactics used to influence agendas and decisions

A range of strategies and tactics have been adopted by organizations and individuals as they have attempted to influence agendas concerning the (un)sustainability of the status quo as well as innovative products and processes. Those agendas and the disputes that are a consequence of the perspectival diversity are typically concerned with issues such as problem identification, causal diagnoses and prescriptions.

In relation to every type of industrial or commercial sector, the first regulatory policy battle has almost always debated whether or not the sector needs to be regulated. Regulations are rarely introduced at the first evidential hint of a problem. While much of the relevant evidence is scientific, judgements about how much evidence, and of which types, are variously necessary or sufficient grounds for restricting or prohibiting industrial practices are normative policy judgements, not scientific ones. Some have argued that only causal proof of harm should be deemed sufficient grounds to 'disrupt' market transactions, while many others have argued from a precautionary perspective that industrial practices and products are almost invariably regulated in conditions of scientific uncertainty. Judgements about how much evidence should be required and how much uncertainty should be tolerated have been the focus of fierce disputes. In practice, regulatory regimes have typically been reactive rather than anticipatory.

Regulatory science: a contested domain

One common source of scientific uncertainties arises as a consequence of the fact that many putative risks are not studied directly, but explored indirectly through the use of models. Thankfully, scientists are sometimes reluctant knowingly to release a potentially harmful product in order to study directly the nature and scale of the harm it can cause. Rather than testing radioactivity or chemicals on human subjects, experiments are typically conducted using laboratory animals or bacterial and cell cultures as models of the effects on people, as well as on flora and fauna. Rather than deliberately changing concentrations of greenhouse gases, the risks of climate change are most commonly examined using computer-based models coupled to available (but incomplete) empirical data. Policy-making is complicated by the fact that we are often very uncertain about the relevance and reliability of the models that the experts develop and deploy to the conditions that they purport to model. It is not that too few models are available; rather, the problem is often to make judgements about the relative reliability of competing models, their predictions and forecasts.

Many protagonists in debates about (un)sustainability assert that they are uniquely in possession of the best science; their assertions can come in two main forms. The first alleges full scientific certainty for their perspective, while the second laments the limitations of prevailing knowledge and the extent and/or severity of scientific uncertainty. The former tactic often requires understating, or maybe even concealing, uncertainties. The latter typically involves overstating, or perhaps exaggerating, them. Both tactics have been used by protagonists on all sides, by those in governments, the corporate sector and civil society. That does not mean that everybody is always dissembling, but it does mean that ostensibly scientific assertions concerning the risks and/or benefits of industrial products and processes such as 'fracking', 'nanotechnology' or 'climate engineering' should not be taken at face value because their apparent scientificity is invariably misleading. On the contrary, questions should routinely be asked about how they were constructed from mixtures of both factual and normative considerations. The fact that they have all been constructed, using forms of hybridization, does not, however, entail that they are all uncertain, let alone that they are uniformly uncertain. Examining how they were constructed, and identifying the elements that contributed and the means by which they were hybridized, can enable scholars, policy-makers and citizens to make well-informed judgements about their relative reliability (van Zwanenberg and Millstone, 2000).

One scientific field that is characterized by profound uncertainties concerns the implications of studies using laboratory animals to try to identify the potential adverse effects of chemicals on public and environmental health. In 1984, a leading US toxicologist explained that: 'Given all the uncertainties, it may seem that the very laborious and expensive tests for assessing safety may be no better than throwing darts at a board full of numbers' (Wodicka, 1984). In the same year I asked the UK's then leading professor of toxicology what was the relevance of tests of rats and mice to humans, and his reply was the one I least expected, namely: 'Your guess is as good as mine' (pers. comm. Guildford, May 1984).

While extrapolations from models may be uncertain, estimates of the magnitude of the attendant uncertainties are rarely provided. In the late 1970s a valiant innovative attempt was made by a US National Academy of Sciences panel to estimate the upper and lower bounds of the carcinogenic risk that the artificial sweetener saccharin could pose to the US population. The panel estimated those bounds by comparing the most pessimistic interpretation of the most worrying evidence against the most optimistic interpretation of the most reassuring study. The resulting estimate was that if, on average, US residents were to continue to ingest ~120 milligrams of saccharin daily for a period of 70 years (which then corresponded to the average level of consumption in the USA) it was unlikely that fewer than 0.22 extra deaths from cancer would occur over that period, while it was unlikely that more than 1,144,000 extra deaths would occur (US NAS, 1978). In other words, estimates of the potential carcinogenicity of saccharin for humans were characterized by uncertainty of *six orders of magnitude*! A remarkable fact about that analysis has been the conspicuous reluctance of toxicology professionals or policy-makers to ever cite that conclusion or acknowledge its implications. Bizarrely, expert advisory committees in the USA, the UK, the European Commission (EC)/ European Union (EU) and at the WHO have subsequently all chosen to assign numerical values to an 'acceptable daily intake' for saccharin in the form of single point estimates, some of which were even specified to one decimal place, rather than as ranges (CEC, 1977; CEC, 1985; MAFF, 1990; WHO, 1993; US FDA, 2013). The practice of ignoring, neglecting and/or concealing uncertainties, and providing single point estimates is unfortunately widespread.

One of the reasons why expert advisers too frequently ignore and/or conceal uncertainties is because there is a 'market' for their misrepresentations. Policy-makers, such as government ministers and European Commissioners, often prefer to use their advisory committees to shield them from having to take responsibility for contestable and contested decisions. When expert advisory committees or panels highlight the existence, and even the magnitude, of policy-relevant uncertainties, policy-makers are obliged to take some responsibility for decision-making in conditions of uncertainty. If no uncertainties are acknowledged and if the expert advisers provide seemingly precise monolithic and prescriptive advice, then policy-makers only have to rubber-stamp the advice, so excusing them from taking responsibility for policy decisions. There is also often a market for such spurious precision from those interest groups that stand to benefit from the resulting policies. If there are no, or few, uncertainties attending the efficacy and safety of your products then the adoption and retention of those products will be relatively uncontroversial.

Profound uncertainties of the types discussed above create the conditions in which broad ranges of scientific assertions can be made; nonetheless, some protagonists try to maintain that they are in possession of a uniquely authoritative scientific understanding (thereby understating or even ignoring the uncertainties), while others emphasize or even exaggerate the uncertainties. The tactics adopted often reflect the interests and beliefs of the particular protagonists as well as the distinctive features of the issues at stake. Abraham has characterized the tactics often adopted by representatives of the pharmaceutical industry, when commenting on the efficacy and safety of their own products, and those of their competitors, as opportunistic and 'consistently inconsistent' (Abraham, 2008). Such practices are, however, not confined to that industrial sector.

One of the most familiar tactics adopted by incumbent authorities in both public and private sectors, when confronted by an unwelcome assertion that prevailing practices or proposed innovations may pose risks to environmental or public health, or some other ecological parameter(s), has been to claim that science has robustly established the absence of risks. Those claims have often been problematic because the relevant sciences have been too uncertain to justify such confident assertions. In many cases, not only had the science not provided sufficient evidence robustly to support such reassuring narratives, but the relevant sciences were not yet sufficiently sensitive, reliable and precise for such claims to be established.

Examples of this tactic are often encountered in the context of regulatory policy-making on some aspect of protecting environmental and/or public health, and this chapter will discuss several examples. The approach has also often entailed understating or even completely denying policy-relevant scientific uncertainties, and portraying the judgement of the official advisers as definitive, and based on the most well-informed expert judgements on the available evidence. As van Zwanenberg and Millstone have explained, that approach could most readily be deployed within closed technocratic institutional regimes (van Zwanenberg and Millstone, 2005). The advantage of a closed regime, at least to those operating within the system, is that the secrecy (or as they prefer to call it 'confidentiality') of the system serves to protect it from scrutiny, and in particular helps to conceal scientific uncertainties and contestable assumptions that guide, in particular, the selection and interpretation of evidence. Regimes of that sort prevailed in the USA prior to the passage of the 1966 and 1976 legislation of Freedom of Information, and in the UK and many other European countries until the BSE crises of the late 1990s (US Congress, 1966, 1976). In those contexts, power was exercised in part by concealing its exercise, which highlights the importance of transparency and accountability in the construction of a global 'sustainability science'.

US legislation on the freedom of information entailed that much of the scientific evidence on which policies were based entered the public domain, with the consequence that many of the uncertainties that characterized the scientific basis of policy-making could no longer be concealed. Once uncertainties became unconcealable, the tactics had to change. The most widely adopted option was to diminish the emphasis on claims that policies were based on, and only on, (sound) science in favour of a narrative asserting that policy deliberations start from value-free scientific assessments of the expected environmental impacts of technological products or processes, which are delivered to policy-makers in the form of quantitative thresholds or targets, along with estimates of such residual uncertainties as may remain. Policy-makers then decide how to achieve the targets, goals or standards that the experts had recommended. For example, scientific panels might specify figures for concepts such as a 'threshold limit value' or a 'maximum residue limit', and then policy-makers might set rules to try to ensure that those figures were not exceeded, or that they were not often exceeded.

The practice of portraying assessments of the risks and/or benefits of technologies, provided by officially appointed panels or committees of experts, as if they were entirely uncontaminated by non-scientific considerations, least of all political or economic considerations, is widespread and entirely orthodox; it is, however, invariably misleading. Representations of such putative risks and/or benefits of familiar or innovative technologies are inevitably constructed by hybridizing normative with empirical considerations. When scientists working for industrial interests are asked if they can provide sufficient data to enable their employers to negotiate their way over regulatory hurdles, they are likely to conduct different studies from those that public-interest scientists could conduct when asked to search for evidence that those products might pose some risks. Not only may those two groups conduct different kinds of studies, they can also be expected to interpret the available data in different ways and to judge them against different criteria.

In a project called *Late Lessons from Early Warnings*, the European Environment Agency (EEA) documented numerous examples in which incumbent authorities had, in the name of science, asserted the absence of environmental risks or hazards, only for evidence subsequently to emerge showing that the initial reassuring narratives had exaggerated the reliability of apparently reassuring evidence, and discounted evidence indicating problems (Gee *et al.*, 2001; EEA, 2013a). Examples included fish stocks, radioactivity, benzene, asbestos, halocarbons, diethylstilbestrol, tributyltin and vinyl chloride.

That pattern highlights a key type of policy judgement – namely, how much of which kinds of evidence are variously deemed necessary or sufficient to recommend or decide to permit, restrict or forbid some technology or practice? One of the devices that has contributed to the persistence of such flawed regimes has been the practice of discreetly leaving it to scientific advisers to decide how much evidence they deem necessary or sufficient for particular types of conclusions, and choosing as advisers those people who could be characterized, in the British cricket-derived idiom, as a 'safe pair of hands'. Those arrangements have allowed hybrid science-and-policy judgements to be misrepresented as if purely scientific. Allowing complacent policy judgements to masquerade as if purely scientific can serve to insulate those responsible for making or defending such judgements from many forms of political accountability; after all, it is (supposedly) only scientific experts who are qualified to adjudicate (Thatcher, 1999).

Incumbent authorities have often not only made misleading claims about the scientific certainty of reassurances that some alleged aspect of unsustainability is mistaken, they have also often claimed that such unsustainability problems as they have acknowledged can be addressed uniquely well with their preferred techno-logical solution. For example, claims are made that genetically modified (GM) crops technology provides a uniquely appropriate solution to chronic hunger and mal-nutrition in developing countries (Pollock, 2013; Anon., 2013a), or that nuclear power provides the uniquely optimal solution to the challenge of decarbonizing the production of electricity (HMG, 2009).

While some protagonists in debates about climate change have offered spuriously precise forecasts of changes that may be anticipated, others have been far more cautious. In its first report, the Intergovernmental Panel on Climate Change (IPCC) did not provide a single point estimate of future changes to average global surface temperatures; rather, ranges were indicated, along with mid-points of those ranges (IPCC, 1990). More recent IPCC reports have qualified the estimates of those ranges with figures indicating levels of confidence in those estimates. No protagonist offering a single point estimate of future changes of climate and/or weather would nowadays be deemed credible by those with professional expertise in climate change debates.

Debates about the safety and acceptability of GM foods and crops

Examples of such tactics and narratives have emerged in the context of the dispute between EU Member States and the European Commission on one hand and the USA on the other, about the safety and acceptability of GM crops (Millstone *et al.*, 2008). In this context, it is remarkable that the biotechnology industry endeavours to portray GM crops as a technology that could contribute to, or even be essential for a 'green transformation' (Shapiro, 1996; Borlaug, 2000). Since the late 1990s, the EU as a whole and/or several EU Member States have restricted imports of some GM products deemed acceptably safe by the US authorities, which resulted in a formal complaint to the World Trade Organization (WTO), adjudicated under the WTO Dispute Procedures. In those cases, the US authorities have argued that since their GM crop policies are based on sound science, any assessment that reaches contrary conclusions must *ipso facto* be examples of either 'bad science' or be entirely unscientific (USA, 2004).

Very similar tactics have been adopted by UK policy-makers. In 2009, a senior official in the Department for the Environment, Food and Rural Affairs (DEFRA), with responsibility for advising ministers on the assessment and approval of GM crops, insisted that UK policy was decided solely by reference to scientific criteria concerning safety, and based on and only on scientific considerations. When I suggested that criteria relating to non-scientific considerations such as economic and social factors could also contribute to policy-making, the official asserted that the policy was, and should only be, decided by reference to scientific factors – beyond that, adoption or rejection of particular products should be decided 'by the market'. When I pointed out that to be judged 'by the market' is paradigmatically an economic criterion, the official was evidently shocked (pers. comm. DEFRA, May 2009). It had never occurred to him that a market-based criterion might not be socially or politically neutral. Nor did he appreciate that the reluctance by UK and EU citizens to accept GM foods could be based on considerations that were not just about safety or transactions of exchange.

Empirical research into disputes about the regulation of GM crops, on both sides of the Atlantic, has shown that when expert advisers reach different conclusions they typically do so, not because only one side is doing good science or because they are reaching contrary interpretations of shared and agreed evidence, but because they are asking and answering different questions, and consequently gathering and analysing different bodies of evidence (Millstone *et al.*, 2008). In October 2013, the European Network of Scientists for Social and Environmental Responsibility (ENSSR) issued a statement in October 2013 entitled: 'No scientific consensus on GMO safety' (ENSSR, 2013). It stated:

> As scientists, physicians, academics, and experts from disciplines relevant to the scientific, legal, social and safety assessment aspects of genetically modified organisms (GMOs) . . . we strongly reject claims by GM seed developers and some scientists, commentators, and journalists that there is a 'scientific consensus' on GMO safety . . . and that the debate on this topic is 'over' . . . the claimed consensus on GMO safety does not exist. The claim that it does exist is misleading and misrepresents the currently available scientific evidence and the broad diversity of opinion among scientists on this issue. Moreover, the claim encourages a climate of complacency that could lead to a lack of regulatory and scientific rigour and appropriate caution, potentially endangering the health of humans, animals, and the environment. Science and society do not proceed on the basis of a constructed consensus, as current knowledge is always open to well-founded challenge and disagreement.
>
> (ibid.)

That document was a response to repeated attempts to pretend that the safety of GM crops, which had been approved by the US authorities, were consequently known for certain to be entirely safe. In the USA, Paarlberg articulated such a narrative in relation to GM foods. In *Starved for Science: How Biotechnology is Being*

Kept out of Africa, Paarlberg asserted that problems of chronic hunger and undernutrition in Africa could and should be solved by cultivating and consuming GM crops (Paarlberg, 2009). His analysis mistakenly assumed that people starve in Africa because too little food is produced, rather than because they are poor. If chronic hunger was merely a technical problem to which technology could provide a solution, it would have been solved long ago. It persists because it is a socioeconomic problem, not a technological one. An irony that Paarlberg and his allies fail to address is that under conditions of severe socioeconomic inequalities, introducing certain kinds of technological innovations can aggravate rather than diminish the underlying problems (Griffin, 1974).

Spurious uncertainties and imprecision

Just as uncertainties can be opportunistically concealed or understated, they can also be exaggerated. The range of issues, to which the tactic of exaggerating the magnitude and significance of uncertainties has been applied, is almost as broad as the range of examples of spurious certainty. One tactic has involved exploiting the ambiguity as between 'there is no proof of harm' and 'there is no evidence of harm'. Evidence is often not conclusive, from which it certainly does not follow that no relevant evidence is available. Policy judgements are invariably informed by assumptions about how much, of which kinds of evidence may be deemed variously necessary or sufficient to sustain decisions to permit, forbid or restrict some products of practices, even though such assumptions often remained implicit.

In the USA, from the 1960s until the late 1970s, for example, the Food and Drug Administration (FDA), Environmental Protection Agency (EPA) and Occupational Health and Safety Administration (OSHA) regularly deemed a compound carcinogenic on the basis of evidence from one variety of one species of laboratory animals. Following the installation of the Reagan administration, the threshold criterion was first increased to evidence from two different species, and then to two different animals species administered the test compound by relevant routes of exposure plus *in vitro* mutagenicity data (Proctor, 1995). Those changes represented political shifts in the criteria that data sets had to meet before US government agencies were allowed to categorize a compound as carcinogenic. It was not the science that changed, but the evaluative benchmarks against which the policy-makers wanted the scientific evidence to be interpreted. In those processes, scientific findings that were previously deemed reliable and sufficient were subsequently reinterpreted as insufficient (Davis, 2007).

The debate in which the greatest efforts have been made to exaggerate the magnitude and significance of scientific uncertainties has been in respect of climate change and the impact of human industrial activities on global climate and local weather. In this case, as indicated previously, there are serious uncertainties, especially when it comes to forecasting future developments, but that is no justification for exaggerating the uncertainties. To combat such exaggerations, a report was issued jointly by the US National Academy of Sciences (US NAS) and the

Royal Society of London (RSL) at the end of February 2014 (US NAS and RSL, 2014). The Foreword to that document asserted:

> It is now more certain than ever, based on many lines of evidence, that humans are changing Earth's climate. The atmosphere and oceans have warmed, accompanied by sea-level rise, a strong decline in Arctic sea ice and other climate-related changes. The evidence is clear. However, due to the nature of science, not every single detail is ever totally settled or completely certain. Nor has every pertinent question yet been answered.
>
> Scientific evidence continues to be gathered around the world, and assumptions and findings about climate change are continually analysed and tested. Some areas of active debate and ongoing research include the link between ocean heat content and the rate of warming, estimates of how much warming to expect in the future, and the connections between climate change and extreme weather events . . . [but this] . . . publication makes clear what is well established, where consensus is growing, and where there is still uncertainty.

The initiative for that report was in response to numerous occasions on which representatives of vested commercial and/or political interests have denigrated claims about anthropogenic contributions to climate change by exaggerating the uncertainties in the relevant science. Oreskes played an important role tracking such occasions in US policy debates, not just in relation to climate change but also in respect of numerous other technological policy controversies. She has documented how:

> for two decades, influential Republicans – initially in Congress and . . . in the White House – in concert with determined allies in private industry . . . have systematically denied, disparaged, and misrepresented scientific information on topics relevant to public policy. The list is long: acid rain, global warming, the efficacy of condoms in preventing the spread of sexually transmitted diseases, the health impacts of excess dietary sugar and fat . . . the status of endangered species . . . the therapeutic potential of adult stem cells, and more.
>
> (Oreskes, 2005, p75)

Oreskes and Conway have contributed by documenting some of the ways in which organizations, and especially corporate interests, have invoked doubts and substantially exaggerated policy-relevant uncertainties in this domain and more widely (Oreskes and Conway, 2010). They reviewed numerous examples of corporate and official responses to evidence that industrial products or practices may be harmful. Oreskes emphasizes that 'Some corporations whose revenues might be adversely affected by controls on carbon dioxide emissions have . . . alleged major uncertainties in the science' (Oreskes, 2004).

That pattern has been especially pronounced in the USA, and while it may be less prevalent in the UK and EU, it is far from absent (Hansard, 2014). Climate sceptics can be found in the UK government as well as in corporations. A careful reading of the four successive reports from the IPCC suggest that while it is not possible to prove beyond all possible doubt that anthropogenic emissions of greenhouse gases are destabilizing the earth's climate, the evidential base has strengthened and the conclusions of the IPCC reports have become increasingly robust, though also reported in increasingly cautious and qualified ways (IPCC, undated).

The task of definitely *proving* that anthropogenic releases of greenhouse gases are responsible for observable changes to climate and weather would require having access to a multiplicity of 'earths' upon which experiments could be performed, but that is obviously absurd. Given that such 'proof' is unobtainable, and given that the Earth is an open not a closed system, there will always be residual uncertainties about the dynamics of global climates and the impacts of human activities. The costs of failing to diminish anthropogenic climate change may nonetheless be unsustainable. If we were to wait until the uncertainties had been substantially diminished, very substantial harm may be a consequence, and by then adverse effects might be irreversible.

Conclusions

The discussion has argued that while scientific knowledge about (un)sustainable practices and technologies provides essential components for any adequate understanding of the need for green transformational changes, and of what will be required to achieve such changes, scientific knowledge can never on its own be sufficient. Moreover, selective portrayals, as well as downright misrepresentations, of what is known and what is uncertain in our understandings are being deployed to delay or prevent green transformational changes. If scientific knowledge and expertise are constructively and legitimately to contribute to green transformational changes, they can do so only if certain social, cultural and political conditions are satisfied.

The claim that 'knowledge is power' has often been attributed to both Francis Bacon and Thomas Hobbes (Bacon, 1597; Hobbes 1651). The assertion is, however, slightly misleading. It is often the case that ignorance entails powerlessness, and while knowledge might be necessary for power, it is certainly not sufficient. If scientific knowledge and expertise are to contribute to green transformations, or even just to enhance sustainability, the knowledge along with the attendant uncertainties and the exercise of expertise, all need to be in the public domain. Research has shown that power can often be exercised by controlling the creation, diffusion and portrayals of scientific evidence. Moreover, power has often been exercised in scientific-seeming deliberations in part by concealing the fact that power was being exercised, which was possible only if those deliberations were conducted secretively in closed meetings, with some or all of the evidence excluded from the public domain. Consequently, transparency is a condition for enhanced authentic legitimacy, both scientific and political, at all levels, local, national, regional and global.

In conditions of transparency, however, it will be evident not just that much of the relevant sciences are incomplete, uncertain and equivocal, but also that particular portrayals of the science, especially monolithic prescriptive portrayals, are framed by crucial non-scientific assumptions. Those assumptions will be concerned, among other questions with: What is to be counted as a benefit or as a risk? What would count as relevant evidence? And how much of which kinds of evidence can/should be deemed sufficient to license inferences to particular types of policy prescriptions? Different assumptions concerning those sorts of issues have often been the source of policy disputes. It is possible that explicit international negotiations over such framing assumptions might diminish rather than exacerbate international policy differences; we'll have to try it to find out.

Stilgoe *et al.* (2006) have argued, in relation to scientific advice to policy-makers, that there is an important difference between opening 'windows' or 'doors'. In relation to the former, citizens may watch and listen to the experts' deliberations, but cannot contribute to them – for example, by asking questions or providing information. In the latter case, they may. Transparency and genuinely open doors may therefore be essential, though they will not be sufficient.

Not only should sustainability-related, policy-relevant scientific evidence and deliberations be in the public domain, but the ways in which scientific studies have been designed, conducted, reported and interpreted need to be seen as framed by non-scientific judgements about what is important and which are the objectives to which the activities are oriented. If those framing assumptions are allowed to remain implicit, politics will still be able to masquerade as if it were scientific; but by making those framing assumptions explicit, the relationships between science and policy can be assessed and, under appropriate conditions, politically legitimated (Millstone, 2007).

If those framing assumptions, or at least the most important ones, were explicitly to be articulated by policy-makers, scholars and citizens could then have a better understanding of how competing claims and analyses have been constructed. Under those conditions they could also make well-informed judgements about the relative reliability of competing assertions about, for example, risks or benefits. In those circumstances, the chances of scientific knowledge and expertise contributing to enhanced sustainability, and even to green transformations, rather than as a hindrance to enhanced sustainability, will be increased.

4

EMANCIPATING TRANSFORMATIONS

From controlling 'the transition' to culturing plural radical progress[1]

Andy Stirling

Introduction

Are green transformations too urgent, deep and pervasive to be reliably achieved by democratic means? As suggested by the iconically influential environmentalist James Lovelock, perhaps 'it may be necessary to put democracy on hold for a while' (Hickman, 2010). Indeed, the main European Commission news website recently queried whether democracy is actually an 'enemy of nature?' (Euractive, 2010). As formally structured procedure, 'democracy' is often caricatured as an obstructive or dispensable 'luxury' (Haan and Sierman, 1996). However, perhaps history teaches instead that the *only* sure way to achieve any kind of progressive social transformation is through unruly democratic struggle. These are the questions on which this chapter will focus.

In short, the argument here will lead to a general heuristic distinction between two ideal-typical forms of radical social change. On one hand, are '*transitions*': managed under orderly control, through incumbent structures according to tightly disciplined knowledges, often emphasizing technological innovation, towards some particular known (presumptively shared) end. On the other hand, are '*transformations*', involving more diverse, emergent and unruly political alignments, more about social innovations, challenging incumbent structures, subject to incommensurable knowledges and pursuing contending (even unknown) ends. By reference to emancipatory struggles by excluded classes, ethnicities, slaves, workers, colonies, women, young people and diverse sexualities, the chapter will argue that it is repeatedly the latter that achieves the most profound (often rapid) radically progressive social changes.

So, apparent contention between different meanings and practices of sustainability and 'democracy' are not so much problems, but crucial parts of solutions. Ecological viability and social justice are not competing ends to be traded off, nor a single integrated and depoliticized 'nexus' of technical imperatives. What makes them seem this way, is the expedient shaping of knowledge (as well as action), by powerful interests. What ecological and social justice challenges actually require, is not controlled 'transitions' driven by incumbent structures, but vibrant agonistic political mobilizations towards more open-ended 'transformation'. Far from democratic struggle being an 'enemy of Nature', then, they may be each other's deepest hopes.

Nexus, necessity and nudge

A starting point lies in a growing body of science warning that the world is faced with a 'perfect storm' of environmental threats. Even if not as existential as sometimes implied for the Earth as a whole, there are grave implications for many populations, livelihoods and societies. The resulting 'nexus' of new vulnerabilities interacts with multiple prevailing forms of insecurity and injustice. As in these long-established but socially remediable patterns, it is typically the least privileged people who remain the most vulnerable.

These new scientifically framed threats are currently attracting unprecedentedly intense attention in global governance. In many ways, this exceeds the consideration afforded to older, more directly politically comprehensible vulnerabilities. The result is unusual high-level willingness to contemplate 'radical transformation' in global practices, institutions and infrastructures for the provision of food, water and energy. If the rhetorics are taken at face value, possibilities are opening up for potentially 'revolutionary' kinds and scales of change.

Such is the intensity of these developments, that leverage is potentially emerging not just for serious technical, organizational and discursive change, but for even more substantive political dislocations. Yet exactly how this leverage plays out, is open to modulation. The changes that occur may act in progressive ways, challenging concentrations of privilege and power. Or they may act more regressively, to entrench some of these incumbent patterns. Crucial here, is that it often remains rather non-specific and ambiguous what exactly will constitute these widely mooted 'green transformations' or 'transitions to sustainability'.

For instance, pressures for transformation towards zero carbon energy practices may instead be redirected towards driving a global transition to climate geoengineering. Visions inspired by distributed renewable resources may yield instead a low-carbon transition based around centralized nuclear energy. Likewise, imperatives for transformations towards ecologically sensitive forms of agriculture respecting the diverse knowledges of farmers as open source innovators in different settings may instead be harnessed towards transitions to 'sustainable intensification' strategies promoting 'monoculture' transgenic crops that maximize rents on intellectual property and global value chains.

Choices between contending institutional and infrastructural pathways like these – each variously claimed to be 'green' – are profoundly political. Yet these choices are typically discussed in much existing 'nexus' or 'green transition' literatures in rather vague and apolitical ways. It is as if the key questions are simply about whether to be 'green' or not, rather than about the radically different political alternatives that make these claims. It is in this depoliticized atmosphere that it becomes possible to pose the questions with which this chapter began – over the relevance of democratic deliberation, contention and struggle.

This increasingly disempowering style of debate is reinforced by a growing climate of 'environmental authoritarianism'. Interventions by prominent global non-governmental organizations (NGOs) help set the mood – for instance, by loudly asserting that there are 'one hundred months to save the planet' (Hulme, 2010). If they are lucky, such polemics will be forgotten before they are refuted. However, they are widely repeated. The result is to further polarize politics simply around compliance or rejection of particular apocalyptic assertions. Little space is left for more nuanced scepticism or challenge over all-important details. Crucially, this negative emphasis on uncompromising technical fears suppresses roles for democratic struggle over contending positive hopes.

Growing authoritarianism is also evident in the ways that many influential institutions in environmental governance are increasingly deprioritizing previously hard-won duties to be transparent, responsive and accountable to *citizens* and *public interests*, in favour of more covert strategies for the 'nudging' of 'users' and 'consumers'. Public, private and civil society organizations alike seem ever more preoccupied with controlling and explaining their prior established ends and means, rather than listening or adapting to criticism. Risk is repeatedly interpreted in terms of reputation. Trust is addressed overwhelmingly as an appropriate response by the powerless in favour of the powerful, rather than the other way around.

Behind this, the roots of environmental challenges are increasingly located in the 'behaviour' of ordinary people, rather than in the powerful vested interests that so actively constrain and condition associated growing individualism, consumerism and materialism. The diagnosis increasingly moves away from explicitly political struggle, towards more apparently technical and psychologistic 'behaviour management'. By emphasizing the centrality of supposedly undifferentiated hardwired 'human nature', appreciation is attenuated for critical argument and democratic struggle. Attention is drawn even further away from the potential for progressive political action to challenge particular incumbent interests. In this 'end of history' illusion, the contrasting environmental and justice implications are lost, even of relatively proximate 'varieties of capitalism'. Conflated into seemingly amorphous depoliticized inevitability, the prospect for more diverse, creative and progressive forms of social transformation are rendered even less imaginable.

The implicit expectation seems to be that the powers doing all the nudging and controlling will somehow be kept benign simply by the manifest gravity of the professed rationales. The more assertive and apocalyptic the envisaged threat, the more desperately necessary this expectation. Yet neither history nor current affairs suggest any guarantee that such expectations will be delivered. Many historic examples can be found, where ostensibly progressive efforts at social transformation actually reproduced familiar kinds of concentrated power structures in new forms, often more entrenched (Arendt, 1963; Skocpol, 1979). When power finds itself credibly able to invoke overriding missions to control (especially under a climate of fear), the results can be even less positive. The disarming effects of superficial appearances can make the dangers especially acute where initial motivations appear progressive.

The world is a complex place and care should be taken with overly simplistic analogies, but there do seem to be many grounds for more careful scrutiny of environmental authoritarianism. The greater the genuine respect for ecological imperatives, the greater this responsibility.

Anthropocene planetary domination

These authoritarian pressures are also reflected in scientific discourse. Here, even geological history is subject to reinterpretations emphasizing the theme of control. For instance, the established epoch of the Holocene is a tiny 11,700-year span, oddly tacked on to the end of the preceding 1.6 million-year Pleistocene epoch. Marking the point where Earth moved out of the last of a long series of glaciations, there is little to distinguish the Holocene from previous Pleistocene interglacials, such as to justify a new scientifically recognized epoch. The sustaining of relative climate stability over such brief periods is not geologically unique. That all previous epochs extend to many tens of millions of years compounds the anomaly. It seems that general scientific considerations are trumped by more parochial anthropo-centric excitement, for it is in the Holocene that specifically human activity greatly intensifies.

The relevance of this to control arises because the subjective human excep-tionalism that helps shape this scientific acceptance of an anomalously tiny Holocene epoch is now being compounded by recent moves to add a further even more eccentrically miniscule 'Anthropocene' epoch of just a few hundred years' duration. Crucially, this is defined explicitly by reference to notional 'human control' – even 'domination' (Vitousek et al., 1997; Crutzen and Schwägerl, 2011; Steffen et al., 2011) – variously of 'Earth's ecosystems' (Vitousek et al., 1997) or wider 'biological, chemical and geological processes' (Crutzen and Schwägerl, 2011). And, as in environmental authoritarianism, these conditions of control are ubiquitously associated with an undifferentiated human 'we'.

Given that 'human control' is already held to be so diagnostic of the Anthropocene, it is paradoxical that much of this literature also calls urgently 'for identification of mechanisms amenable to human control' (Ehlers and Krafft, 2006). If such mechanisms have not yet even been identified, one wonders how current 'control' is already exercised? And why, if 'control' is so negative in retro-spect, should it be seen so optimistically in prospect (Lövbrand et al., 2009)? In a similar way to the 'crisis of capitalism' in Marxism, or ideas of grace in Christian theology, a paradoxical conjunction appears here of described actuality with prescribed urgency. It seems that the Anthropocene is framed from the outset as much as a normative doctrine as a scientific analysis.

This leads to a further telling feature of 'the Anthropocene'. As with 'the Nexus' more widely, it is clear that the aggregate environmental impacts of diverse global economies are truly devastating. However, for humans to exert *unintended impacts* is very different from exercising *collectively intentional control*. Indeed, some Anthropocene literature does acknowledge that even 'self-control of mankind' remains a speculative scenario (Faroult, 2009). Serious wider questions are raised not only over what is meant by control, but who is doing it, how it is supposedly enacted and on exactly what systems. After all, when has humanity as a whole even undertaken – let alone controlled, still less achieved – any single explicitly and collectively deliberate end?

Perhaps the confusion might be alleviated by redefining the problematic Anthropocene concept in terms of human *impacts*, rather than notional human 'control', or substituting it with a similarly more careful definition of the Holocene? There is anyhow a case for tracing global-scale human impacts back to the very early Holocene (Zimov *et al.*, 2011). And the difference between a starting point a few hundred and a few thousand years ago is well below the chronological resolution for comparable geological epochs. That this rather obvious course has not been adopted confirms that 'Anthropocene' discourse is fulfilling a rather particular political function. Crucially, this new category moves beyond the implicit subjective acknowledgement of human impacts to a direct (ostensibly objective) assertion of human 'control'.

To be fair, a growing 'Earth systems governance' literature (Biermann, 2007) is often more qualified in its treatment of notions of 'Anthropocene' control, referring instead to apparently less deterministic notions of 'governance' and 'stewardship' (Chapin *et al.*, 2011). However, substitution of more nuanced terms does little to reduce the substantive tensions. 'Governance' is still frequently addressed in terms of integrated knowledge, formal procedures, coercive instruments and individualistic leadership. And, implying 'control in absence of overarching authority', even 'stewardship' is arguably not so much about diminished control, as diminished accountability (Anon., 2013b).

What remains under-addressed is the general paradox that the more intensely desired the control, the greater the necessity to comply with conditions for tractability. Even an engineered artefact works only if designed in accordance with inherent material constraints and propensities. No matter how much a governance model might emphasize 'polycentric' coordination (Biermann *et al.*, 2012b) (rather than top-down hierarchy), then, if it remains subordinated to a particular agency and ends, then the process is equally about control. And there are few more effective means to assert iniquitous managerial control invisibly than by rhetorics of equal collaboration. So, superficial shifts in terminology do little to alter the substantive dynamics.

It is here that preoccupations with 'planetary boundaries' further illuminate Anthropocene narratives (UN, 2013). These define the 'safe operating space' within which global governance must strive to navigate a path (Rockström et al., 2009). Despite resting on the supposed indeterminacy of 'catastrophic tipping points' (Hoff and Rockström, 2013), planetary boundaries are routinely asserted as determinate and precisely known (Rockström et al., 2009). Indeed, they are typically presented as 'non-negotiable' imperatives, raising 'absolutely no uncertainty' and brooking 'no compromise' (Rockström, 2010). It is on this basis that 'manuals' are issued (Newton, 1998) for taking charge of the 'control variables of the Earth' (Rockström et al., 2009) and so achieving not just governance in the loosely coordinated sense, but unprecedentedly ambitious forms of 'planetary management' (Faroult, 2009). Presumptions of undifferentiated controlling agency are reinforced. Ends are further subordinated to means. The discursive constraints on space for democratic struggle seem more restrictive even than the material boundaries.

It is by appreciating this discursive dimension that the paradox may be reconciled that 'control' is viewed retrospectively as negative, but prospectively as positive, for – as in the other political and religious doctrines mentioned above – this is how a retrospective diagnosis of 'planetary domination' can be recruited seamlessly into a narrative prescribing prospective 'planetary management'. Of course, such pre-laden politicized implications are not unique to Earth systems governance. Other areas of policy-relevant science and 'global assessment' are also widely recognized to be similarly shaped by the cultural conditions under which they are produced (Scoones, 2009). The Anthropocene narrative is just one particularly acute instance of a general pattern that emerges when knowledge itself is recognized as political.

So, it is not as if such dynamics are entirely avoidable, nor do they somehow necessarily render the implicated science thereby invalid. In no way do these political dynamics in the presentation and interpretation of contemporary Earth science detract from the need to question very seriously contemporary economic and technological trajectories. Indeed, it is precisely where imperatives for political transformation are taken most seriously that the lesson takes a different form. In short, science for policy holds responsibilities not only to be accurately reflective of the objective systems it is concerned to represent. It is at least equally obliged to be reflexive about the ways these representations are conditioned by subjective systems in which 'the science' is produced. Without this, there are dangers that Anthropocene rhetorics of uncompromising leadership, non-negotiability, certainty and control will be taken much too literally. Planetary management should be careful what it wishes for.

Democracy, sustainability and emancipation

So what of the queries with which this chapter began? Is democracy really an 'enemy' of transformations towards sustainability – a 'luxury' that should be 'put on hold'? Or is it rather sustainability that is vulnerable to longstanding powerful forces that find associated transformative emancipations so threatening? If so, maybe the real questions are about whether authoritarian appropriations by incumbent interests, can make environmentalism itself an 'enemy' of the very forms of democratic struggle that it gave rise to?

In the above spirit of reflexivity, these queries require careful thought about the forces and conditions under which the answers themselves are shaped. And this is as true of general talk of 'democracy' and 'sustainability' as of more specific concepts like 'the nexus', 'the Anthropocene' or 'planetary boundaries'. In all these areas, understandings supposedly *informing* practice are typically at least as much *formed* by it. In other words, knowing and doing are not so much distinct as inseparable – especially when it comes to transformation.

One crucial initial reflection, then, concerns how to interpret 'democracy'. It is easy for loose usage to be misunderstood, appropriated – or strategically subverted – by specific traditions, institutions or interests (Agamben *et al.*, 2011). Any wider understanding of democracy wishing to transcend such parochialisms (Li, 1997; Sen, 2005; Leib and He, 2006) must relate at root to the general dynamics of power, as featured prominently in the discussion so far. Here, the implications are as profound for knowledge and discourse as for material practice.

In short, despite the plural, multidimensional and multiscale faces of power, a constant common element shared across many different historical and cultural settings is that power is about 'asymmetrically structured agency' (Stirling, 2014c). Social norms, institutions and discourses concentrate diverse flows and experiences of social agency in greatly varying ways. As a reaction to this, 'democracy' in the broadest of senses can be seen not as any formal procedural end-state, but as a complex, distributed never-ending *struggle*, for 'access by the least powerful, to the capacities for challenging power' (Stirling, 2014c). Although the dynamics of power doom any such success to be constantly provisional, the greater this access and the stronger the capacities for challenge, the more effective the democratic struggle might be judged.

Far from being in tension, then, this characterization of democracy as struggle displays especially strong affinities with sustainability. Sustainability historically came about through democratic struggle and remains formally defined by reference to it (Brundtland, 1987). After all, sustainability was not elevated to the present highest levels of global governance by the kinds of integrated, polite, orderly apolitical procedures currently highlighted in elite planetary management literatures. Just as in other transformative processes of democratic struggle for the emancipation of classes, ethnicities, slaves, workers, colonies, women, young people and diverse sexualities, this occurred through diverse, protracted, radically challenging and overtly political agonistic struggles by subaltern social movements (Mouffe, 1999).

Take, for instance the development of issues around occupational hazards, resource degradation, consumer chemicals, ionizing radiation, atmospheric pollution, water contamination and climate change (Gee *et al.*, 2001; EEA, 2013b). All were typically pioneered by subaltern communities of workers or affected people, then picked up by social movements. In each case, it was recognition of uncertainties that advanced progressive causes, not assertions of 'uncompromising', 'non-negotiable' certainties. Indeed, these imperatives were at each stage strongly contested by precisely the authoritarian language now used by the kinds of mainstream science and high-level governance institutions, which currently profess to champion sustainability as 'planetary management'.

The same is typically true not only of the problems highlighted by sustainability concerns, but also of the prescriptions. Innovations such as wind turbines, ecological farming, super-efficient buildings and green chemistry all owed their pioneering origins and early development to subaltern social movements (Smith et al., 2013). All were systematically marginalized, if not actively suppressed, by incumbent interests in science, government and industry. These transformative responses were nurtured not by controlling management, but by adversarial struggle. That so many of these innovations have now become central elements in prospective transformations to sustainability is despite, rather than because of 'sound scientific', 'evidence-based' elite policy discourse.

It was for all these reasons that early visions of sustainability went beyond merely highlighting environment and social justice as outcomes. Increasingly forgotten nowadays is that the Brundtland Commission, for instance, also made direct reference to the agonistic processes through which these ends are best pursued. For Brundtland, the entire sustainability vision was about achieving 'greater democracy' (26: 16) through 'effective citizen participation' (26: 58). This was picked up and strongly developed in the subsequent Agenda 21 programme. However, this theme of democratic struggle has become increasingly subordinated to local level implementation. Contemporary instruments like the Millennium Development Goals (MDGs) also sideline this crucial process of agonistic struggle, amidst the clamouring instrumental concerns with metrics and outcomes (Griggs et al., 2012).

In conclusion, the links between democracy and sustainability are not just contingent. At root, both are driven by, and towards, emancipation. And this is as true of knowledge and discourse as of material practice. It is in this light that it looks most dissonant, that contemporary high-profile debates about 'sustainability transitions' should display such increasing preoccupations with contradictory attributes like 'certainty', 'leadership' and 'control'. It seems that the greatest need is to emancipate understandings of transformation itself.

From transition to transformation

So much for the background in the general history and practice of sustainability, but what has all this got to do with particular real-world prospective 'sustainability transitions' on the ground? Even if the above account is right, does it really matter that environmental authoritarianism tends to emphasize control over accountability? What is the harm in a little over-egging of notions of Anthropocene 'planetary domination'? Might not a measure of over-assertiveness concerning the certainty and non-negotiability of planetary boundaries at least help galvanize attention? As has been emphasized, it is not as if existing efforts have hitherto been so conspicuously successful.

The thrust of all the previously raised concerns is not to belittle the gravity or urgency of the current nexus of imperatives around social justice and ecological disruption. The crucial challenge is not *whether* to achieve the necessary radical technological, political, economic and cultural changes, but *how*? Here, though, particular care needs to be taken in the light of the preceding discussion, because the shaping effects of incumbent power act on knowledge and discourse as well as on more material structures. This means that neither words nor actions may always be what they seem, sometimes even entailing their apparent opposites. It also means that interventions expressly and sincerely motivated by progressive interests (in the senses defined here by reference to power and democratic struggle) may nonetheless sometimes end up being regressively counterproductive in their effects. Analysis and action must get below expedient surfaces.

This is where there arises the importance of the distinction touched on in the Introduction – between 'transition' and 'transformation'. Transitions, it may be recalled, are managed under orderly control, through incumbent structures according to tightly disciplined technical knowledges and innovations, towards a particular known (presumptively shared) end. This typically emphasizes integrated multidisciplinary science directed at processes of instrumental management through formal procedures in hierarchical organizations sponsored by the convening power of government. Transformations, on the other hand, involve more diverse, emergent and unruly political alignments, challenging incumbent structures, subject to incommensurable, tacit and embodied social knowledges and innovations pursuing contending (even unknown) ends. Here there is a much stronger role for subaltern interests, social movements and civil society, conditioning in ambiguous and less visible ways the broader normative and cultural climates in which more explicitly structured procedures are set.

Of course, the utility of this distinction is heuristic (provocative and catalytic), rather than formal or definitive. The real value lies in considering implications on a concrete case-by-case basis, by reference to real-world examples and settings. Crucial devils will lie in details and positive or negative evaluations in the eyes of beholders. And the point here is not to insist on particular definitions for specific words. It is the implications of the ideas that matter. The contrast between transition and transformation is also not a dichotomy, because both real- world dynamics and salient models will typically lie somewhere in between, and the two concepts are not mutually exclusive – there are several ways in which each dynamic depends on (and is partly constituted by) the other. The central point is rather that if the distinction is not made (by whatever names), then governance knowledges and discourses (as well as practices) in any given sector are vulnerable to systematic subversion by incumbent interests to channel more around expediently controlled transition than inconveniently emergent transformation.

Explored more thoroughly elsewhere (Stirling, 2014a and b), there is sadly not the space here to develop examples in the desirable detail. However, the point is nonetheless readily made by considering the radical implications of 'transformations', potentially displayed, for instance, by ecological agriculture, zero carbon energy futures in general and renewable energy in particular. As already touched on, these can be contrasted with characteristics of 'transitions' towards 'sustainable intensification' based on agricultural transgenics, or nuclear power (or even climate geo-engineering) as large-scale responses to climate change. These latter transitions are typically propounded by powerful incumbent interests within existing sectoral regimes. The former possible transformations reflect knowledges, values and interests that are more marginal to the current constituting of these regimes. Characterized, then, as a contrast between orientations for radical change driven alternatively by powerful incumbent or relatively disempowered subaltern interests, it is only the latter kinds of transformation that depend on clear roles for democratic struggle that are worthy of the understanding adopted here.

More fine-grain features of this contrast between 'transformation' and 'transition' can be illuminated by considering in more detail the much-proclaimed global 'renaissance' in nuclear power (Nuttall, 2005; Toke, 2013). Of course, when consideration is given to the actual patterns of investment and their relation to other energy technologies, the objective reality of a global nuclear renaissance is rather dubious, but the success of this rhetoric is unquestionable. Promulgated at the highest political levels and by scientific authorities ostensibly unrelated to nuclear supply chains, the effect is to condition wider knowledges and expectations in powerful ways. The result in many countries is that political pressures for green transformations in the energy sector, originally driven largely by public concerns over nuclear power and sympathy for renewable energy transformations, are in fact systematically channelled by apolitical 'management' discourse into transitions more towards nuclear power (Stirling, 2014c).

Of course, general claims that nuclear power is 'green' or 'sustainable' remain strongly criticized in any sense other than low operational carbon emissions. Nuclear waste, weapons proliferation and accident risks – and their associated authoritarian control structures – have long made nuclear an iconic target of the green movement (Dorfman, 2008). The Brundtland Commission and follow-on intergovernmental processes also generally treat this technology with suspicion, so the language of 'sustainability transitions' is typically not used directly of nuclear power. Although displaying many key diagnostic features of a controlled 'transition' outlined here, initiatives explicitly identified as 'transition management' in the energy sector are typically linked with more popular renewable technologies. However, it is precisely the central point here that it is the attributes of power dynamics in knowledges and practices constituting 'transition' (by contrast with 'transformation') that lead nuclear power in many countries to be the perverse beneficiary of authoritarian inflections of decades of subaltern pressures that were typically formatively forged disproportionately in opposition to nuclear power.

Further revealing examples of similar dynamics can be found in emerging global governance of climate change – arguably (as documented elsewhere in this book) the principal high-level arena within which issues of 'green transformation' are currently played out. Key issues arise most acutely in the concluding paragraphs of the recent summary for 'policy-makers' by the Intergovernmental Panel on Climate Change (IPCC, 2013). That such an influential body chose (tentatively, but nonetheless momentously) to highlight a possible transition involving the diverse technologies of 'climate geoengineering' indicates the depth of the dissonance and contradiction. So important is this for understanding the contrast being drawn here that it is worth briefly recalling the magnitude of this disjuncture.

A 'progressive' global transformation towards zero carbon energy would harness diverse proven viable renewable resources and innovations to deliver energy services at the same time as eliminating carbon emissions and realizing other sustainability benefits. Although the challenges of such transformations are undoubtedly ambitious and daunting, it is clear that there exists a diversity of possible pathways through which to address them. The obstacles to an entirely renewable global energy system are not – as often claimed – about intrinsic limits on resources, technologies or economics. Repeated detailed assessments show that the energy service needs of a more heavily populated and equitable world enjoying radically higher levels of well-being, can be cost-effectively met, entirely and solely through diverse currently available technological and organizational innovations around wind, solar, biomass, hydro, ocean and geothermal power (PwC, 2010; GEA, 2012; IPCC, 2012).

However, the climate geoengineering alternative raised by the IPCC (IPCC, 2013), by contrast, would use an array of speculative technologies and unprecedented global institutions aimed solely at assuming human 'control' over the planetary climate (Shepherd et al., 2009; Fleming, 2010; Ridgwell et al., 2012; Ruddiman, 2005). Although requiring economic and political investment on a scale similar to that required for direct transformation of energy infrastructures, most forms of climate geoengineering would leave energy needs entirely unaddressed (Morgan and Ricke, 2009; Bracmort and Lattanzio, 2013). And it is this manifestly more speculative alternative that is gaining strikingly increasing high-level worldwide attention beyond the IPCC as well. That a regressive transition built around climate geoengineering is asserted in some quarters to present a somehow more tractable governance challenge to a progressive transformation based on renewable energy is an indication not only of the strength of entrenched vested interests in this sector, but of their impact on wider structures, knowledges and expectations.

These examples illuminate a general factor of enormous importance for considering these contrasting dynamics of transition and transformation: the 'fallacy of control' (Cunha et al., 1999). This can be found in various areas of psychology, organizational studies and politics, where simple deterministic pictures of control are all variously problematic. They are often better understood more as instrumental fictions necessary for the assertion of privilege than as disinterested accounts of actuality (Aldrich and Pfeffer, 1976; Krackhardt, 1990; Thornton *et al.*, 1999; Mintzberg and Waters, 2009). When stripped of this expediency, any real-world instance of 'control' decomposes (in the same ways discussed earlier with respect to the Anthropocene) into complex conditions of diverse mutually adapting intentionalities and (in)tractabilities. As in that example, the possibilities of many alternative accountings for causality among proliferating multitudes of nested implicated factors leaves any particular tracing of 'control' in any given instance significantly in the eye of the beholder (Power, 2000). And this is at least as true in wider governance, as it is within organizations (Pfeffer, 1992; Parry *et al.*, 1997).

In energy pathways, agricultural futures and climate change strategies (as elsewhere), care must be taken that analysis of social dynamics does not – under instrumental pressure of patronage to 'see like a state' (Scott, 1998) some particular favoured 'transition' – simply entrench and perpetuate these misleading fallacies of control. As the examples above suggest, such self-reinforcing channelling by incumbency can all too easily lead to the opposite of the envisaged transformation. Crucially, this applies as much when contemplating the exercise of nominally democratic, as of autocratic, power in 'social control'. The difference lies not in the notional source of legitimacy, but in the nature of 'control' itself. In other words, even in the constituting of the concepts themselves, incumbency has a habit of subverting the deepest understandings of what human 'agency' is all about.

For interests committed to achieving substantively radical transformation rather than expediently aligned transition, then, political creativity and effort are perhaps better invested instead in the diverse, unruly, agonistic interventions that are suppressed by structures and discourses of control (and which they themselves subvert). And since knowledge and action are not as separate and sequential as prescribed in this same expedient fiction of control, truly transformative interventions are better seen as combining both. Freed from such instrumental mythologies, then, the formative energy of these 'knowing doings' lies not in their purported direct controlling force, but in the combined effects with their wider reflexive social reactions.

Drawn from underdocumented repertoires of subaltern movements, examples of such potentially transformative 'knowing doings' might include 'Trojan horses' (Stirling, 2011). This is where an exercise in subaltern policy analysis or political action which ostensibly takes one form, actually exerts its effects in entirely different ways. Or – learning from past experience of insurgent struggle – there are various forms of 'political judo' (Popkin, 1970), where it is the very strength of incumbency that offers the principal opportunity for less powerful actors to successfully contend against it. Also relevant is the potential for the 'civilising effects of hypocrisy' (Elster, 1995). This is where incumbent power is conditioned reluctantly to reorient itself in new directions by the incremental ratcheting of tensions between discourse and practice.

Now is not the place to detail these kinds of distributed political moves. The point is that just as 'deflection by walls' differs from 'steering by compasses', these kinds of 'knowing doings' are not subject to the controlling force of a coordinated transition. Instead, they involve more emergent distributed realignments around diverse, but spontaneously shared aims. The parallels between ecology and society strike another chord, for the transformative results quite closely resemble the exquisitely abrupt shifts in direction arising in the autonomous and internally directed flocking behaviours observable in many animals.

Similar patterns are arguably visible in culture change, where comparably radical alterations of direction can occur without any overarching framework (either of codified knowledge or structured action) simply by emergent coordination. Indeed, this is arguably more characteristic of crucial dynamics in the most impressively progressive of historical transformations also mentioned in this chapter – in struggles for emancipating excluded classes, ethnicities, slaves, workers, colonies, women, young people and diverse sexualities. Recognizing that such processes are more like the dynamics of grassroots culture than high policy – and more active than determined – the processes of transformation envisioned here might be thought of more as the 'culturing' than the controlling of radical social change.

Conclusions

This chapter took its cue from growing tendencies for high-profile actors in sustainability governance debates to question (not only implicitly) the value of democratic struggle. With unfeasibly short periods to 'save the planet', participation is seen as a threat. Acknowledging any uncertainty is a weakness. Scepticism is a pathology, dissent an unaffordable 'luxury'. Responsibility is increasingly externalized away from particular political and economic structures and towards 'human behaviour' in general – or humanity in an undifferentiated sense. Emphasizing multiple kinds of catastrophe, there is a suggestion 'to put democracy on hold'.

This chimes with emerging scientific discourses that emphasize and assert the need for various kinds of domination and control. The Anthropocene is expressly defined in these terms. Associated planetary boundaries are described as the 'control variables' of the Earth. This is a world of 'non-negotiable' imperatives, raising 'absolutely no uncertainty', brooking 'no compromise' and requiring strong leadership. Governance is addressed not as a political process, but as a more instrumental procedure for 'planetary management' . . . 'taking control of Nature's realm'. Democracy, in this light, can become the 'enemy of nature'.

However, this emerging picture is strikingly at odds with the realities of sustainability and the progressive social dynamics that gave rise to it. Both in its prioritized outcomes and its constituting processes, sustainability has always been centrally about democratic struggle. And though the two are mutually conditioning, this is more about rudely unruly political contention *against* power than the kinds of power-driven (and -constrained) 'integrated knowledges', 'invited engagements' and polite policy etiquettes of 'planetary management'. Just as it was arguably only in agonistic contention by social movements that high-level recognition of environmental and social justice imperatives ever came about, so too is this the best hope for sustaining them towards their promised aims.

It is this crucial lesson that current planetary management initiatives are most in danger of forgetting. Without it, there is a serious vulnerability to 'fallacies of control'. These exaggerate the efficacy of intentionally structured determinism, not because it is particularly effective in achieving radical social change, but because the idea merely helps sustain existing patterns of privilege. The prevalence of this fallacy is thus a particular example of how knowledge not only informs power, but is profoundly shaped by it. If aspirations to radical social change are to have real prospects for success, actions must be as transformative of these regressive patterns in knowledge as of more material relations.

Perhaps transformation is better understood in terms of mutual relations of 'care' than of dominating 'control' (Bowden, 1997; Cluff and Binstock, 2001; Noddings, 2002; Frankfurt, 2004; Pellizzoni, 2004; Hagedorn, 2013). Deliberately enacted this way, the 'knowing doing' of care can transcend the context-free absolutes, assertive dualisms and idealized subjugations of control (Gilligan and Richards, 2009) − of neatly subordinated subjects over objects; relations after categories; actions based on knowledge; effects determined by causes; ends driving means; structure over agency (Held, 2005; Slote, 2007). The obdurate realities of the world remain. However, in its rebalancing of relations between subjects and objects of practice, a caring approach accommodates better than control the ways in which transformative understandings and actualities are symmetrically co-produced with action (Felt *et al.*, 2013).

The knowing and doing of transformation are thus not separate, but intimately interlinked. Neither alone is sufficient. As in the exquisite changes of direction seen in flocking behaviours in nature, real social transformation is arguably only truly achieved through a dynamic of diversity, creativity and democratic struggle − equally in knowledge and action. Radical social change is therefore not about controlled structures in knowing and doing, but about fractal patterns of 'political judo', Trojan horses' and 'civilizing hypocrisies' in turbulent flows of 'knowing doings'. Transformation is not achieved by deterministic structurings of social control, but by counterpointing these with the subversive mutualities of care, yielding more distributed *culturings* of radical change.

Where instead sustainability is addressed as a determinate technical end, rather than as an emancipatory process for determining plural human and ecological ends, it betrays its own foundations. Hope for genuinely progressive 'green transforma-tions' are not about fear-driven technical compliance, but hope-inspired democratic choice. This is the challenge of 'emancipating transformation'.

Note

1   A longer, fully referenced version is available at: http://steps-centre.org/wp-content/uploads/Transformations.pdf, accessed 2 July 2014.

5

THE POLITICS OF GREEN TRANSFORMATIONS IN CAPITALISM

Peter Newell

Introduction: from transitions to transformation

> The 'Great transformation' – the ecological conversion of industrial societies into a climate compatible, resource-conserving and sustainable world economic order, requires far-reaching and manifold tasks to shape it, which, in their make-up, are neither purely scientific and technological nor purely social or political. The transformation process should lead to just and sustainable governance over the use and management of global, regional and local commons.
>
> (Heinrich Böll Foundation, 2013)

Talk of great transformations is back in vogue. Though in some circles it never went away, of course, human-induced climate change, in particular, is at the epicentre of renewed attention to the need for (another) 'great transformation' amid calls for a new, or third, 'low carbon' industrial revolution, new models of 'green growth' (NEF, 2010; UNEP, 2011; OECD, 2011) or a 'green deal' (Lipietz, 2013). The point of departure for such calls is the requirement for disruptive change in the form of radical reductions in emissions and large-scale technological breakthroughs as part of the pressing need for transition to a low- carbon economy (WBGU, 2011; Heinrich Böll Foundation, 2013). For this reason there is increasing interest in historical precedents of deliberate, large-scale orchestrated change in the face of crisis (of the sort called for in the quote above), of when concrete strategies for moving from one sociotechnical system and set of practices to another have been successfully deployed that might offer relevant parallels to grappling with the contemporary climate crisis.

It is around this twin sense of transformation both as historical process and contemporary challenge that this chapter seeks to enlighten current discussions about the politics and possibilities of change with historical lessons about how, when and why such change has taken place previously. It does so by situating contemporary debates about transitions to a 'green economy' within a broader historical context of change within global capitalism. In particular, it offers some reflections on what previous reorganizations in production and technology reveal about how, when, why and for whom transformations occur under capitalism and what this suggests about the prospects of today's attempts to restructure the global economy along low-carbon lines.

The world is not short of initiatives that claim to be pursuing such a goal (Hoffman, 2011; Bulkeley *et al.*, 2012). However, despite rhetorical embracing of the concept of green transformations by governments, businesses and international organizations, applied analysis of what a dramatic shift in the structures of production and consumption would imply for alignments of political and economic power that will be required to achieve and sustain a low-carbon economy is sorely lacking. The premise of this chapter, then, is that much of the policy debate so far, as well as existing academic scholarship on these questions, has understandably focused more on the governance of transitions than the politics of transformation (Loorbach, 2007; Scarse and Smith, 2009; Verbong and Loorbach, 2012). Interestingly, other literatures on different kinds of transitions place politics and system change more centrally. In political science work on democratization, 'transitions' refers to wholescale upheaval or even revolutions in a political system and mode of governing society, and the development industry often talks about 'economies in transition', meaning the wholescale reorganization of socialist economies along capitalist lines, while for many Marxist scholars 'the transition debate' is about the transition from feudalism to capitalism (Wood, 2002). The point, however, is that current debates about green transformation adopt a more apolitical reading of what is at stake. They have failed to adequately analyse either the role of social forces in *how* change occurs in contemporary capitalism or to provide a fuller political analysis of historical precedents about the politics of *when* organized large-scale sociotechnical and economic change has occurred in the past (albeit in pursuit of very different ends) and *what lessons* might be deduced for our current predicament. It is precisely such a framework for political and historical analysis of 'green transformations' that is proposed here.

I draw on work within different strands of political economy literature to develop an understanding of the politics of green transformations and the relations of power which enable and frustrate change. This approach is used to highlight the importance of the following social forces in the politics of green transformations.

First, competition between different *fractions of capital*[1] and their reliance on particular types of energy for the success of their accumulation strategies (Newell and Paterson, 1998). This builds on the idea that a key challenge of enabling green transformations is to assemble 'coalitions of the winning and the willing': of actors, including powerful fractions of capital, that will materially benefit from a new wave of low-carbon growth and which compete to promote their role in enabling such growth (Newell and Paterson, 2010). Put more bluntly, someone has to win (or believe they can win) in capitalism for change to be realized and working out who this is likely to be and how they can be mobilized for lower carbon trans-formations is a key task.

Second, the historically central *role of labour* in struggles to constantly 'revolu-tionalize the means of production'. While the power of labour movements has been reduced in a globalized economy, the potential of green transformations to threaten or create employment is a key battleground and will significantly affect their chances of state and public support as the examples below illustrate.

Third, *the state* has a key role to play in enabling or frustrating transformations as historical and contemporary evidence shows clearly (Mazzucato, 2011). This is true not just in terms of supporting innovation and 'picking winners', but also mediating the above struggles and conflicts between fractions of capital and between capital and labour. The state also plays a central role in shaping and being shaped by global institutions which potentially circumscribe (or globalize) their control over energy (politics) through interventions in power sector reform and liberalization processes (Tellam, 2000; Cho and Dubash, 2005).

Fourth, the *role of finance* in enabling technological revolutions and unsettling incumbent regimes, in particular from the Industrial Revolution onwards (Perez, 2002). Given the heightened power of finance capital in the current phase of capitalism, a key strategic challenge is whether and how this power might be har-nessed to the goal of green, in this case low-carbon, transformations.

Highlighting these dimensions provides a basis for exploring what the role of these social forces and relations of power in previous periods of capitalist restructuring imply for current efforts to reorganize the energy base around what regulation theorists refer to as a new 'regime of accumulation' and its associated 'mode of regulation'.[2] Reference to 'Great Transformations' in these debates also invites reference to Karl Polanyi's (1980 [1944]) insights into the disembed-ding and re-embedding of the economy from society that began with the rise of economic liberalism in nineteenth-century Britain through efforts to create 'self-regulating markets' in land, labour and money by subjecting them to market exchange, and the reaction this laissez-fair approach provoked in the form of a 'double movement' for the protection of society. Indeed, many scholars have sought to underscore the relevance of these insights for contemporary debates in environ-mental political economy (Dale, 2010; Peck, 2013; Prudham, 2013), although less so around questions of environmental transformation per se. While it is possible to argue that a Polanyian approach needs to include a wider range of forms of domination and exploitation to effectively shed light on the nature of the current triple crisis (financial–social–ecological) (Fraser, 2012; Selwyn and Miyamura, 2013), it remains a valuable point of reference for thinking about how the balance of social forces in particular historical epochs has a profound impact on the 'nature' of transformation that is considered possible and desirable at a particular conjunc-ture.

Taken together, a political economy approach provides the sort of understanding of power and structure that is absent in much of conventional theorizing about transitions and green transformations. A more explicitly political and historical analysis allows us to move beyond glib statements about 'green growth' and 'win–win solutions' to reveal the conflicts, trade-offs and compromises that are implied by a fundamental restructuring of an economy and the relations of power which will determine which pathway is chosen. The 'incumbent' regime of existing actors and interests that benefit from ongoing reliance on a fossil fuel economy and that have played such a decisive role in the development of capitalism over the last century and beyond will not give up their position easily. Nor in all likelihood will states that depend indirectly on the revenues generated by these actors and that have, so far, shown little appetite for initiating structural change. Since energy use, in particular, is closely correlated with growth, there is tremendous political sensitivity around proposals to transform its provision and distribution. So what will it take politically to create powerful coalitions of the 'winning' and the 'willing' that are able to shift the balance of political and economic power in favour of those that stand to benefit from a low-carbon economy? What historical precedents are there for such reorganizations in production and political power, and what can we learn from them? Which historical, political and economic conditions appear to be necessary for such change to occur and, more importantly, can they be replicated given the current alignments of power in the global economy?

Lessons from history?

History teaches us how quickly industrial transformations occur through waves of technological development, such as the introduction of electricity, based on innovation and discovery.

(Stern, 2014)

In order to inform the discussion below about the contemporary politics of green transformation, I briefly refer to a series of pertinent historical examples so as to reveal the confluence of forces that appear to be critical to enabling large-scale deliberate sociotechnical, economic and political change. This builds on previous histories of transitions (Correlje and Verbong, 2004; Geels, 2005b, 2006; Fouquet and Pearson, 2012; Grubler, 2012; Pearson and Foxon, 2012), which emphasize factors such as the role of prices, science and human capital (Allen, 2012), or, as in the quote above from Nicolas Stern, 'innovation and discovery'. However, rather than view the technological and the social context which supported a particular sociotechnical transition in isolation, the emphasis here is on identifying the underlying political, historical and material factors that enable large-scale transformations to take place which will inform our understanding of contemporary developments. This means being attentive to prevailing systemic conditions and alignments of power given, for example, that 'The transition to coal was punctuated by the Atlantic social revolutions and the Napoleonic wars; the transition to oil by two great wars and a mighty world depression' (Moore, 2009, p6), underscoring the links between energy, production and world order (Rupert, 1995). As well as reading politically the significance of these types of examples in terms of the actors and interests that propelled them, the analysis will also reflect on the extent to which they have contemporary resonance and application.

One obvious challenge to drawing such parallels lies in the basic fact that no larger scale transformation (as opposed to a more discrete shift in technological or social practices) to date has been motivated explicitly by the imperatives of dealing with environmental crises per se, even if dwindling access to resources, for example, has been a key driver of innovation and social change (witness the push for alternative and renewable energy as well as energy conservation provoked by the 1970s oil crisis). Another challenge is around the role of intent, design and vision in relation to these transformations and what this implies about the role of the state in particular: whether the key transformations in capitalism have really been steered (rather than enabled and enforced) by the state, and what this suggests about the willingness and ability of contemporary states to assume such roles. With the benefit of hindsight, it is easy to ascribe motivations and read plans into key changes, but it is unclear that reorganizations of the economy, even as drastic and unprecedented as the Industrial Revolution, were done by conscious design or implemented 'from above'. Restlessness on the part of capital was the key. Likewise, while in retrospect it is tempting to ascribe linearity and unity of purpose to them, in the historical moment in which they were unfolding, as now, pathways are experienced and understood as multiple, contested and competing trajectories whose destiny or success cannot be anticipated or known in advance. This uncertainty structures the way in which different actors engage with transitions and which transformations they hedge their bets on and invest in, or seek to resist, as we see below in relation to the role of finance capital and the state in particular. By invoking historical examples, the point is not to underestimate what might be novel or unique about the nature of the challenges associated with 'green' transformations in terms of their scale (across regions, sectors, levels of decision-making and involving such a breadth of actors) and the time-frames within which they have to occur, or in relation to the particular role of expert knowledge, for example. It is rather to shed light on how capitalism has been transformed previously, and particularly its energy base, in ways that it is now being called upon to do again.

The Industrial Revolution

The transition to coal was driven both by its cheapness and abundance, and the fact that wages were relatively high in Britain at the time, creating a demand for labour-saving energy technology (Allen, 2012, p17). Marx recognized the superiority of coal over water from the point of view of capital in the following terms:

> The flow of water could not be increased at will, it failed at certain seasons of the year, and *above all it was essentially local* . . . Not till the invention of Watt's second and so-called double-acting steam-engine was a prime mover found which drew its own motive force from the consumption of coal and water, was entirely under man's control, was mobile and a means of locomotion.
>
> (1974 [1867], p499, emphasis added)

Likewise, the drive for the creation of a railway infrastructure was the need to enable exchange on an increasing scale. Marx called the railways the 'crowning achievement' of the industrial economy for their ability to connect a single inter-acting economy, just as the steamer enabled the multiplication and intensification of the capitalist economy incorporating ever more parts of the globe, providing the basis for a 'gigantic export boom' in which world trade increased by 260 per cent between 1850 and 1870 (Hobsbawn, 1997, pp48–49). Central to the expansion of manufacture and trade were improved systems of transport and the 'new sources of energy and raw materials opened up in response to the appetites of industry' (Cox, 1987, pp143–144). Thus, an expansion in productivity and technological development under capitalism increased the quantity of energy throughput that was required to expand the accumulation of capital, and the operations of capitalist production became dependent on a constant supply of raw materials that could sustain its operations on an ever-greater scale. Whereas previous modes of pro-duction primarily operated within the 'solar-income constraint,' which involved using the immediate energy captured and provided by the sun, by mining the earth to remove stored energy to fuel machines of production, capitalist production broke 'the solar-income budget constraint, and this has thrown [society] out of ecological equilibrium with the rest of the biosphere' (Daly, quoted in Clark and York, 2005, p406).

For Huber, then, 'fossil fuel represents a historically specific and internally necessary aspect of the capitalist mode of production' whereby the late eighteenth-/early nineteenth-century 'energy shift' from biological to fossil modes of energy – at the time meaning coal – coincided with the dramatic *social* shift toward the generalization of capitalist social relations (Huber, 2008, pp105–106). This helps us to understand energy as a 'social relation enmeshed in dense networks of power and socio-ecological change' (Huber, 2008, p106), such that changes to those relations of power will inevitably be required to displace an energy order. At the pinnacle of the networks of power resting on this base of production in the nineteenth century was the British state, which assumed a central role in under-pinning an expanding world economy and liberal world order on its own terms: the Pax Britannica (Cox, 1987).

There is a sense here in which the embrace of new energy sources was born of both the frustration with the limits of existing energy systems (to the ambi-tions of capital in terms of productivity and labour costs) and the abundant availability of an alternative. Whereas in the current situation the interests of capital in general are, for the most part, well served by an ongoing dependence and even expansion of fossil fuels as discussed below, even in the face of pressures to leave large reserves of them 'in the ground'. There is a degree of carbon 'lock-in' (Unruh, 2000) that has resulted from the creation of trading and transport infrastructures dependent on and requiring the type and scale of energy inputs that arguably only fossil fuels can supply. Anticipation of a new wave of accumulation will be vital to future shifts from one energy source to another.

Fordism

Besides production, what about transformations in consumption? Perhaps unsurprisingly, transformations in consumption have generally aimed to increase the consumption of resources and material products, as with the Fordist era, which brought with it the need for new systems of transportation and a reorganization of the production process. If the Industrial Revolution laid the foundations for 'industrial civilization', then the era of Fordist mass production also brought with it a requirement for mass consumption of the goods being produced in the factories of mid twentieth-century America.[3] This mass consumption has come to be ultimately dependent on the provision of cheap energy 'to power privatized automobile transport and electrified/heated single-family homes' (Huber, 2008, p110). The specific underpinnings of the Fordist model, however, were the twinning of a model of economic expansion based on mass production: the manufacture of standardized products in huge volumes using special purpose machinery and unskilled labour with the creation of a consumer base to absorb the fruits of this up-scaling of production. Higher wages had the by-product of giving workers the means to become customers, which nurtured a culture of consumption necessary to reproduce the 'cycles of production/consumption necessary to sustain the regime of accumulation' (Paterson, 2007, p107).

The pursuit of 'auto-mobility' and mass car ownership, for example, in the form of the Volkswagen dream for all German workers to own a car, or President Hoover's 1924 election promise to provide 'a chicken in every pot; two cars in every garage' (quoted in Paterson, 2007, p115) helped to cultivate a mass consumer base for oil (as petrol and its by-products) through individualized transport, even at the expense of the deliberate destruction of urban infrastructures. Part of this history involved deliberate campaigning to dismantle and disband rail and other mass transit public transportation infrastructures in order to force greater reliance on and demand for cars. Peter Dauvergne shows how entrepreneurs such as Henry Ford and Alfred Sloan at General Motors 'vastly expanded markets by reducing profit margins, lobbying policy makers, advertising new models, designing cars for obsolescence and destroying alternative forms of transport such as the electric trolley' (2008, p35). The latter was achieved by the 'auto-industrial complex' forming holding companies to acquire transit firms, demolish trolley lines and then replace them with GM buses, providing financial and technical assistance to municipalities to switch from rail to road systems and financing supportive politicians. The state then played its part in realizing 'the car's potential in accelerating accumulation' (Paterson, 2007, p115) by providing motorway infrastructure and banks provided the credit and loans to enable debt-fuelled consumption.

In terms of lessons for the current predicament, first the drive to stimulate increased consumption by states and corporations is notable as a way of addressing crises of overproduction, cast in the Fordist era and repeated many times since, and presents a huge challenge for more radical green transformations. The way in which increased consumer spending and consumption has become the default mode for getting economies out of crises was observable once again in the wake of the latest financial crisis from 2008, where the appeal to consumers, almost as their primary duty as citizens, was to spend more to buoy the economy, even if this implied increased personal indebtedness. This highlights the scale of the challenge facing anti-consumerism groups such as Rising Tide and Enough and other movements seeking to challenge unsustainable patterns of consumption, especially given that the introduction of new sources of energy has historically tended to increase overall consumption (Fouquet and Pearson, 2012, p2). Histories of energy transition also point to the fact that consumer willingness to adopt new technologies and accept new energy sources depends on the enhanced benefits they are perceived to provide (Fouquet and Pearson, 2012, p2). Yet it will be very difficult for renewable energies to compete with the comfort and reliability of fossil fuels. The same is perhaps true for the alleged personalized freedom that the car provides.

Second, the importance of assuring a social contract or pact between capital and labour emerges as key to attempts to reorganize production, and has implications for debates about the prospects of a 'just transition' and, in particular, how labour might benefit from a switch of industrial base to lower carbon forms of energy: the US$4tn industry that is sustaining a large number of jobs and growth according to some estimates (Jacobs, 2012b). Pursuing the 'just transition' means making sure the transition to a lower carbon economy is a fair one (Swilling and Annecke, 2012). This is often about bringing on board the potential losers from a transition to a low-carbon economy, those whose jobs and livelihoods are dependent on fossil fuels (such as in the mining, oil and car sectors that have been so central to previous and the current regime of accumulation),[4] and being explicit about the trade-offs, compensation and forms of retraining that may be required to make transition socially just and palatable. There are emerging cases of how fossil-dependent economies have tried to do this (Evans, 2010), for example, of cities in Germany losing jobs in coal and setting up solar industries, but clearly it has to go beyond how individual communities blighted by deindustrialization adapt or seek to identify new accumulation strategies on to wider decoupling strategies of energy use from growth. On the positive side, it can be about selling the potential of renewable energy that 'renewable energy is poor people's energy', as groups like Earthlife South Africa do, demonstrating job-creation potential of different energy pathways (2013). However, it needs to be explicit who gains what in such transitions.

There is perhaps also a great, but thus far largely unrealized potential for alliances with potential losers from climate change, such as farmers who might lose out from declining yields and unpredictable rainfall patterns, for example, which are often mobilized in powerful unions such as the UK's National Farmers Union. Or with potential winners such as public sector transportation workers who would benefit from large-scale investments in public transport. This is why it is so important to get mass movements on board, such as trade unions, those with extensive reach, mass appeal, perceived legitimacy and reach (Obach, 2004). Indeed, there are examples of localized emerging collaborations between environmental groups, 'green business' and trade unions (Newell and Mulvaney, 2013). For instance, the Just Transition Alliance (JTA) is a coalition of environmental justice and labour organizations based in California, in the US. Together with frontline workers, and community members who live alongside polluting industries, it seeks to create healthy workplaces and communities. It focuses on contaminated sites that should be cleaned up, and on the transition to clean production and sustainable economies (JTA, 2011).

Third, the example of 'auto-mobility' above shows how powerful actors sought to destroy one set of infrastructures and build another which 'locked in' use of their preferred technology. In the current context we can see both how incumbent regimes work hard to discredit support to niches around claims of their incompatibility with existing infrastructures, as the gas and nuclear industry is doing at the moment with regard to wind and solar energy around claims of problems with intermittency and transmission (Leggett, 2014), but also how an overriding commitment to preserving a particular infrastructure of grid-based energy privileges some energy providers over others, particularly the fossil fuel and nuclear industries.

Globalization

What is the significance of the fact that green transformations, if they are to take place, will have to unfold in an increasingly globalized and integrated global political economy? By the mid to late 1960s pressure was mounting to reconfigure the landscape of power between states and capital, and to renegotiate the Fordist compromises between capital and labour around full employment and union rights. The push was towards more flexible forms of accumulation in which the social forces of production would be recast once again, this time along more transnational lines aimed both at disciplining labour and accessing new sites of accumulation (Robinson, 2004). The current neoliberal order subsequently emerged from the late 1970s onwards, but whose project of monetary discipline and global integration has deepened and intensified during the 1980s and 1990s (Cox, 1994; Harvey, 2005). In terms of green transformations, what is significant is the intensification of resource exploitation associated with the spatial and temporal reorganization of capitalism, alongside which a disciplining of state autonomy was required to lock in states to an integrated neoliberal world order, overseen in particular by the hegemonic power of the US (Panitch and Gindin, 2012). As with the Industrial Revolution before it, this required increasingly expansive and efficient networks of commodity circulation, especially revolutions in the means of transport and the competitive struggle to reduce the costs of circulation to an absolute minimum.

The contemporary neoliberal context in which transformations have to occur is significant, among other things, for its potential impact on the autonomy of states to pursue green transformations. In particular, there is the obvious need for regulation and steering at a time when many states have relinquished, or been forced to relinquish, control over the key parts of their energy sectors (such as generation, distribution and transmission) as a result of energy and power sector reform programmes promoted by the World Bank in particular (Tellam, 2000; Cho and Dubash, 2005). The role of 'disciplinary neo-liberalism',[5] practised by key international institutions and multilateral development banks, in constraining the policy autonomy and developmental space of poorer countries over whom they exercise control through their lending practices (Gill, 1995; Gallagher, 2005), raises key questions about what instruments states have available to address the challenges of decarbonizing their economies when many have ceded direct control over their energy sectors. At the same time, as host to a suite of Climate Investment Funds and serving as the trustee of the Green Climate Fund, the World Bank and other donors are in a position to use their structural power in ways that promote lower carbon energy pathways, even if the record to date is mixed at best amid continued large-scale lending for fossil fuels (WRI, 2008). Either way, these examples pose a challenge to assumptions in debates about transitions management about how much autonomy and power most states have in reality to pursue their preferred transition pathways, or to manage transitions on their own terms.

Given the unequal and uneven global economy in which green transformations will have to occur, the uncritical pursuit of the 'green economy' also runs the risk of reproducing injustices of the fossil fuel economy unless attention is paid to inequities and injustices in the production or supply of energy technologies. Examples include the use of toxic chemicals by immigrant and female labour in the production of solar photovoltaics (PV) cells (Newell and Mulvaney, 2013); green grabs for biofuels (Fairhead *et al.*, 2012); displacement for carbon-financed wind-farm projects (Böhm and Dabhi, 2009) or the lithium rush in Bolivia for batteries for electric cars. This is about addressing the creation or exacerbation of poverty in the production of energy technologies and reducing scope to displace and allocate burdens in unequal and uneven ways within the global political economy between and within states.

Financialization

It may also be the case, however, that shifts in power as a result of the global reorganization of capitalism might create opportunities to destabilize incumbent regimes. I am referring to the interest that powerful actors in this current phase of neoliberalism – global finance – have shown in decarbonization. The centrality of finance in the making of global capitalism has already been emphasized in general terms. Its role in the era of post-Fordism has also led to claims of a finance-led regime of accumulation being the dominant growth model in the contemporary global economy from the late 1970s and early 1980s (Aglietta, 2000). This section seeks to reflect on the historic role of finance in literally fuelling the industries and underwriting carbon-intensive infrastructures, and what this suggests about the role it may play in supporting and benefiting from a shift away from a structure of production based largely on the extraction and consumption of fossil fuels. Although current debates about transitions and transformation place technology centrally in their vision of how to move towards a lower carbon model of development, Perez (2002) shows that finance capital is crucial to the Schumpetarian 'waves of creative destruction' that challenge and dislodge the power of incumbents. Here it is suggested that this will be vital to disinvesting in fossil fuels, such that the twist in the story could yet be about the rise of a finance-led regime of accumulation and its role in accelerating decarbonization.

Historically, finance capital has been vital to unsettling existing technologies, industries and bases of political power. Carlota Perez's (2013) work reminds us of the key role of finance in supporting previous historical transitions – the 'grand experiments' she refers to 'when unrestrained finance can override the power of the old production giants and fund the new entrepreneurs in testing the vast new potential'. Examples include the technological revolutions produced in the Industrial Revolution, what she refers to as the 'age of steam and railways', and around 'oil, automobile and mass production' in the Fordist era described above, for example (2002, p11). Indeed, as Arrighi notes: 'Throughout the capitalist era financial expansions have signalled the transition from one regime of accumulation on a world scale to another. They are integral aspects of the recurrent destruction of 'old' regimes and the simultaneous creation of new ones' (2010, ppxi–xii).

This raises the question of whether the interests of different fractions of capital – finance or money capital on the one hand, and productive capital concentrated in fossil fuels on the other – can be played off against one another for the purposes of producing a shift in the energy regime. While certain 'base technologies' (Storper and Walker, 1989) may characterize eras of capitalism, as Buck notes, it is important not to 'confuse particular manifestations of capitalism – that is, particular historical social formations – with capitalism itself, thus under-estimating the flexibility of the beast' (2006, p60). If there is 'one essential feature of the general history of capitalism', Braudel claims, it is 'its unlimited flexibility, its capacity for change and adaptation' (1982, p433). Might it be possible, then, that climate change can be reworked as an opportunity for growth where fossil fuels can be replaced by, for example, a 'solar revolution' (Altvater, 2006, p53)? As Marx and Engels famously stated, the bourgeoisie 'cannot exist without constantly revolutionizing the means of production' (1998 [1848], p28). Technological dynamism is at the heart of capitalism and, as a consequence, its technological trajectories are not necessarily set in stone. 'Capital, as value in motion, does not care about what it makes, the machinery used or the motive source. It cares only about its own self-expansion and valorization' (Buck, 2006, p63). These are the incessant waves of creative destruction that need to be harnessed towards the goal of a low-carbon economy.

Recognizing the heightened power of finance in this phase of capitalist development means asking questions about the dilemmas and opportunities of trying to harness that power to the project of decarbonization, which include some of the following. First, the pressure to disclose: from the US Securities and Exchange Commission rulings, for example, forcing companies to disclose information about greenhouse gas (GHG) emissions alongside their financial reporting. Or from the UK Companies Act 2006 (Strategic Report and Directors' Report) Regulations 2013 which require all UK quoted companies to report on their greenhouse gas emissions as part of their annual Directors' Report, which affects all UK incorporated companies listed on the main market of the London Stock Exchange. Or from the wave of shareholder activism that has emerged over the last ten years. The year 2005 saw a record number of shareholder resolutions on global warming. State and city pension funds, labour foundations, religious and other institutional shareholders filed 30 global warming resolutions requesting financial risk and disclosure plans to reduce GHG emissions. This is three times the number for 2000–2001 (Newell, 2008).

Disclosure is the first and necessary step to applying and enforcing pressure on corporations to disinvest in fossil fuels, and there is growing evidence of successful disinvestment campaigns targeted at governments, corporations and universities. To date, 22 cities, 2 counties, 20 religious organizations, 9 colleges and universities and 6 other institutions have signed up to rid themselves of investments in fossil fuel companies, and Norway's US$815 billion sovereign wealth fund – the world's largest – has already halved its exposure to coal producers. In addition to these disvestment announcements, many major banks and financial institutions have limited or halted their lending to coal projects (Ecowatch, 2014).

There is also evidence of some interesting alliances emerging between environmentalists and finance capital. Examples include the Carbon Disclosure Project (CDP) that works with 655 institutional investors holding US$78 trillion in assets to help reveal the risk in their investment portfolios and aims ultimately to sensitize investors to climate change as an opportunity as well as a threat. Michael Jacobs (2012b) refers to the 'stranded assets' that many investors may be left with if states get serious about climate change and force companies to leave the 'oil in the soil' and the 'coal in the hole' if ambitions to keep warming below 2 degrees are to be achieved. By some calculations, between 60 and 80 per cent of coal, oil and gas reserves of publicly listed companies are 'unburnable' if the world is to have a chance of not exceeding global warming of 2°C. Disclosure strategies such as these provide one means of repositioning investments currently viewed as assets rather as liabilities (Newell and Paterson, 2010). In the words of Carbon Tracker which is advancing this approach, 'the two worlds of capital markets and climate change policy are colliding' because major institutional investors are starting to think about these issues such that 'there will be increasing pressure from stakeholders for explanations about how capital is being allocated' (Carbon Tracker, 2013).

It is not that these actors do, or have to care about climate change. The question is whether most investors care what they are investing in as long as they get a return. Some 60 per cent of trading on stock exchanges is high-frequency trading where automated systems are used to track price changes and follow them (MacKenzie *et al.*, 2012). If technologies and services in the low-carbon economy are seen to be the promising investments, the money will flow. However, it needs a strong steer, as Kirsty Hamilton's work with financiers, aimed at establishing what it would take to really shift investments into renewable energy, makes clear. *Long* (long-term time-frames so commitments are not reversed by change of government or political expediency), *loud* (strong price signals) and *legal* (regulation and legal lock-in) were the key messages that came through about what would be required to bring about such a shift in strategy (Hamilton, 2009). And powerful though these actors are, governments for the most part have not been bold enough to chart a clear course out of fossil fuels. Witness, for example, the deletion of text at Rio + 20 calling for reductions in fossil fuel subsidies that currently stand at around US$600 billion a year.

In terms of the analysis here, the key point is that finance, as one powerful fraction of capital whose interests might yet be delinked from the idea that the interests of capital in general, in most cases continue to view their interests as best served by an accumulation regime largely dependent on fossil fuels. In this sense, the strategies described above build on a longer history of attempts by activists to engage financial actors as a way of breaking up the bloc of industrial power traditionally opposed to action on climate change (Leggett, 1996; Paterson, 2001).

Theories of change

> *The crisis consists precisely in the fact that the old is dying and the new cannot be born; in this interregnum a great variety of morbid symptoms appear.*
>
> (Gramsci, 1971)

> *We are entering the declining decades of the fossil fuel era, that brief episode of human time when coal miners and oil workers moved an extraordinary quantity of energy . . . up to the earth's surface, where engines, boilers, blast furnaces and turbines burned it at an ever increasing rate, providing the mechanical force that made possible modern industrial life . . . electrical power and communication, global trade, military run empires and the opportunity for more democratic forms of politics.*
>
> (Mitchell, 2011, p231)[6]

It is clearly too early to call time on the current fossil fuel energy regime and assume the confidence to attribute it the characteristics of a temporary, transient phase in the history of socioecological evolution, as Tim Mitchell does in the quote above. Or to have the luxury to look beyond it, sure that a new energy order is in the process of being born out of the current interregnum (to borrow a phrase from Gramsci in the quote above), even if we are not yet sure what form it will take. While the 'morbid symptoms' produced by the old order are clear for all to see, the new order still lacks a powerful author. Gramscian scholars often refer to such a moment as an interregnum: a period between the decline of one order and the rise of another. Likewise, claims in some quarters that the 'liberal–productivist' model is experiencing a 'great crisis' (including tightly interwoven financial, social and environmental aspects) which 'marks the end of a capitalist model of development' (Lipietz, 2013, p127) seem premature, even if we might have sympathy with the claim that 'there will be no exit to this great crisis without a change in the whole model and in particular without a strong shift in the climate-energy nexus' (Lipietz, 2013, p134).

The examples of positive change above should not detract from the issue of what to do about the intransigence and resistance of what is referred to in the transitions literature as the 'incumbent regime': those actors that benefit from the status quo and are thus likely to resist change. In many ways, it is business as usual for the world's most powerful companies that continue to operate as if climate change is not a serious constraint on their activities. The Greenpeace report *Point of No Return* (2013) looks at how a group of 14 giant 'carbon bomb' projects that are currently in planning and development is on track to single-handedly increase global greenhouse emissions 20 per cent by 2020, making it near impossible for the world to avoid runaway climate change. This includes proposals for giant open-cast coal mines in China and Australia, plans to increase offshore oil and gas extraction in the Arctic and off the coast of Brazil, and plans to expand development of Canada's tar sands. We have seen far less discussion of putting limits on these plans. The actors behind them are not threatened by the green economy debate. They will invest in a 'green economy' too and hedge their bets, as with BP's commitment to go 'Beyond Petroleum' in which renewable energy amounts to 1 per cent of their portfolio. It is worth sharing a quote from former Shell chairman director, Lord Oxburgh, where he stated:

> If you look at it from oil companies' point of view, effectively what they're doing at the moment is continuing business as usual, and sticking toes in water in a number of areas which might become important in future. But at present there is a relatively poor business case for making significantly greater investment in these new areas . . . so when I agree that they may not be investing enough, that is if you like the point of view of a citizen of the world rather than a shareholder in one of the companies.
>
> (Strahan, 2009)

This is a far more difficult political economy. Neither the climate change regime, which is still seeking to develop a post-Kyoto legally binding agreement, nor carbon markets (where prices of carbon are at record lows), nor governments are sending powerful signals to the worlds of finance and industry that the future lies in sustainable low-carbon energy. This will be key. While it continues to be profitable and legitimate to increase exploitation of new reserves of fossil fuels – even in the most extreme ways and with the most devastating consequences (tar sands, fracking, drilling in fragile arctic environments, etc.) – finance will not shift with the speed or at the scale required for more radical lower carbon transformations. As noted above, we need loud, long, legal signals about the direction of change, the like of which have not yet been forthcoming – in fact, quite the opposite. The dash to gas and the advent of fracking may relieve the US of some pressure to use warfare to secure future supplies of oil, but we would be wise not to underestimate the resilience of the fossil fuel energy regime, nor the power of the interests that sustain it and benefit from it, whatever its social and environmental costs. This should chime a note of caution with regard to Mitchell's optimism about the imminent demise of the fossil fuel order. As Huber notes: 'Any analysis of a mode of production beyond capitalism, or the possible emergence of an "alternative energy economy", must come to grips with the deep embeddedness of fossil-energy in the most basic forms of commodity circulation' (Huber, 2008, p112). As the current political economy attests, energy issues are at the epicentre of not only the geopolitics of empire and the global climate crisis, but also the more banal, everyday reproduction of capitalist social life.

Such an account also implies a critique, however, of the idea that transitions, or indeed transformations, can be largely organized from above through 'transition management', visions or blueprints without the acquiescence of powerful fractions of capital. This is not to downplay the role of the state per se, given its willingness to intervene on behalf of capital in the ways described in the examples above. Rather, it is to suggest that the 'animal spirits' of capitalism in their restless pursuit of profit through innovation and (creative) destruction will be decisive. There was no blueprint for previous industrial revolutions. We run the risk, therefore, of having a mismatch between the theories of change implicit in many understandings of what is implied by low-carbon energy transitions and what historical experience seems to suggest about how, when and why change occurs in capitalism.

Hence, a reading of the landscape of power exposes the enormity of political lock-in: the interests and the durability of the order, but also the scope for radical change as we have seen with the shift from coal to oil and now as the oil economy faces a growing challenge from a renewed 'dash to gas' and the spectre of climate change. In doing so, however, this chapter has also highlighted the danger that capitalist inequalities and patterns of exploitation will persist in the constitution of a lower carbon green economy unless there is serious attention to the need for a 'just transition' involving new social compacts and deals involving capital, labour, state and civil society. The evolving nature of the global capitalist system has both intensified and rescaled the processes which have brought about the current predicament for society and constitutes the terrain on which near-term strategies aimed at addressing climate change and challenging the energy order which fuels it, will have to be developed. It is precisely an understanding of this terrain, how it has been formed historically through innovation, exploitation and struggle, disembedding and re-embedding, that highlights the dilemmas and contradictions facing progressive movements today. Although signs of immediate and drastic change are not abundant, there is significant movement from below, and it is worth recalling that transitions, let alone transformations, take decades or often centuries.[7] Widespread public and political engagement with climate change is only 30 years old at best and in its heightened form probably only 10–15 at most, which, set against the long durée of capitalist development, is a very short space of time indeed.

Given the abundant problems and apparent limits of the ability of the existing economic system to adequately oversee a 'green transformation', the contours of what such a transformation might look like are unclear. While we can observe 'moves' in a Polanyian sense, it is harder to discern a 'double-movement' at work.[8] Despite a level of common buy-in to the language of transition and transformation, it is evidently a contested and deeply politicized terrain. Discourses of green growth naturally seek to reduce transformation to technological innovation and hype about the possibilities of a new round of 'greener' accumulation (Wanner, 2014). As well as critiques of the inherent impossibility of a truly 'green capitalism', given the tendency to deplete the very resource base upon which the economy depends to reproduce its own conditions of existence (what has been called the second contradiction of capitalism) (O'Connor, 1998), green growth narratives downplay the politics of the transformation. Indeed, one reading of the current situation would interpret much of the current discourse about win–win opportunities for growth that is 'green' as precisely an attempt to depoliticize critique and attention to the limits of growth and its destructive environmental effects (Brand, 2012a; Wanner, 2014). There is an intense debate unfolding about whether technological trans-formation and market innovation are enough to produce the radical shifts that are acknowledged to be needed, or whether in the proper sense of transition (in its political rather than sociotechnical meaning) a change of order is required and will inevitably result from a reordering of production and finance, for example. The political struggle is, on the part of the incumbent historical bloc, to render climate change and associated nexus challenges as entirely manageable within a global-ized capitalist political economy, albeit one in which nature is properly priced and the animal spirits of capitalists suitably shepherded, and on the part of critics to suggest that a growth-oriented market-driven economy is structurally incapable of addressing these challenges, and that the idea of a green transformation within capitalism essentially amounts to a contradiction in terms. In other words, a great deal of political work goes into establishing the boundaries around the terrain of *what* is up for discussion and *by whom*.

An account such as this might rightly be accused of privileging macro transformations by only focusing on episodes of major restructuring and reordering of the economy because of its attempt to link contemporary calls for a 'green industrial revolution' to relevant historical examples. It is certainly the case that this discussion has downplayed the role of smaller scale, bottom-up, inadvertent or disorganized transformations – in values and norms, behaviours, and sites of resistance – which might challenge prevailing structures and orthodoxies. By engaging with existing power structures and alignments of interests and incentives, other sites of potential transformation are inevitably obscured or neglected. However, it is the case that the terms of transition are currently being set *by* and *for* a set of existing regime and landscape actors whose power to enable and frustrate particular types of green transformation needs to be understood and challenged.

Rather than look for evidence of the circumstances in which political revolutions come about as a more radical account might demand, I have assumed here that capitalism will form the context in which green transformations will have to emerge, at least initially and embryonically, and therefore that they will be subject to the dynamics of power pertaining to this model of organizing the economy. To be clear, though, the starting point was explicitly to look for precedents of more radical reorganizations in the structure of the economy of the sort I believe are required again now. I do not share the view, therefore, that a combination of appropriate market signals and improved technologies or better governance will be sufficient to produce a serious, deep or lasting green transformation of the sort that is required to properly create a sustainable economy. That is not to say that technological transformation will not be possible or that effective responses to some aspects of sustainability challenges could not be forged. It is possible to envisage a project of decarbonization that is made compatible with the growth imperatives of capitalism, a form of 'climate capitalism' (Newell and Paterson, 2010), but across the range of resource limits which a growth-obsessed capitalist economy pushes up against, where rebound effects means that resource savings are often reinvested in greater resource use, and the way responses to these challenges tend to employ spatial and temporal fixes to move crises around rather than resolve them, the picture is less optimistic. The longer term goal, therefore, has to be a transformation of capitalism rather than a transformation within, but that we have to start the analysis on the terrain of the here and now and the actually existing political economy, as it is, not as we would like it to be.

Notes

1   Marxists use the concept of fractions of capital in different ways to refer to a particular stage in the circuit of capital – i.e. 'finance capital', 'commodity capital' etc. or sometimes in relation to sectoral interests – i.e. 'mining' or 'agricultural capital' where interests are understood in relation to their political representation within policy processes (Clarke, 1978; van der Pijl, 1998, p3).
2   The concept of the regime of accumulation refers to the way in which production, circulation, consumption and distribution organize and expand capital in a way that stabilizes the economy over time. The modes of regulation required to stabilize these regimes include the law, state policy, corporate governance and cultures of consumption.
3   The term gained prominence when it was used by Antonio Gramsci in his essay 'Americanism and Fordism', in his *Prison Notebooks*.
4   Lipietz claims that 'creative destruction' through a green transport revolution would suppress 4.5 million jobs in the production of individual cars but create 8 million jobs in collective transport (Lipietz, 2013, p13).
5   Disciplinary neoliberalism refers to the ways in which the scope for legitimate state action and progressive democratic politics is circumscribed by global trade, and investment accords and the rights of capital over states begin to take the form of a 'new constitutionalism', protected by international law (Gill, 1995).
6   Mitchell's claim is based on the fact that the era of abundant oil appears to have ended, given that the world is using up stores of petroleum faster than new supplies can be discovered and the need to reduce fossil fuel consumption in order to tackle climate change (Mitchell, 2011, pp231–233).

7   Individual sectoral and service energy transitions typically unfold over 40–130 years while aggregate transitions involving the whole economy could take centuries (Fouquet and Pearson, 2012, p2).

8   As Mittelman suggests, the term 'move' rather than movement is used by Polanyi to indicate the proto forms by which social forces 'waxed and waned' before ultimately giving birth to a political organization that begot a transformation (Mittelman, 1998, p867).

6

THE POLITICAL DYNAMICS OF GREEN TRANSFORMATIONS

Feedback effects and institutional context[1]

Matthew Lockwood

Introduction

Why do green transformations in some countries appear to have more momentum than in others? As other contributions in this book make clear, there are multiple interpretations of what transformations to more sustainable economies and societies might look like. However, even with relatively limited and mainstream conceptualizations, such as decarbonization of the economy or the growth of renewable energy, there are large variations between countries in how far they have progressed over the last two decades.

Whatever form green transformations take, some basic features of their political dynamics will be common to all. There are some fairly obvious factors that help determine where such transformations are more likely to start – for example, the absence of a powerful coal lobby (Steves and Teytelboym, 2013) or a more green-minded population (Harrison and Sundstrom, 2010). However, sustainable transformations are likely to take some time – for example, at least two or three decades for decarbonizing energy systems and economies. A key corollary of this is that successful transformations not only require instigation, but also have to be politically sustained for long periods. Coalitions need to be created around a number of different objectives (see Schmitz, Newell, this book), but they also have to be kept together and expanded over time. Eventually, as the costs of more sustainable technologies and processes come down, green transformations should become economically self-sustaining, led effectively by a new green demand paradigm (Perez, 2013). However, until that stage is reached, public policy is needed to lead the transformation. Such policy will tend to be highly political because it effectively involves a process of creating and managing rents to pay for the development of greener products and processes (Schmitz *et al.*, 2013).

In this chapter I argue that the sustainability of green transformations depends heavily on the *political effects of policies* aimed at bringing about transformation. These effects in turn either strengthen or weaken support for such policies, causing positive or negative feedback effects and divergent policy paths. In the political science literature such knock-on effects are known as 'policy feedback'. My focus here is on public policy-making, since this will inevitably be needed for large-scale transformations of economies, but I would argue that the same set of issues also apply to campaigns and other actions by social movements or civil society organizations. Unless they create some form of positive feedback through their actions or ideas, such movements and organizations will not be able to lead significant transformations. Especially for transformations relating to global sustainability problems (including most 'planetary boundaries'), this dynamic is crucial, since such problems in themselves are not seen by the majority of people as sufficiently urgent to prioritize action, or pose severe collective action challenges that block change.

The political effects of policies depend in part on how policies are designed. However, both policy design and their political consequences will also be affected by the nature of *underlying institutions and dominant ideas*, which vary between countries (Morgan *et al.*, 2010). The factors of policy feedback and underlying institutions are likely to play a major role in shaping the speed and likely success or failure of transformations, since they help determine the political dynamics of transformation. They also point to the possibility of trying to accelerate transformations.

Below, I explore these issues through a number of comparative examples, a particularly useful approach, since it allows the examination of divergent pathways. In the following section, I focus on renewable energy policy, so it is useful first to briefly consider the political forces and relationships at work in the energy sector. I then examine the concept of policy feedback and how it can be a useful analytical tool for understanding the dynamics of renewable energy policy in Germany, the UK, India and China. The role of institutional context is then discussed and the case studies revisited. The chapter concludes with some reflections on the approach, its relation to the issue of social justice, and implications for accelerating green transformations.

The politics of energy

In modern energy sectors there are broadly three groups of actors that are important for political dynamics: *energy providers, policy-makers* and *users of energy* (e.g. Scarse and Smith, 2009, p710). The relationships between these groups of actors ultimately determine investment, technological change and outcomes such as greenhouse gas emissions, all of which will have further feedback effects on actors (Figure 6.1).

Energy providers can in principle be of any size, from individuals to multinational corporations, and privately or state owned, although in most contexts the politically important incumbent actors are large companies. Their investment decisions, especially for new technologies, will be shaped heavily by incentives, risks and regulations set by policy-makers. Once made, these decisions create vested

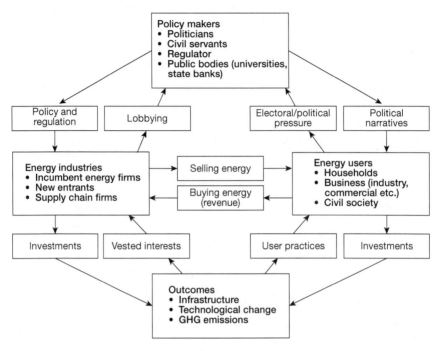

FIGURE 6.1 Political and economic dynamics in the energy system

Source: Lockwood *et al.*, 2013.

interests that shape the subsequent actions of incumbents in energy markets. This is particularly so in the energy sector because infrastructures are so long-lived, and so give a heavily path-dependent nature to regimes and transitions. However, large energy firms are rarely passive and usually seek to influence policy actively through a range of means, including direct lobbying, secondments to government and sitting on technical committees that shape markets, all backed up with the threat of investment strikes (Jessop, 1990) or divestment leading to the lights going out. In privatized and liberalized markets, a key objective for incumbents in influencing regulation and policy will often be to maintain high costs of and barriers to entry in markets (e.g. Stigler, 1971), meaning that new and potentially innovative new companies will find it harder to enter the energy sector.

However, in addition to being lobbied by energy providers, politicians will also pay attention to the relationships they have with energy users, which encompasses both the general public and businesses outside of the energy sector. Political elites may also be concerned about climate change and want to see change towards low-carbon energy, either because that is what the public want, or because of personal conviction. Among businesses, large, energy-intensive users tend to lobby strongly against policies that increase energy costs, while other businesses may support transitions because they see opportunities for revenue in low-carbon products and services, and in owning renewable energy assets. This split in views can even run within a single company – for example Siemens, which manufactures both wind turbines and conventional turbines for coal and gas power plants.

Overall, much of the process by which policy-makers shape the institutions that govern the energy system is effectively a balancing act between the perceived interests of energy users with those of energy provider incumbents (Peltzman, 1976). This is what makes a sustainable energy transition so challenging, because policy-makers have to find some way of managing this balance through a process of profound change.

This framework is very general. The actors and relationships in any actual case will depend on the institutional context. For example, in many OECD (Organisation for Economic Co-operation and Development) countries, the energy sector has been liberalized, and incumbents are large (often multinational) private corporations. In countries like China and India, most energy companies remain state-owned, giving their relationships with policy-makers a different quality. There will also be differences in the relationship between policy-makers and energy users, determined especially by differences in the nature of politics between countries. This can apply even between countries with apparently very similar polities. For example, Germany and the UK are both mature European democracies, but Germany's proportional representation electoral system means that environmentally minded voters have enjoyed much stronger political representation through its Green Party, whereas in the UK the first-past-the-post system prevents this, and the route to influencing policy goes via environmental campaign organizations. In non-democratic systems, such as China's, the relationship between political elites and mass publics is obviously different again, as political pressure comes not through voting but through different kinds of demands from a range of actors, from urban communities protesting about pollution, to local governments seeking to maximize economic growth (Lampton, 2014). However, even in authoritarian China, ensuring that energy is available at an affordable cost will still be a major concern of political elites (e.g. Yuan and Zuo, 2011a).

Feedback effects and renewable energy policies

Policy feedback effects

The idea that policies can have political effects is now a well-established idea in political science, with a number of applications in areas such as welfare and pensions policy (e.g. Béland, 2010). As Skocpol puts it, 'Policies not only flow from prior institutions and politics; they also reshape institutions and politics, making some future developments more likely, and hindering the possibilities for others' (quoted in Patashnik and Zelizer, 2009, p1).

In a classic essay on such effects, Pierson (1993) distinguishes a number of potential routes for such effects. One is that policies distribute resources and create material incentives, which can work to create or strengthen particular *social interest groups*: 'Public policies often create "spoils" that provide a strong motivation for beneficiaries to mobilize in favor of programmatic maintenance or expansion' (Pierson, 1993, p599). Second, policies can also transform *state capacities and institutions*, changing the administrative possibilities for government initiatives in the future and affecting later prospects for policy implementation. For example, policies that involve the collection or generation of new types of information then make possible other kinds of policies dependent on that information.

Most importantly, feedback effects can work via what Pierson calls the 'mass public', transforming the interests, identity and political participation of large groups of people. For example, the introduction of social security in the US created the conditions for the invention of a new social category ('retired people') and the formation of the politically powerful American Association of Retired Persons (AARP). Another important mass public policy feedback effect can occur where a policy induces large numbers of people to make commitments or investments that it subsequently becomes 'both expensive and politically perilous' (Béland, 2010, p575) to reverse, thereby 'locking in' the policy decision (see also Pierson, 1993, p610).

As well as the allocation of material or political resources, there are also what Pierson calls 'interpretive effects' (1993, p611), where policies may produce 'cues' for parts of the electorate that 'help them develop political identities, goals, and strategies' (ibid., p619). Particular policies can become iconic of particular political approaches and help mobilize support for or opposition to that approach, above and beyond any material effect. Given the complexity of modern life, policies can generate 'focusing events' or cues for social actors, but in that process also 'heighten the visibility of some social and political connections while obscuring others'.

Much of the policy feedback literature has tended to focus on cases of *positive* feedback, not least because it is in these cases that policies become successfully entrenched. As Pierson (2000, p259) notes, positive policy feedback is one of the drivers of *increasing returns* in politics, which by analogy from economics (e.g. Arthur, 1989) creates the lock-in noted above. Increasing returns also make political processes path-dependent, in the sense that small details of policy design or institutional context will lead to rapidly diverging paths if one involves positive feedback and the other does not. By contrast, *negative* political feedback effects undermine policies and limit their transformative reach (Pierson, 1993, p600; Béland, 2010, p575). This is particularly important for understanding the political dynamics of attempted green transformations, since such transformations often involve additional financial costs and challenges to vested interests, which can quickly create opposition.

Overall, whether and how quickly transformation occurs depends on the balance of positive and negative effects, whether policies can be amended to improve that balance, or indeed whether new and more transformative policies are feasible (Weaver, 2010, p138). Where policies have strongly positive feedback effects they become successfully locked in, but where there are both potential negative and positive feedbacks there can be a 'snakes and ladders' pattern whereby what appear to be similar policies can diverge according to which feedback effect dominates (Weaver, 2010).

These considerations clearly apply to the example of renewable energy raised above. Most countries have some kind of support policies for renewable energy, yet in some countries these have not gone very far, whereas in others they have taken off. It might be argued that contrasts are simply due to the extent or generosity of subsidy, but this in itself begs the question of how higher levels of subsidy (which are clearly seen in countries like Denmark and Germany) are politically sustained.

One factor which might be expected to have an influence on the knock-on effects of policies is *policy design* (Pierson, 1993; Patashnik and Zelizer, 2009). Apparently small differences in policy design may lead to quite big differences in who can access the benefits from the policy, how those benefits are distributed, what the cost is and who bears that cost. Different policy approaches can also have varying interpretive effects, resonating strongly or falling flat with existing or new constituencies, and leading to large divergences in political sustainability. In the case of renewable energy policy design, a key issue is how different designs affect the political dynamics of the energy sector discussed above, and in particular the balance between producers and users.

Germany and the UK

Germany and the UK provide contrasting examples of how policy feedback has produced different pathways in the growth of renewable energy. At the start of the 1990s, neither Germany nor the UK generated significant amounts of electricity from renewable sources. In Germany, policies adopted from 1990 onwards led to rapid sustained growth in renewable electricity capacity, which actually accelerated after 2000. In the UK, renewable electricity was also eligible for support from around the same time, but growth has been much slower. By 2012, total renewable generation in the UK was around 11 per cent of total demand, less than half the share in Germany. The growth of renewables has generated negative feedback effects in both countries, especially opposition on grounds of cost. However, a key difference is that Germany's policy approach created considerable positive feedback effects which are largely absent in the UK, leaving the policy there far more politically exposed and currently in some trouble.

The growth of renewables in Germany has undoubtedly benefited from higher levels of environmental awareness and stronger opposition to nuclear power than in the UK. However, the nature of the policies adopted in the two countries has also been distinctively different. Germany's policies have offered stable, technology-specific prices to renewable generators (fixed prices from 2000) and a guaranteed market. By providing attractive returns with low risk and ensuring grid connection (Mitchell *et al.*, 2006), a key aspect of the feed-in tariff was that its benefits could be accessed by a range of groups, including farmers, households, cooperatives, schools, small businesses and municipalities, rather than large energy companies, which were, in fact, excluded from the policy. The policy supported a range of technologies, not only wind but also solar photovoltaics (PV), biomass and anaerobic digestion. The fact that conservative farmers in areas such as Bavaria benefited from the policy was particularly important for keeping Germany's centre-right political party on board.

A coalition of political support for renewable energy rapidly grew through the 1990s (Jacobsson and Lauber, 2000, p266), created partly by the development of vested interests, with 340,000 Germans having invested around €12 billion in renewable energy projects by the early 2000s (Sawin, 2004, p25). There were also political effects that worked via the strengthening of interest groups, with an increasing professionalization of renewable energy associations, amid strong support from the Green Party and the Ministry of the Environment (Laird and Stefes, 2009). In addition, because renewables policy was linked to industrial policy, especially from the late 1990s onwards, employment in factories producing wind turbines and solar PV panels created a new constituency in favour of a strong renewables policy, especially in the former East Germany.

This wide coalition helped to maintain and strengthen renewables policy – for example, it was the involvement of municipalities in the 1990s that prevented the collapse of solar PV (Jacobsson and Lauber, 2006, p266). When the first renewable energy law was threatened by legal action by the large utilities in the late 1990s and the government proposed a reduction in feed-in rates, the Green Party mobilized a wide coalition of environmental groups, solar industry associations and companies, trade unions and regional politicians to successfully oppose the changes (Jacobsson and Lauber, 2006, p265).

Germany's renewable policy has not been without negative feedback effects. It provoked strong opposition from the incumbent energy companies and over time the overall cost to energy consumers has grown, despite sharp falls in the prices of wind turbines and solar panels. At the same time, some of the employment benefits have evaporated as solar PV producers have been undercut by Chinese imports. Nevertheless, despite current debates about cost, the growth of renewable energy in Germany looks set to continue to enjoy broad support. The main political party opposed to further expansion lost all its seats in the 2013 parliamentary elections, and the German government pressed strongly for a national renewables target to be part of the European 2030 package in early 2014. The new government has introduced reforms to reduce some subsidies and spread their costs more widely, but planned growth in renewables remains unchanged.[2]

In the UK, policy took a different course. From 1989, renewable energy was in theory eligible for support through an auctioning policy, although in practice very little capacity was built (Mitchell and Connor, 2004). In 2003, a Renewables Obligation (RO) was introduced, which placed an obligation on large energy companies to source a certain proportion of generation each year from renewables. This created a market for renewables, but with a price that was not certain, and one which basically rewarded the cheapest technology (on-shore wind). As a result, almost all investment in new renewable energy under the RO was by large companies able to bear the price risk, and was concentrated in wind only (Mitchell et al., 2006). In terms of Figure 6.1 above, while German policies had begun to transform the structure of relationships in the sector, breaking down the distinction between providers and consumers, UK policy reinforced those structural divisions. A small and badly run grants programme supported a trickle of investment in solar PV by households, but this was at a tiny level compared with Germany. Eventually, in 2010, a feed-in tariff for small-scale renewables was introduced, but following explosive growth in solar PV, tariff rates were quickly scaled back. Only in 2013 has the desire to reduce risk for larger investors led the UK to finally embrace a version of feed-in tariffs more widely.

The policy design of the RO has created weak positive feedback effects, and left the growth of renewables in the UK exposed to considerable negative feedback effects. Large energy companies have made the largest investment in renewables, but they also have existing high-carbon assets, and the companies have been half-hearted advocates for renewables at best. Their ambivalence has also affected interest group formation, with one organization (RenewableUK) representing larger companies and another (the Renewable Energy Association) the small-scale renewables lobby. During the debate about the introduction of a feed-in tariff in the UK, these two groups were unable to agree. The UK has also so far failed to develop a strong industrial policy and supply chain for renewable energy, meaning that employment effects are nowhere near as politically important as they have been in Germany, and that a narrative about the importance of 'green jobs' is not yet taken for granted.

At the same time, the dominance of large corporate interests in renewables has produced stronger negative feedback effects. One issue is planning. Whereas in Germany around half of onshore wind turbines were owned by farmers or local cooperatives in the late 1990s, in the UK 98 per cent were owned by large energy companies or developers, which have no link to or stake in the local society and economy (Pollitt, 2010, p36). Szarka (2006, p3046) argues that 'It is clear from fieldwork contacts with anti-wind protesters in Britain . . . that one cause of rejection is the feeling of injustice engendered by outside firms who exploit a local resource and impose burdens, but offer no community benefit or compensation'. Moreover, and again in contrast with Germany where tariffs were adjusted to help investors in less windy sites, the RO has incentivized developers to seek out the windiest sites, which often tend to be in ecologically and visually sensitive areas.

The fact that much of the financial benefit from renewables policy has been captured by large energy firms, which have become extremely unpopular since the mid-2000s due to price rises, suspected profiteering and high executive salaries, also leaves UK policy particularly exposed to the negative feedback effects of cost. Germany's renewable electricity support programme has so far cost about four times what the UK has spent, as a share of national income (OECD, 2013, p48). Despite this, rifts on the future of renewable power in the political elite and the media are stronger in the UK – with, for example, proposals to halt and even reverse on-shore wind expansion – creating considerable political uncertainty and a chilling effect on investment.

Overall, in Germany, renewables policy appears to have maintained a dominance of positive over negative feedback effects through spreading the benefits of the policy widely through society. Policy-makers, not without controversy, have tried to solve the problem of how to manage interests during transformation discussed above not so much by balancing them but by beginning to transform energy users into producers and challenging incumbents directly. It was not clear that this was intended at the start of the policy, but it has evolved in such a way as to produce this outcome. In the UK, by contrast, policy has benefited incumbent producers, but the problem of balancing this approach with the interests of users has become increasingly fraught over time.

India and China

This framework can also be applied in the very different settings of countries like India and China. These countries are still at a relatively early stage of transformation in terms of renewable power. For example, despite rapid growth (Lewis, 2011; Sharma *et al.*, 2012), wind power as the leading technology in both countries still only provided 2.5 per cent of total electricity generation in India in 2011 and 1.5 per cent in China. Policy feedback effects are likely to be much weaker at this stage. However, both countries also have ambitious targets for renewable energy, and the policy feedback approach can help identify how far, and where, these ambitions are likely to encounter political problems.

Investment in wind power in India has historically been driven by capital subsidies and tax incentives, including accelerated depreciation (AD). This policy has drawn in investors from a wide range of businesses (who also seek on-site power generation given the unreliability of the Indian grid), and also fostered substantial development of wind farms by wind-turbine manufacturers themselves in a so-called 'vertically integrated' model (Benecke, 2011; Shrimali, 2014). Interestingly, in terms of Figure 6.1 above, this policy approach means that the distinction between energy providers and consumers is again broken down, but unlike as in Germany, only for industrial and commercial customers, not for domestic customers, and with quite different political effects. Additional support mechanisms have also been introduced over the 2000s, including feed-in tariffs at the state level, a 'generation-based incentive' offered by the central government and a renewables obligation on (largely state-owned) electricity companies, but not all of these are functioning particularly effectively (Shrimali and Tirumalachetty, 2013).

The cost of feed-in tariffs for wind is incurred by state utilities and passed on to customers. While the relatively small role of wind means that this is not yet a major problem, in some states, utilities and regulators have begun to worry about the sustainability of such costs and are pressing for a move to an auctioning policy (Kanchan, 2013), which has been successful in bringing down generation costs in solar PV (Deshmukh *et al.*, 2011).

At the same time, support via accelerated depreciation has also produced negative feedback effects, not so much via electricity consumers as via the federal budget. In theory, this route leads ultimately to taxpayers, but the nature of Indian politics means that mechanisms of accountability are limited and the pressure for cuts to support mainly comes from reformist policy-makers themselves. Accelerated depreciation covers other investments in addition to wind farms, but overall it is responsible for almost half of India's foregone tax revenue from the corporate sector (Bandyopadhyay, 2013), and has come under increasing pressure from a government interested in fiscal reform. In 2012, the allowance for wind investments was slashed and the generation-based incentive was cut, leading to a sharp slowdown in new investment.[3]

If wind, and indeed large-scale solar PV investments grow on the scale envisaged by national targets for renewables, a further negative feedback effect may arise through competition for land. Early so-called solar 'ultra-mega power plants' are being sited on government-owned land, but clashes over the siting of renewables in farming communities are not unknown and informed observers argue that without benefits for local communities this will be a potential problem for the growth of renewables in future.[4]

Against these negative feedback effects, positive effects are also likely to play some role. India has favoured local turbine manufacturing through import duties, although its industrial policy for wind has been nowhere nearly as active as China's (Lewis, 2011). The leading turbine manufacturer, Suzlon, estimates that the wind industry is creating around 40,000 jobs a year. Also important, as in Germany, will be popular ownership of, or participation in renewables, with a large increase in solar PV on domestic roofs anticipated, partly financed and/or owned by energy services companies.

China's wind boom originates from 2003, when the government introduced a policy of auctioning opportunities to build wind farms on pre-selected sites, with preferential loans and tax conditions, grid access and other infrastructure provided, while at the same time placing obligations on state-owned power generation companies to generate a certain proportion of electricity from wind, and on state-owned supply companies to buy a certain proportion of electricity from renewable sources (Lema and Ruby, 2007; Lewis, 2011). The approach has incentivized a very rapid expansion of investment in wind capacity, with less attention to quality. There have been problems with poor turbine performance, lack of grid access and poor maintenance, and increasingly frequent incidents of turbine failure (Wang et al., 2012; Zhang et al., 2013). From 2009, a feed-in tariff policy was introduced to try to address some of these issues.

The key success of China's policy has been in building up what is now a globally successful wind industry through a highly active industrial policy (Lewis, 2011; Wang et al., 2012; Lema et al., 2013). This has led to positive feedback effects both through employment (in 2008 an estimated 1 million people were employed in the Chinese renewables industry, mostly in wind (Li, 2010)) and export earnings. These effects can be expected to grow further if the Chinese wind industry can further develop its position and if global wind markets hold up.

As in India, much of the political dynamics of the wind energy boom in China play out between large energy companies and policy-makers. At the national level, the state has been keen to promote a wind industry that is now a major exporter.

Local governments are often keen promoters of smaller wind farms, which do not require state-level approval because they bring tax revenue, provide jobs and help local industry (Zhang *et al.*, 2013, p338). Energy companies, meanwhile, have mixed interests. Grid and supply firms have to buy wind energy, but to some extent have been allowed to pass costs through to consumers and in any case have soft budget constraints as state-owned enterprises. State-owned generation companies have invested heavily in wind power because of the requirement on them to meet their portfolio targets, which affects their ability to obtain permission to build more conventional (coal and nuclear) capacity. Such companies own more than 80 per cent of China's wind capacity (Zhang *et al.*, 2013, p338).

The costs of wind and other renewables in China are now financed from a fund set up by a surcharge on consumers' bills (Yuan and Zuo, 2011a). The surcharge is still fairly low, but has been increased several times since the mid-2000s. In spite of this, the renewables fund is still facing shortfalls and, as a result, there have been delays in payments to wind developers since 2010 (Davidson, 2013). The most recent increase to the surcharge has involved a doubling for industrial customers but no change for domestic customers, a reverse of the German policy by which most industrial users were exempt from such charges. At the same time, feed-in tariffs have been somewhat scaled back, especially for solar PV. However, the overall political effects of negative cost feedback are likely to be limited. This is because the Chinese government sets electricity prices centrally and consumer prices have been kept low, including for industrial users (Rutkowski, 2013).

In China, then, policy has been kept on track by strong positive feedback via the development of wind as industrial policy and by more direct control of energy companies by the state. The potential negative feedback effects of costs falling on electricity consumers is likely to remain small as long as the state continues to keep power prices low. In effect, in terms of Figure 6.1 above, the Chinese state is using its huge fiscal resources to act as a buffer between providers and users.

The role of institutional context

Diversity in social and economic institutional systems

In addition to the nature of policies themselves, we might also expect the wider discursive, institutional and political context in which policies are made and implemented to also have an influence (Pierson, 1993, p602; Patashnik and Zelizer, 2009, p3). As discussed above, it is these contexts that determine the exact nature of the structural relationships between energy providers, users and policy-makers (see Figure 6.1 above) in different countries.

First, the range of options for policy design which are acceptable in any particular context will to a great extent be prescribed by what are sometimes called 'policy paradigms' – i.e. interpretive frameworks of ideas and standards that are 'embedded in the very terminology through which policy-makers communicate about their work . . . influential precisely because so much of it is taken for granted and unamenable to scrutiny as a whole' (Hall, 1993, p279). Particular policy paradigms are in turn often associated with particular institutional systems. For example, Schmidt (2002) argues that in Britain policy has been dominated by a neoliberal paradigm, linked to a liberalized market institutional system and a politics deeply influenced by Thatcherism. By contrast, Germany's distinctive 'social market' paradigm complements a set of more deliberative economic institutions, while France's paradigm of *dirigisme* is a good fit for an institutional system in which the state plays a prominent role.

Beyond policy design, institutional systems may also influence the articulation of policies and political effects – i.e. how far positive and negative feedback effects are likely to arise, and whether these effects are amplified or dampened. Many policies for green transformation are essentially economic policies, involving taxes, subsidies and other forms of state or institutional support, so economic institutions are particularly important. For example, a renewable energy support policy can offer a subsidy, but how far investment in renewables actually takes place depends on how far financial institutions complement that policy and provide credit on acceptable terms. Equally, a country with labour market and welfare systems that produce high levels of poverty and inequality may find it hard to place the costs of renewable energy support on energy bills, as this amplifies the political effects of a negative policy feedback to the point of crisis.

The importance of context for policy feedback effects suggests that differences in speeds and paths of green transformation in different countries may be related to *institutional diversity* across countries. There are many approaches to understanding such institutional diversity (see e.g. Crouch and Streeck, 1997; Schmidt, 2002; Morgan *et al.*, 2010), and considerable debate over whether it is possible to classify countries into particular 'varieties of capitalism' (Hall and Soskice, 2001; Crouch, 2005a; Hancké *et al.*, 2007) or the relevance of those models for countries outside of Europe (Carney *et al.*, 2009; Schneider, 2009). However, common to all these approaches is the idea that different countries do have distinctive systems of social and economic institutions that complement one another and which evolve over time (Crouch, 2005b; Streeck and Thelen, 2005). We can therefore expect such systems to have significant implications for the speed and path of a green transformation.

Germany and the UK

Returning to the cases of Germany and the UK, there are several contrasts in institutions and discourses which may help explain why Germany adopted a policy that had the potential to create stronger positive feedback effects, and also why that potential was realized more fully.[5]

The Renewables Obligation (RO) was chosen in the UK explicitly as a mechanism that attempted to mimic a market – i.e. not setting a fixed price – and avoided an explicit technology-specific focus. It was seen as superior to the German feed-in tariff specifically for these reasons. This approach was entirely consistent with a policy-making environment in the UK dominated by a neo-classical, and often neoliberal, economic paradigm. In Germany, the neoliberally minded finance ministry was also opposed to a technology-specific feed-in tariff. However, the wider German policy paradigm was more influenced by the concept of 'Ordoliberalism', a social market approach developed in Germany after the Second World War, which laid much greater emphasis on active government intervention to ensure competition and prevent monopolistic or oligopolistic market power (Toke and Lauber, 2007).

Ordoliberalism also turned out to be far more consistent with the idea of an active industrial policy – and therefore a mission-oriented green industrial policy (see Mazzucato, this book) – than the UK's policy paradigm. In the UK, governments since the 1970s have largely been sceptical of any directed form of industrial policy, with the Treasury in particular a major opponent. More widely, many comparative analyses of economic institutions placed emphasis on the much greater degree of coordination among industrial companies and the state in Germany compared with the UK (e.g. Hall and Soskice, 2001; Schmidt, 2002).

Other aspects of Germany's institutions have also turned out to play important roles in facilitating both the implementation of its renewable policy and in increasing its net positive political feedback effects. Much of the investment by non-corporate actors in renewables has been supported by state finance in the form of the KfW bank, channelled through a network of local and regional banks which know their clients personally. The UK has no equivalent financial institutions.

In Germany, higher energy costs for consumers have not produced quite the same political backlash as in the UK, partly because higher levels of welfare and lower inequality in Germany make fuel poverty and squeezed incomes in the middle less acute problems (Crepaz 1998; Iversen and Soskice, 2006).

Below the level of national political economy, German federalism and decentralization has also meant that municipalism is strong, at least compared with the UK's currently highly centralized system. Both municipal and regional government in Germany have been highly supportive of various aspects of renewables growth, and many municipalities in Germany still own energy supply and generation businesses that have given them a vehicle for investment. In the UK, such companies disappeared after the Second World War.

India and China

In the case of India and China, there are similarities as well as differences in institutional context, which partly explains why they initially adopted similar support policies for wind that focused on capital costs and directed subsidy towards those institutions that play a leading role in their respective political economies – state-owned enterprises in China and family-owned corporations in India (e.g. Taylor and Nölke, 2008). Both countries have also historically embraced significant state intervention on the economy (although China to a greater extent than India), including active industrial policy. Chinese provinces and many Indian states also have state-owned energy utilities with soft budget constraints, a situation which has given policy-makers more room for manoeuvre in the balance between providers and users, and has also softened negative policy feedback that might work through private sector incumbents.

However, one key difference between the two countries that helps explain why the pace of wind expansion is currently faltering in India and not in China is the unwillingness of policy-makers in India's central government to continue to subsidize wind via accelerated depreciation. This unwillingness can be explained in part by the policy paradigm of the current Indian government led until 2014 by Prime Minister Manmohan Singh, who has pursued a series of reforms over the last decade aimed at liberalization, tax simplification and fiscal consolidation clearly influenced by the ideas of orthodox economics.

Conclusion

What constitutes a green transformation will be open to contestation, but for any kind of transformation actually to occur it must be politically sustainable. Alliances for transformations need not only to be formed but also maintained and expanded. In this sense, if policies (or actions or campaigns by social movements) are to be successful in bringing about green transformations, they must be self-reinforcing, creating constituencies for their own implementation and expansion.

In terms of the concepts explored here, this means that policies must have a preponderance of positive feedback effects over negative ones if they are to become 'locked in'. For many sustainability problems, including climate change, this represents a major challenge, since transformative policies fly in the face of existing high-carbon lock-in and will challenge existing vested interests, norms and institutions. In that sense, policies for green transformations are always likely to encounter negative feedback.

Here I have argued that an important factor in the balance between positive and negative feedback effects is the design of policies, using a number of comparative case studies. For example, Germany's policy approach has been to distribute subsidies from policy relatively widely and use industrial policy to create employment, both of which have created important positive feedback effects to offset the inevitable negative feedback on the costs of the policy. This is not so much a case of grassroots innovation from below (see Smith and Ely, this book) as mass appropriation of innovation from above. The UK's renewable support mechanism has done neither of these things, leaving subsidy to be captured by large and highly unpopular energy incumbents and the policy exposed.

I have also argued that both policy design and political effects in turn will depend in part on institutional systems and dominant policy paradigms present in a country. Again, taking the contrast between the UK and Germany, a technology-neutral, market-mimicking policy was the natural fit for the liberal policy paradigm in the former case, whereas an industrial policy for renewables was very difficult to get going, in contrast to Germany's more managed, coordinated institutional system and discourse.

Most of the analysis in this chaper focuses on two sets of comparisons, one between Germany and the UK, and the other between China and India. However, it is also worth briefly considering what can be learned from comparing Asia with Europe. The first region has fast-growing rising powers with young populations, whereas the second is now economically sclerotic and fiscally constrained. This implies that, for a number of reasons, we might expect renewable energy policy to have a greater degree of political sustainability in the Asian countries, especially China. The Chinese state has deep pockets, which enables it to limit the negative feedback arising from costs to consumers. Both India and China can expect to create exporting industries in renewable energy on a greater scale, certainly than the UK. Both are at a much earlier stage of mass deployment. However, they could still learn from the different experiences of Germany and the UK, and be aware of both the political opportunities and potential traps that arise from policy design.

What are the lessons from this approach, if any, for accelerating green transformations? One is simply that climate policy-making, which is dominated by economics, should include more consideration of the political implications of policy. To some extent, policy-makers already do this in a self-censoring way, avoiding policies they think will be too controversial with some groups, but they rarely think about deliberate strategies for positive feedback. In this sense, we should learn from the German experience. The creation of positive feedback effects in renewable energy policy in Germany was not an initially explicit aim; rather, this aspect emerged as an unintended consequence of policy design. However, this does not mean that feedback aspects of policy should not be thought about from the start; indeed, there is precisely an opportunity to do so. As the political dynamics of policy unfold over time, a strategy of adaptive management may also be important, responding to opportunities for positive feedback or the threats of negative feedback as they arise. To some extent, the German case again provides a fairly successful example of this.

A second implication is that countries with institutions that are less supportive of positive feedback effects should seek to change their institutions or develop new ones. This is a controversial area, with some arguing that institutional systems cannot be changed and others that they can. The key thing seems to be that what matters for learning from others is institutional function rather than form.

Finally, the approach taken here also throws some light on the relationships between social justice and green transformations. Policies which spread the benefits of transformations more widely – for example, Germany's employment in renewable supply chains in the deprived north and east of the country, are likely to produce valuable positive feedback effects and be more sustainable. A different perspective on the issue is to pose the question the other way round – i.e. does greater social justice make green transformation easier? Again, the experience of Germany and the UK would suggest that it does, because the better off are the poorest in society, the more able they are to bear some part of the costs of transformation and able to claim some share of the benefits

Notes

1 I am grateful to Carlota Perez, Hubert Schmitz and the other contributors to this book for comments on earlier drafts, and to Ashwin Gambhir for discussions on India's wind-energy policies. The framework used here for analysing the politics of energy was jointly developed with Caroline Kuzemko, Catherine Mitchell and Richard Hoggett. This work was supported by The Engineering and Physical Sciences Research Council (EPSRC) [EP/K001582/1].

2 Available online at: www.carbonbrief.org/blog/2014/04/germany%E2%80%99s-renewables-reforms-are-a-step-towards-giving-energy-sector-back-to-big-corporations/. Accessed 16 June 2014.

3 Available online at: www.business-standard.com/article/companies/restore-accelerated-depreciation-scheme-for-wind-sector-suzlon-114020900114_1.html. Accessed 16 June 2014.

4 Personal communication, Ashwin Gambhir, PRAYAS.

5 See also Laird and Stefes (2009) for a similar analysis of Germany and the US.

7

GREEN TRANSFORMATIONS FROM BELOW?

The politics of grassroots innovation

Adrian Smith and Adrian Ely

Introduction

Throughout the history both of modern environmentalism and development there has existed an insistent undercurrent of practical, grassroots initiatives seeking socially just and environmentally sustainable forms of production and consumption (Smith, 2005; Hess, 2007; Rist, 2011). In North and South, in cities and rural settings, networks of activists, development workers, community groups and neighbours have been generating bottom-up solutions for sustainable development – solutions that respond to the local situation and the interests and values of the communities involved. Initiatives have flourished, and struggled, in sectors as diverse as water and sanitation, housing and habitats, food and agriculture, energy, mobility, manufacturing, health, education, communications, and many other spheres of activity. We call this grassroots innovation (Gupta *et al.*, 2003; Seyfang and Smith 2007).

Some grassroots innovations have developed into widespread practices, such as car clubs across many cities in Europe. In a few cases, what began as grassroots activity has evolved into substantial green commercial activity in new industrial sectors, such as wind energy, whose dominant designs can be traced back to grassroots activism and alternative energy cooperatives. On occasions, the mainstreaming of grassroots innovation can involve input from and hybridization with research and development in more conventional institutions for science, technology and innovation (Ely *et al.*, 2013). Hybrid forms emerge through scaling-up that, while sometimes denuded of the grassroots vision, remain novel to other adopters, such as socially responsible corporations operating to different frameworks. In the case of wind turbines, while smaller scale, community-based initiatives continue, engineering development and commercial mainstreaming has scaled up into the form of much larger turbines in utility-scale wind farms relatively less disruptive to adoption within prevailing energy institutions.

On other occasions, grassroots organizations pioneer, adapt and develop novel uses of new (high) technologies emerging out of more conventional innovation systems. An example here is vibrant explorations into new forms of commons-based, peer-produced goods and services using versatile digital design and fabrication technologies in FabLabs and Hackerspaces today.

Policy and business is slowly taking notice of this bottom-up innovative activity. Agendas for inclusive innovation, open innovation and social innovation (highly relevant to green transformations) are drawing grassroots innovation to the attention of elite national and international agencies (OECD, 2012; World Bank, 2012). Grassroots activity attracts interest as both a source of potentially inclusive or socially valuable ideas and practices, worthy of scaling up, and as a relevant field of experience from which programmes for inclusive, social or green innovation might learn.

Not all business and policy incumbents welcome such developments. Policies for promoting corporate renewable energy models have been resisted by fossil energy interests, for instance. Neither does everyone in the grassroots welcome main-streaming either, where there can be reactions to elite co-option and distortion of visionary innovations. The resurgence of citizen and community energy initiatives in recent years is a countervailing example in energy, for instance.

Such political features in grassroots innovation can go much further and much deeper. Grassroots innovation movements can pursue an active and critical alternative to elite trajectories of innovation. Innovative initiatives in agroecology, for example, resist the encroachment of corporate-led agricultural biotechnology. Movements experimenting with commons-based, peer-production in grassroots digital design and fabrication, and their vision for open hardware and software within a knowledge commons, are actively opposing and resisting the institutions of proprietary intellectual property at the heart of conventional innovation institutions. In cases such as these, grassroots innovations are not simply contributing novel ideas and practices for green transformations, but contesting the very principles and character of these transformations.

So the questions guiding this chapter are, what transformations are envisaged and contested from 'below', and how does the politics of grassroots innovation manifest itself? In answering these questions, green transformations from below become infused with a politics that involves issues of autonomy and institutional-ization, ingenuity and contested knowledges, and objects and mobilization.

This chapter illustrates its argument with examples from grassroots innovation movements at different times and places. In the following section we introduce grassroots innovation by exploring three different framings and approaches to the phenomenon evident in practice and research. We then contrast grassroots innovation with more conventional innovation approaches, which typically involve research institutions, firms and investors. The politics of grassroots innovations in green transformations is understood through relationships with conventional approaches to innovation. Then follows consideration of the political dynamics generated by attempts to insert appropriable ideas and practices arising through grassroots innovations into mainstream innovation processes. We then look at how, in contrast, grassroots innovators can sometimes be less pliant and fit into mainstream agendas, and instead mobilize and press for transformations to mainstream innovation processes. This leads to questions about power and struggles for democracy in innovation processes, before we return the question of how green transformations emerge from below.

Grassroots innovation: between policy fixes and political mobilization

Grassroots innovators have been present at all the high-level summits devoted to the environment and development. They were at the 'hog farm' at Stockholm in 1972 and in 2012 were at Rio+20 at the Cúpola dos Povos in Flamengo Park. Displays at these events exhibited practical examples of how human needs could be defined and met more sustainably. Whether through their decentralized renewable energy designs, agroecological practices, eco-housing techniques, water and sanitation services, community workshops and remanufacturing facilities, complementary currencies, fair trade and solidarity economy arrangements, or a myriad of other initiatives, these grassroots innovations present practical anticipations of more sustainable societies (Ely *et al.*, 2013). In the context of this book, we might say they suggest green transformations from below.

Grassroots ingenuity

Some approaches towards grassroots innovation frame activity as a reservoir of ingenuity to be supported and tapped into. At its most precise and circumscribed, grassroots innovation is defined as a process generating creative solutions to development challenges arising within local communities, through the knowledge and inventive activities of individuals or groups in those communities. Social movements and policy institutions can help cultivate this activity by scouting for grassroots ingenuity and supporting innovators in the development of their initiatives. Development support can involve the provision of financial, technical and marketing resources. It can bring the innovator into contact with more conventional development and technology institutions, where expertise helps formalize the innovation into a form that can diffuse more readily or transform it into a scaled-up form. Arrangements are made for the original innovator to benefit from this process – for example, through some form of intellectual property provision. Assistance is provided for meeting regulatory or commercial standards requirements.

Examples of grassroots innovation of this kind include the thousands of examples documented by the Honey Bee Network and associated Society for Research and Initiatives for Technologies and Institutions, and Grassroots Innovation Augmentation Network in India, now supported by government through the National Innovation Foundation. Specific innovations include agroecological approaches reducing the need for irrigation or synthetic inputs (Gupta, 2013), or a particular kind of clay fridge that is now patented and on the market (Fressoli *et al.*, forthcoming 2014). Broader examples include movements that have seen small-scale turbine experimentation in communities in Denmark to develop into the multimillion dollar wind-power industry that we see today (Ely *et al.*, 2013).

Under this ingenuity framing, innovations move from inside grassroots activity outwards: it is the ingenuity and knowledge of individuals and groups in their local communities where the process begins (to the extent that it is possible to locate beginnings). Innovation arises in a specific, grassroots socioeconomic location. Support and assistance translates the innovation into more mobile, diffusible forms that work in other socioeconomic locations, including perhaps markets or larger scale applications.

Grassroots empowerment

A broader and more expansive definition of grassroots innovation includes ideas and innovations whose origins may have begun outside a grassroots setting, but whose appropriation and adaptation to local communities and their socioeconomic situations is carried out with grassroots groups in control over the process and deciding who benefits from the outcomes (Smith and Seyfang, 2013). Here the initial movement is more from the outside coming into the grassroots (Bell, 1979), and with the intention of providing grassroots innovators with new resources and capabilities that empowers them. Such a definition includes those strands of the appropriate technology movement, or attempts in participatory design, where the intended beneficiaries are put at the heart of the development process.

The Social Technologies Network (STN) based in Brazil involved until recently over 900 organizations (as of 2011) from across Latin America collaborating in the generation, dissemination and reapplication of innovations for sustainable development. An important aspect of the STN is the recognition of the need for local learning and innovation when attempting to replicate a social technology in a different place from where it was developed (Miranda *et al.*, 2011) – a focus on grassroots empowerment rather than scaling up in which the communities in question are passive recipients.

It can be argued that the more expansive view weakens the notion of grassroots innovation by opening it up to the kinds of consultancy-driven, participatory development already prevalent in many places, and whose good intentions are confounded at times through unreflexive application that disempowers communities, or empowers them selectively in ways not welcomed by the recipients. Anil K. Gupta founded the Honey Bee Network precisely because he was frustrated with his experience in development consultancy that ended up extracting and undermining knowledge and innovation in local communities. Donor-driven projects can impose or develop models (for the next job) through their grassroots engagement, rather than helping grassroots ingenuity flourish. Honey Bee's development of scouting techniques, working in the languages of the communities concerned, careful recognition of individual inventors by name, etc. (Gupta, 2013) reflect this concern to focus and build grassroots ingenuity, rather than expropriate it.

Certainly, the risks exist. Grassroots innovation can be co-opted as the latest term for the development industry, providing a new way of thinking about a relatively passive *site* for either appropriating ideas or inserting ready-made solutions, with little reflection on the grassroots as active subjects in innovations and appropriations of their own.

In our view, however, this is a criticism that calls for greater reflexivity towards grassroots innovation processes rather than circumscribed definitions. Even tightly defined notions focusing on grassroots ingenuity can involve encounters beyond the communities concerned. Even well-intended assistance for grassroots ingenuity can transform it through, for example, the introduction of intellectual property for the purposes of protecting benefits, standardizing for purposes of scaling up, and commodification for the purposes of attracting investment and marketing. All are processes that decontextualize the innovation and turn it into an object removed from the originating grassroots processes. More positively, the inevitable tacit knowledge and local experience required to domesticate any technology can provide some levers for local communities to influence the introduction and development of 'solutions' arising initially from beyond. This can include resisting or neglecting the innovation and in practice, we find that many grassroots innovations involve a bricolage and hybridization of indigenous and imported knowledge, skills, objects, resources, and so forth.

So another framing of grassroots innovation focuses not so much on the location of ingenuity, as on the power relations involved in developing solutions and the ways that grassroots actors can be empowered or build their own power to exert greater influence over developments in their social worlds, but also co-opted and overwhelmed by more powerful agendas. Certainly, appropriate technology projects in the past were intended to empower the target beneficiaries (in some cases whether the beneficiaries wanted them or not), and included instances where this was done clumsily and failed to attend fully to local power relations, or served to co-opt certain groups and issues.

One example illustrating this dynamic is the Cisterna (or 'One Million Cisterns') programme that sought to bring water to rural communities in Brazil. As originally conceived, the initiative introduced possible designs and materials for rainwater harvesting to communities, but it was the communities themselves that developed their capabilities through the build process and who exercised autonomy over the water they provided for themselves. Building the power to do grassroots innovation can be a strongly held aspiration. When the Brazilian government sought to accelerate the provision of rainwater harvesting by distributing more rapidly installed plastic water-butts, the pioneering social movement organized protests to remind the Cisterna programme about the ethos behind the original self-build process. Simply installing this technology provided neither the space nor processes for development workers and local community members to address issues that affect how the systems would be used. Unlike the government view on scaling up, the grassroots initiative was about more than providing families with water. There was a desire to address local power relations that affected not only access to water (and the injustices arising from reliance on water tanked in by vendors) but to expand it to other development issues too. In its original form, Cisterna attempted, through the organization of the self-build process, to build up capabilities for addressing social change, thereby giving people the confidence and power to organize themselves, articulate demands, do projects and coordinate their maintenance. Protests in the region subsequently reinstated a self-build track into the programme (Fressoli *et al.*, 2014).

A similar ethos can be found among some participants and promoters of FabLabs and Hackerspaces, and the grassroots use and development of digital fabrication technologies. It is argued the development of technical proficiency in specific projects is accompanied by the cultivation of wider and deeper social capabilities that have wider application, and can build among participants the power to do further grassroots innovation and participate practically in other developments. However, the processes of empowerment do not stop with capabilities. The experience of the initiatives within the People's Science Movement in India indicates how the organization of alternative economic arrangements can be an important underpinning to the subsequent effectiveness of any grassroots capabilities realized through innovative initiatives (Abrol, 2005). Specific improvements in productive processes in rural sectors like leather and food processing, required concomitant adaptations and developments in economic organization, such as creating co-operatives and negotiating new relations between occupations (and sometimes having to transcend cultural divisions of caste) in order for the innovations to be put to work by people. We pick this point up on below.

Encountering institutions of science, technology and innovation

Grassroots innovation movements present contrasting approaches to innovation compared to conventional science, technology and innovation (STI) institutions. The protagonists involved, their priorities and practices are typically distinct from the actors and processes policy-makers envisage when, say, promoting innovation systems for clean technologies. The mechanisms for developing innovations, through incentives, investments and forms of appropriation, look and operate differently. And there are contrasts in the forms of knowledge production emblematic for each. Table 7.1 provides a schematic contrast between mainstream STI institutions and grassroots innovation movements.

While the emphasis among grassroots innovation movements is 'exercising control over the innovation process' (Letty *et al.*, 2012, p1), in practice such control can require engagements with more powerful STI institutions. These encounters can take the form of partnerships with investors and firms in the scaling up of an innovation, for example, or with public research laboratories in the upgrading of

TABLE 7.1 Mainstream STI institutions and grassroots innovation movements' approaches to innovation

	Primary actors	Priority values	Principal incentives/drivers	Sources of investment	Forms of appropriability	Sites of innovation	Predominant forms of knowledge	Emblematic technological fields
Mainstream science, technology and innovation	Universities, public labs, commercial firms, ministries and other public institutions, international funding agencies	Scientific advance, for-profit innovation/ not necessarily focused on social inclusion	Market demand and regulation/ science competence	State/ corporate funded, venture capital	Intellectual property framework strongly biased towards patent-based innovation	Laboratories and R&D institutes, boardrooms and ministries, market-based firms	Scientific and technical knowledge	Biotech, ICTs, nanotech
Grassroots innovation movements	Civil society, NGOs, social movements, cooperatives	Social justice/ not necessarily focused on for-profit innovation	Social needs/ cooperation and community empowerment	Development aid, community finance, donations, state funding	Not appropriated by individuals – seen as common goods	Community projects and participatory processes, social movements	Local, situated knowledge/ indigenous knowledge	Organic food, small-scale renewable energies, water sanitation

Source: Fressoli, M., Arond, E., Abrol, D., Smith, A., Ely, A. and Dias, R. (2014) 'When grassroots innovation movements encounter mainstream institutions: implications for models of inclusive innovation', *Innovation and Development*, Vol. 4, No. 2, pp277–292.

designs and techniques, and inclusion in the programmes of governments, aid agencies and business initiatives to assist marginalized groups (Cozzens and Sutz, 2014).

So the two worlds characterized in Table 7.1 actually interpenetrate one another. In practice, we see a much more dynamic, complex and messy field of hybrids and contestations working across the poles of grassroots and conventional STI presented in Table 7.1. Much of the politics of green transformations from below will derive from where participating groups are coming from in approaching a grassroots innovative activity, how they are seeking to push and shape developments, as well as the political strengths and creative capacities of the groups involved in these negotiations, and how they are situated in terms of wider power relations.

Nevertheless, the analytical simplification in Table 7.1 points to a basic political dynamic in green transformations from below: whether one is seeking to insert the grassroots innovation into conventional STI institutions, or whether one is seeking to mobilize around the grassroots innovation as emblematic of an insistent need for new forms of innovation institutions, and new processes for doing innovation. So even though grassroots innovations are perceived, understood and approached by various actors in multiple ways, at heart tensions emerge between strategies for bottom-up innovative activity that seek to adapt it into forms amenable to assistance from prevailing STI institutions, and more overtly political sensibilities whose aims are to transform the institutions of innovation and to open them up through mobilization of grassroots innovation activity.

As Fressoli *et al.* (2014, p6) elaborate, insertion of grassroots innovations has more of a technical, policy fix temper to it:

> From the point of view of grassroots innovation movements, insertion means fitting into prior spaces of innovation and playing by or adapting to the rules of dominant institutions, technologies, regulations, etc. The reverse side of the same movement may happen at the locus of top-down engagement, where mainstream institutions seek to insert and capture ideas, elements and even models from grassroots innovation movements, adapting them to their own agendas and practices.

The scope for doing green transformation differently and pursuing alternative pathways in grassroots innovation is reduced by insertion. Fressoli *et al.* (2014, p7) go on to argue:

> If this occurs, giving way to policy disagreements, or if mainstream STI institutions are impenetrable to GIM [grassroots innovation movement] proposals, a second mode of engagement can arise. This happens when there is *mobilisation* or resistance of grassroots to incumbent regimes, with the aim of developing pathways toward alternative innovation systems. In this way, mobilisation implies direct attempts to transform the spaces of innovation by challenging the dominant practices, technologies, power relations and

discourses . . . [that] may eventually force the incumbent regimes to change *their* models, and/or lead to autonomous experimentation with new socio-technical arrangements.

Where the former, insertion view positions grassroots innovation as generating appropriable object solutions (technological artefacts or social innovations), often accompanied by a desire to select and scale up those that look promising under prevailing institutions of science, technology and innovation, the latter, more political view interprets grassroots innovation as an attempt to recast institutional priorities through mobilizations that entail a politics-of-doing, and whose awkwardness or unfamiliarity to elite institutions underscores how the latter exclude and marginalize many people and perspectives in innovation. Such 'technological agit prop', as Mike Cooley once called it, suggests not just why but how institutions need to change. An alternative way of framing grassroots innovation arises, which is to view it as expressing a grassroots politics of sustainability through the processes of practical reasoning.

Note that politics is involved in both forms of encounter. Insertion generates a politics through the particularities of its selective approach to grassroots innovation, just as responses to political approaches to grassroots innovation generate a wider politics too. One can see this in the appropriate and alternative technology movements in the 1970s. One can glimpse it today in maker movements for grassroots fabrication. Pressures to conform and provide solutions on elite terms, and grassroots reactions to the criteria and norms of any appropriations to scale are argued to underpin the politics of grassroots innovation. And one can witness a push back or resistance to this in attempts to mobilize alternative principles for innovation, such as commons-based peer-production, and renewals of practice that recuperate more holistic grassroots solutions following selective insertion, such as in some forms of agroecology. Indeed, one can argue that a dialectical relation between these two positions is what drives grassroots innovation movements over time. It is also likely to shape any future green transformations from below.

Inserting the grassroots into mainstream innovation

Policy interest has returned to grassroots innovation in recent years against a backdrop of growing attention to inclusive innovation. The OECD (2012), World Bank (2012) and many national governments have produced reports, held events and set up initiatives to try to promote models for more inclusive innovation. Levels of attention have been paid to innovation beyond more formalized institutions and systems – a situation not seen since appropriate technology in the 1970s and 1980s, and when the OECD had its own Centre for Appropriate Technology, like many other organizations.

Aspirations for supporting grassroots ingenuity and promoting innovation processes that empower have to be unpacked into questions about empowering for whom, to do what and why, questions about the credit or recognition for solutions that emerge, and about the distribution of costs, benefits, risks and uncertainties involved. While well-designed initiatives need to be clear on these matters, and the best involve the intended beneficiaries themselves, encounters that adapt and insert grassroots innovation unreflexively into STI institutions ignore the way engagements are framed in the first place. So, for example, it is often presumed that grassroots innovations need to be scaled up or replicated widely, and this then feeds back to become a criterion for supporting particular grassroots initiatives.

Or, to put it another way, the performance of a grassroots innovation may be associated narrowly with a particular artefact of the initiative and measured according to conventional policy criteria, such as a community energy initiative being assessed in terms of the quantity and costs of electricity provided. What these instrumental readings of grassroots innovation miss is some of the purposes and framings of the people involved in the initiative. In the case of community energy initiatives, this can include feelings of community identity, a sense of justice and claim over local renewable resources like the wind and sun, and promoting a degree of social and economic self-determination in matters of (electrical) power.

Beyond individual artefacts, approaches such as the number of designs, patents or other forms of intellectual property provide an indicator of the volume of 'grassroots ingenuity' (combined with the attention and support paid to it). Aggregating the value added from such grassroots innovations provides another (economic) output metric. It is common, for example, to hear arguments made about the potential to scale up a grassroots innovation or to replicate across a great number and variety of locations. Alternatively, calls have been made to develop indicators and other measures of grassroots innovation (Letty et al., 2012). A reasonable point is made that policy interest in grassroots innovation will be attracted only when the scale and significance of grassroots innovation activity is quantified in some general way. And if this can be done using metrics already appreciated by policy-makers, such as jobs or value added, then so much the better. Such activity may help raise the profile and credibility of grassroots innovation in the eyes of elite innovation institutions, but it also represents grassroots innovation in particular ways familiar to elites, and not necessarily how all activists promoting alternative innovation pathways would wish it to be represented.

The emerging world of grassroots digital fabrication is an example of where multiple framings and metrics converge, clash and contest one another. The increasing accessibility of relatively affordable, yet increasingly versatile machine tools (such as laser cutters, 3D printers, milling machines) and design software (such as computer-aided design freeware and hacked scanners) are increasingly being taken up by a grassroots maker movement that is connecting on-line through social media platforms and physically at meet-ups, maker faires, and in community workshops such as hackerspaces, makerspaces and FabLabs. Ideas, designs and collaborative projects are shared on-line and off-line in these digital and physical spaces.

In some cases, this activity is self-organized, in other cases it receives institutional impetus and support through universities, or charities, or government programmes.

In the latter case, interest in grassroots digital fabrication rests in concerns to engage people (especially younger people) in design, manufacturing and entrepreneurship. Institutions frame makerspaces and digital fabrication as a useful way for future workers to experiment in what they see as an industrial transformation and renaissance. For others, however, such as hacker activists drawing parallels with the free software movement, grassroots digital fabrication is about the democratization of production and consumption, and a contribution to a knowledge commons that includes open hardware designs. Others concerned about sustainability see grassroots digital fabrication offering the promise of a closure of localized production–consumption loops, and through hands-on, collaborative involvement in material processes of provision, it is hoped that post-consumer values may be cultivated (Thorpe, 2012).

So with grassroots digital fabrication, as with other areas of grassroots innovation, we see multiple framings in play that contain institutional insertion in some cases, but also involve aims for political mobilization. Grassroots digital fabrication provides a new stream of talent, ideas and innovations for appropriation for capitalist institutions, but at the same time, the seeds of an alternative, commons-based, peer-produced, sustainable and democratic future. The kinds of resources flowing to these spaces of grassroots digital fabrication, the agendas attached, the ways they are governed, the meaning and symbolism involved, and their consequences, will be contested through these framings. However, as we see in the next section, those contests for grassroots innovation are shaped also by their interplay with broader and deeper political economies.

In sum, the institutional insertion of grassroots innovation looks to initiatives through prevailing institutions for the environment, development and innovation. Grassroots innovations are selected as promising and worthy of support, or marginal and neglected, on the basis of their fit to STI institutional priorities and pressures for reforming fixes. Under such circumstances, grassroots innovation is transformed rather than being transformational.

Mobilizing a grassroots politics of practical reasoning

Grassroots innovators and innovation movements can sometimes welcome institutional support and assistance. Indeed, grassroots innovations can arise for very similar instrumental reasons – a fix to a problem, meeting a need unserved by markets or states. Mutual ground can be found between the grassroots innovation and the resourceful STI institutions that can help it to scale or diffuse. However, this is not always the case. At times, it is the norms, assumptions, aims and practices of prevailing institutions that are precisely the problem, and which the grassroots innovation is responding to through creating an alternative norm, assumption, aim or practice. Other forms of social mobilization for changing norms etc., such as protests, strikes, boycotts, media campaigns, litigation, manifestos, and so on seek rights and recognition from societal institutions. In contrast, grassroots innovation movements involve people in the practical development of alternative activities.

They are engaged in a politics of doing, as much as discussing. In working on the social and technical aspects of alternative ways of, say, harvesting rainwater, they undertake a practical reasoning in the politics of water supply in development.

Formal institutions have a hard time recognizing, let alone accommodating this more political appreciation of grassroots innovation. Indeed, the whole point of some grassroots innovation movements is to challenge and unsettle prevailing institutions for innovation and development. When workers at Lucas Aerospace developed an alternative corporate strategy for their company in 1976, for instance, they were deliberately challenging not just company strategy, but also the wider political economy of technology development. Arising through grassroots trade union organization, the alternative plan was a novel response to management announcements that thousands of manufacturing jobs were to be cut in the face of industrial restructuring, international competition and technological change. Instead of redundancy, workers argued their right to socially useful production. In promoting their arguments, shop stewards at Lucas attracted workers from other sectors, community activists, radical scientists, environmentalists, pacifists and the Left. The Plan became symbolic for a movement of activists committed to innovation for the purposes of social use over private profit. Supportive polytechnics, union organizations and local governments provided resources and spaces for activists to develop their ideas, products and argument.

The Lucas Plan, and others like it, included designs and prototypes for alternative, socially useful products, but they also went much further. These plans included market analyses and economic argument; proposed employee training and the development of new technologies, such as computers, that enhanced and broadened skills; and suggested reorganizing work into less hierarchical teams that bridged divisions between tacit knowledge on the shop floor and theoretical engineering knowledge in design shops.

Business and government rejected the plans. The idea that a grassroots movement of workers, their communities and social activists had a democratic right to participate in the design, production and marketing of goods and services seemed simply incredible to business and government elites, or, more seriously, was discomforting, unwelcome and even threatening. Even leaders in the trade union establishment were reluctant to back this grassroots initiative, wary that its precedent would challenge privileged demarcations and hierarchies. The critical point here is that the practical process of developing prototypes – in community workshops, for instance – was seen as an activity in and for political mobilization.

Recalling the movement now, what is striking is the importance that activists attached to practical engagements in technology development as part of their politics. The movement emphasized tacit knowledge, craft skill and learning by doing through face-to-face collaboration in material projects. Practical activity was cast as 'technological agit prop' for mobilizing alliances and debate. Some participants found such politicization unwelcome. However, in opening prototyping in this way, activists tried to bring more varied participation into debates and enable wider, more practical forms of expression meaningful to different audiences, compared to speeches and texts evoking, say, a revolutionary agent, socially entrepreneurial state or deliberative governance framework.

Activism in socially useful production dissipated in the face of industrial restructuring and relocation, and an emerging Thatcherite political agenda antithetical to active industrial policy. With hindsight, the movement was swimming against the political and economic tide. At the time things looked less clear cut. Ultimately, however, the alliances struck, the spaces created and the initiatives generated were swept aside as concern for the social shaping of technology was left to market decision. Some practices had wider influence, such as in participatory design, albeit it in forms appropriated to the needs of capital rather than the intended interests of labour. Conventional institutions took instrumental advantage of the diversity of novel practices opened up by a more politically inspired burst of grassroots innovation activity.

Today, in FabLabs, Hackerspaces and other forms of makerspace discussed above, people are coming together under very different circumstances to work materially on shared technology projects, using digital fabrication and design tools. Social media opens these engagements in distributed and interconnected forms. Web platforms and versatile digital fabrication technologies allow people to share open-hardware designs and contribute to an emerging knowledge commons. The sheer fun participants find in making things often in personal projects is imbued by others with excited claims, for the democratization of manufacturing and ushering alternative principles for innovation through commons-based peer production. There is a political mobilization to some of this doing.

Grassroots digital fabrication rekindles ideas about direct participation in technology development and use. Grassroots projects, involving the cultivation of tacit knowledge and skills, are also about crafting solidarities. Project-centred discussion and activity is linked to debate and mobilization around wider issues. In the context of green transformations, it is argued by some that these facilities not only help localize sustainable production–consumption, up-cycling, fixing and repair, but they might also promote post-consumerist cultures. Getting involved in design and fabrication shifts a sense of well-being away from the consumption of objects, with attendant chains of short-lived satisfaction and repetition, and towards the cultivation of skills, knowledge and collaborative relationships in differently satisfying, less alienated processes of social production (Thorpe, 2012). However, as pointed out, there are other interests in makerspaces less attendant towards such cultural or political mobilization, and see instead participatory incubators for prototyping and experimenting that will help bring on stream a new generation of entrepreneurs, designers and engineers. And, of course, participants in these spaces may simply be there for the fun of doing their personal projects, unaware or indifferent to these wider social inscriptions and mobilizations.

Other recent attempts to mobilize community ingenuity to serve environmental (especially climate change) and social (inclusion and cohesion) goals have emerged from local experiments in Europe. Again with long historical precedents, the emergence of the 'transition towns' and 'energy descent action plan' narratives, and the growth of the 'transitions network' (www.transitionnetwork.org) over the past decade points towards grassroots innovation as a force for green transformations from below in the global North. Despite the profound structural barriers holding back these initiatives from generating wider political change, proponents continue to celebrate 'the power of just doing stuff' (Hopkins, 2013).

Studies of community agriculture projects, a 'grassroots innovation' as defined by Seyfang and Smith (2007), have pointed to the plurality of objectives motivating communal growing – beyond environmental sustainability to include support for disability, education, health and community, confidence, welfare and skills (White and Stirling, 2013). Under these circumstances, the authors point to external funding programmes as 'windows of opportunity' that brought diverse intermediary actors together in collaborative ways – even if conflicting positions re-entrench once funding comes to an end (White and Stirling, 2013). Such examples can be seen either as inserting policy fixes (public support for non-government actors to work towards policy objectives) or instances of political mobilization (the opportunities that such initiatives present for communities and wider actors to position themselves in relation to oppositional regimes that perpetuate structures of unsustainable and socially exclusive systems of food production).

Power to do innovation, power over innovation and democratic transformations

Historical reflection on earlier grassroots innovation movements, like those for socially useful production, turns attention to the power relations that will matter for these more recent initiatives and a need to address power when considering green 'transformations from below'. Grassroots innovation can range from a necessary response to social challenges, to an accessible and fun way to express creativity. Across this diverse range of activity, people are exercising a power to innovate. However, when some of those grassroots innovations seek wider influence (and not all do), then the same people can still struggle to obtain spaces and resources to be innovative because they lack power over the agendas of elite innovation institutions, such as those determining which innovations attract investment for production and marketing, and under what social criteria.

Of course, in trying to go about innovations for sustainability in ways quite different from elite institutions, and struggling precisely due to the power of those prevailing institutions, then grassroots innovations reveal in very visible and practical ways some of the structural constraints to green transformations from below. Grassroots innovations provide a practical critique of prevailing economic, social and political relations in innovation, but they also point to some alternative possibilities, were those structural constraints to be challenged more powerfully and effectively. It is no coincidence that some grassroots innovations have in the past become emblematic for wider social movements seeking wider and deeper changes, such as environmentalists, feminists, post-development activists. Socially useful production was emblematic in its time, but others have included wind energy, organic food and rainwater harvesting, traditional medicines, manufacturing, free software, and others. Today, campaigners for a knowledge commons, campesino rights, socially just sustainability transitions, and so forth evoke emblematic grassroots innovations also. The travails but also possibilities of grassroots innovations in tune with movement aims point to both critique and alternative at the same time. This dual feature of grassroots innovation movements allows them to switch between insertion and mobilization strategies and vice versa, or even combinations, in ways that not only respond to the context, but also as a deliberate attempt to retain autonomy and exercise influence (Fressoli *et al.*, 2014).

Shifting power relations are thus significant for grassroots innovation: the power to do innovation and power over innovation agendas (cf. Holloway, 2002). Insertion involves power relations between the grassroots and innovation institutions through the way grassroots novelties are selected and developed. Who is in control of these processes? What principles are in play over decisions and selections? This can be articulated as questions of mobilizing for more democratic innovation.

Drawing on grassroots debate and experience as presented in this chapter, then, a democratizing innovation agenda would address the opening up and transformation of innovation institutions towards deeper and more meaningful grassroots participation. Practically, that means thinking of more democratic arenas for establishing research agendas, funding decisions, universities, research institutes, venture and investment capital, training and skills programmes, prototyping infrastructures, marketing, and so forth. It also means building networks and coalitions between these arenas, where the potential can be demonstrated through acts, amplified by lobbying, and win influence through alliances. These are political challenges about opening up innovation systems and making systems accessible to citizens.

What this means, in our view, is that even as we witness the gradual reorientation of dominant techno-economic paradigms and sociotechnical regimes towards a low-carbon agenda, or some other international priority mediated by markets, such as resource efficiency and the circular economy, the wider sustainability of such 'top-down' activity will not go uncontested. We may see an unfolding of 'clean technology' promoted by large investors, corporations and entrepreneurial states, and an attempt to install a co-evolving framework for sustainable development by elites. However, if we look carefully enough, then we will also notice it is accompanied by a more unruly, anarchic and messier exploration of everyday sustainabilities involving the kind of practical reasoning evident in grassroots innovation. Indeed, the latter may continue to be the fount of genuinely creative sustainability solutions, just as it has been in the past.

The practical challenges for these grassroots innovation mobilizations remain considerable and uncertain. One practical possibility arising from some grassroots initiatives suggests lobbying for a scaling down of innovation systems (cf. scaling up of innovations), and providing innovation facilities and institutions where people live. This has been attempted a little with science shops and technology networks in the past, for example, and is being rediscovered and explored through makerspaces and citizen science initiatives today. None of this is a panacea. Other, more demanding and difficult practical steps need to be explored also. There is not space to develop them here, but it connects to other chapters in this book (e.g. see Stirling, Leach and Scoones).

Whatever gets considered, experience suggests that we need to guard against idealizing or even romanticizing grassroots activism in design, experimentation and development of innovations. People do not respond automatically to the provision of a material facilities and training programmes. The spaces need to be in tune with the contexts in which people live; they have to be designed and cultivated carefully, through on-going community development processes. People have to be supported in gaining confidence within these more structured spaces. Nor will everyone wish to take up this support. Questions of inclusion, exclusion, participation, and so forth are just as pertinent in these grassroots spaces as they are in mainstream innovation institutions. Issues abound around expertise, knowing how and knowing what skills, tacit knowledge and practices that push the scope and flexibility of both high and low technological options. The point is that the kinds of networked spaces and grassroots innovation activity flourishing today allows experimentation and learning in democracy itself and what democratizing innovation can mean practically.

Conclusions

The questions motivating this chapter were about what kinds of transformations are envisaged and contested from 'below', and how does the politics of grassroots innovation manifest itself?

Grassroots innovations involve very heterogeneous, dynamic and messy processes. Frameworks for thinking and action in this area include those of 'grassroots ingenuity' and 'grassroots empowerment', but they are not the only ones, and we touched on a structural critique framing towards the end of the chapter, but there are others too. Within these different framings, grassroots innovation movements often aim to challenge and transform existing systems that fail to serve social needs across localities, or to enable 'greener' (see Chapter 1) directions of development neglected by elite agendas. As such, movements for grassroots innovation are driven by a plurality of visions and purposes, including those emerging from within the grassroots itself, but also from beyond in the domains of formal innovation, environment, and development institutions and structures. Our argument tried to simplify and introduce some analytical clarity by drawing a contrast between these policy insertion and political mobilization views of grassroots innovation. Each can emerge from within or beyond the grassroots, as has been illustrated by examples from diverse national contexts and current attention paid by international organizations.

What distinguishes these two broad approaches to grassroots innovation is their relationship to prevailing institutions. Looking to grassroots innovation within existing institutional frameworks and seeking to insert promising ideas and practices results in the transformation of grassroots innovation processes into object forms. Conversely, a more political approach to grassroots innovation seeks to transform wider institutions through the possibilities that grassroots innovation activities offer for mobilization. Only the latter is really about green transformations from below. Whether in the global North or South, these imply more anarchic, messy and ongoing processes of change in contrast to the ordered and mechanical transitions envisaged within 'green economy' narratives.

Historical studies suggest that structures of political economy are vital in enabling or constraining the possibilities envisaged for 'transformations from below'. The potential for communities to exercise their power to 'do' innovation is made so much easier by concurrent power 'over' innovation agendas, pointing to the centrality of struggles for democracy in green transformations. At the same time, the actual process of innovating at the grassroots itself serves to shift the democratic balance and to (re-)position power at the grassroots level.

Thus the perspective on grassroots innovation developed in this chapter views it as expressing a grassroots politics of sustainability through processes of practical reasoning across local activities. The politics of grassroots innovation manifests itself through practical experimentation, learning, organizing and mobilization that enables communities to position themselves in opposition to the unsustainable and unjust systems that to a significant extent characterize our world, and to build up their power to develop alternatives. In continuing to negotiate and attempting to enact 'transformations from below', grassroots innovation movements are challenging the conventional boundaries, definitions and agendas of more elite innovation institutions, e.g. elite emphasis on a capital-intensive 'cleantech' and financialized green economy. At heart, this is a struggle over the democratization of innovations and green transformations.

Acknowledgements

Research underpinning this chapter comes from a variety of projects funded by UK Research Councils. We are grateful to colleagues collaborating in these projects. For their collegiality and insights we wish to thank Dinesh Abrol, Elisa Arond, Jacob Barnes, Rachael Durrant, Tom Hargreaves, Sabine Hielscher, Mariano Fressoli, Mari Martiskainen, Jin Park and Gill Seyfang.

8

MOBILIZING FOR GREEN TRANSFORMATIONS

Melissa Leach and Ian Scoones

Introduction

In building green transformations, vital sources of energy, imagination, knowledge, experience and practice lie in citizen action and mobilization. However, such movements take on different forms in different places and at different moments in history. As argued elsewhere in this book, there are clearly multiple green transformations required today, but how can they come about, and what role do collective organization, mobilization and activism play in this process?

Social movement theory identifies the framing of issues, the construction of identities, the mobilization of resources and the galvanization of networks as key features of movements (Leach and Scoones, 2007). Yet the capacity to contribute to green transformations also depends critically on the relationships between movements, networks and their institutionalization, and on the relationships between particularistic, locally grounded practices, and claims and action focused on wider forms of transformation. Green transformations, as argued elsewhere in this book, involve challenges to investment and infrastructure, practices and power relations that involve both private and public sector actors, and extend up to global scales. We argue here that the effectiveness of mobilization in the politics of green transformation hinges on how far vibrant local action and agendas that make space for citizens' own concerns are able to articulate with and mount challenges to global forces.

In this chapter, we explore and evaluate these dimensions in relation to case studies where movements have emerged to urge green transformations of different sorts – in small farm production and markets, in agricultural technology, and in urban design and living. In each of these cases different types of movements have formed and evolved, framing the green transformation challenge in different ways and navigating tensions along the movement institutionalization and particularism wider transformation, local–global axes in different ways. We also note other contexts where a quieter, more hidden form of transformation occurs through shared practice, linked to particular cultural–political modes of organization. We conclude with a brief discussion of the implications of these differences for alliance building for green transformations and the political challenges this suggests.

Green movements: a simple typology and a very brief history

Not all movements conform to the banner-waving activist image of the media stereotype. Indeed, there is a wide variety of forms and styles, some more resonant with this image, others much less visible. A movement can be defined broadly as a collective response binding different people in 'practised engagement through emergent solidarities' around a particular issue, or set of issues (Leach and Scoones, 2007, p16, drawing on Ellison, 1997). Green movements have often been theorized as exemplars of new social movements (Della Porta and Diani, 2006), and there is a large literature that explores such dynamics of contentious politics (e.g. Tilly, 1978; Tarrow, 1998; McAdam *et al.*, 2001, 2003). Today, at least three types of 'green' movement are evident (cf. Szerszynski, 1997; Jamison, 2001).

First, there are those green movements associated with lifestyle change, focusing on shifts in individual behaviour and practice. Such movements are usually rooted in local networks and often part of 'alternative' lifestyles, linked to other movements associated with, for example, food and housing. They may be more broadly linked through wider networking and, while clearly political in the sense of a personal commitment to change, many do not overtly campaign in the public political sphere, arguing that change must be emergent from individual, community-based and local efforts. There has been a long tradition of such lifestyle-centred movements in Europe and North America from the 1960s onwards, while in other parts of the world they have been associated with protecting the political and cultural autonomy of particular groups (e.g. indigenous people's movements, peasant movements) as well as religious organizations (e.g. Buddhist retreats, Ghandian ashrams), often with much longer traditions.

Second, there are activist organizations and networks that form around particular issues. These are more confrontational and aim to tackle wider policy issues through direct action and protest. From the classic Greenpeace whaling protests of the 1970s to the climate justice or anti-GM campaigns of today, such movements have had high visibility, often with visible impacts. In many ways these have symbolized the environmental movement in the global North that came to prominence in the late 1960s and early 1970s, and led to the creation of organizations from Friends of the Earth to Greenpeace to the Sierra Club. Many of these organizations have themselves changed, responding to shifts in the cultural and political landscape, but the radical, activist edge has not been lost. From the late 1990s, certain green movements and campaigns became increasingly allied to anticapitalist movements, including those convened by the World Social Forum from its founding event at Porto Alegre in 2001, and more recently the 'Climate Justice', 'Occupy' and 'Anonymous' movements. Such movements, even if focused on a particular environmental or social issue, have developed a larger critique of the way that contemporary neoliberal capitalism has affected the environment, and social and political life, and has acted to undermine rights, producing inequality and poverty.

Third, some green movements over time, or through splits in original groupings, have become increasingly professionalized, forming more formal organizations, and arguing for a place at formal policy tables and intergovernmental negotiations to put the green case. An important spur to this was the major UN Conference on Environment and Development held in Rio in 1992. Its predecessor in Stockholm in 1972 had hailed the arrival of the environmental movement on the international stage and was the moment when many organizations formed, led by visionaries such as Barbara Ward, author of *Only One Earth* (Ward and Dubos, 1972) or inspired by the likes of Rachel Carson, author of the classic environmentalist text, *Silent Spring* (Carson, 1962). However, it was in 1992 that environmental issues hit the mainstream, backed by detailed analysis and argument in the World Commission in Environment and Development report, *Our Common Future* (Brundtland, 1987), and then crystallized in the establishment of international conventions and the bottom-up process Agenda 21 (UNEP, 1992). Such institutionalization has, of course, presented strategic and tactical challenges, with co-optation and reformist managerialism being balanced against access and influence. However, since the 1990s and the rise of environmental concerns in national and international policy arenas, such organizations have become increasingly influential, striking up important achievements in a range of areas from biodiversity protection to climate change to sustainable development goals, and even making inroads into business through organizations such as the World Business Council on Sustainable Development.

Whether such groups can be classified as 'movements' is a moot point, however. Some self-define not as such, but as non-governmental organizations (NGOs). Many in the more activist groupings will dismiss organizations that engage closely with the mainstream as co-opted 'sell-outs', no longer grounded in real citizens' concerns or challenges to the status quo. However, whatever the classification, the important point is that today there is a huge array of groups, more or less formally organized, committed to green transformations of different sorts. They have different organizational forms, different framings of the problem and different proposed solutions; they have different strategies and tactics in respect of the politics required, and they are networked in different ways, not always working together harmoniously.

Drawing insights from the Honey Bee Network in India, Anil Gupta (Gupta, 2013) usefully argues that movements (grassroots action) must interact with networks (that link different grassroots forms) in order to embed and spread ideas and change, and must be supported by institutions (embracing larger organizations) if there is any hope of sustaining change within bureaucratic and policy structures. Each cannot achieve a successful and radical transformation alone. There are inevitably tensions, but Gupta argues that these are productive ones, as long as the movements can hold the more formal institutions to account and the network continues to serve the movement participants. The challenge is how to avoid new institutions becoming separated from their network and movement base, and how to keep the networks active so that they are continually generating new ideas and innovations, and avoid getting co-opted by increasingly formalized and powerful institutions in the mainstream. The movements we discuss below have embraced such networking and institutionalization challenges and opportunities to different extents, and in different ways, shaping their abilities to contribute to transformational change.

These case study mobilizations, like many others, are reflective of a particular social–political–cultural process that emerged in Western Europe and North America in the late 1960s, while picking up on other traditions of protest and mobilization, notably Ghandian organization and philosophy in India, and radical social movements protesting against dictatorship in Latin America. Today, such traditions often blend with Western environmentalisms, as new forms emerge through global networking and linkages afforded by international travel, Internet-based communication and global networking, especially among a politically vocal, globalized middle class. Yet in other settings, with a different history, culture and politics, there may be other forms of organization whose 'green' features and commitment to transformation are less recognizable – at least to Western-influenced commentators. We turn to these instances later, asking if there are other forms of less visible but potentially transformative mobilization that are important, and need attention and support if a truly global set of green transformations is to unfold.

Towards green transformations: three cases

In the following sections, we discuss three different cases of mobilization, exploring how four dimensions of social movements identified in the literature – framing, identity, resource mobilization and networks (Leach and Scoones, 2007) – play out in practice in different cases and settings, in interaction with dynamics along a spectrum from movement to institutionalization, and a focus on particular local issues, to wider global concerns. It is in relation to these interacting dynamics that we address the politics of mobilization in each case, and the contradictions and tensions as well as opportunities and challenges that arise in creating green transformations.

La Via Campesina and food sovereignty

La Via Campesina – the peasants' way – emerged in the late 1990s around a constellation of groups, particularly in Europe and Latin America, wanting to defend the rights of small farmers in the face of pressures from large-scale corporate agriculture supported by government and international policy (Desmarais, 2007). A vision of small-scale peasant farming rooted in local markets and economies was developed that adopted the term 'food sovereignty' as its rallying cry (Rosset, 2003). A particular strand of this argument, confirmed in a series of statements and declarations, urged the adoption of 'agroecology', which posed a distinctively green agenda. Agroecology emphasizes working with nature not against it, and using low external inputs that are non-polluting, and that do not rely on large-scale corporate input suppliers of seeds, fertilizers, and so on (Altieri, 2009). There are overlaps, of course, with the longer established organic movement and other agri-food movements (Jamison, 2012), but the emphasis here is on the process of farming, its groundedness in local ecologies and its relationships with economic structures, as well as the product itself.

Since its origins the movement has grown, with some suggesting that today it is the largest social movement in the world.[1] This growth has meant the movement has encompassed more and more interests and issues, including linking up with indigenous people's movements, the women's movement, migrants' movements, workers' unions, consumer groups, and more. This 'big tent' approach has enabled articulation with a range of global forces and challenges. However, it has brought with it tensions, and for some a lack of strategic focus, and failure to concentrate on particular political actions. The Nyeleni declaration, produced through an intensive negotiation among movement participants, is the nearest thing that exists to a political manifesto, and it presents a utopian ideal across a huge range of issues.[2]

As an organization, La Via Campesina has evolved from a very loose federation of groups that found common ground in and around the World Social Fora and other events, to a more structured arrangement, with a General Coordinator (currently from Zimbabwe, previously from Indonesia), a central committee, advisory groups, training events, demonstration sites and a regular series of meetings where members from across the movement gather. With its powerful slogan, 'Globalise the struggle, globalise hope', there is an attempt to forge a united alliance across diverse groups around a global issue. Focused campaigns on particular issues, whether around 'land grabbing', 'GMOs', or corporate agriculture more generally, provide moments for mobilization (Borras et al., 2008).

Together with others, there has been considerable energy invested in recent years in two major international policy processes. First was the International Assessment for Agricultural Science and Technology for Development (IAASTD) that culminated in a report in 2009 that, while presented in the language of an international report sponsored by the World Bank, reflected many of the aspirations – and some key language – of the movement. The IAASTD, or at least selected sections of it, has become a focus for mobilization, and a source of authority and legitimacy (Scoones, 2009). Second has been the UN Food and Agricultural Organization's Committee on Food Security (CFS). This is the first UN process where non-governmental representation (not just observer status) is permitted. This has allowed movement activists to become involved in intergovernmental negotiations – for instance, around the 'Voluntary Guidelines on Land Tenure' that were passed in 2013, as well as the High Level Panel of Experts' discussions around such issues as 'land grabbing'.

Thus, movement framings centre on the themes of food sovereignty and agroecology, and the associated challenge to corporate control of the agri-food system. It is argued that small-scale, peasant farming can indeed 'feed the world' through agroecological practices, if only the system was more just and less skewed towards incumbent corporate interests. Identities are constructed in relation to a somewhat idealized notion of the 'peasant' or 'small-scale farmer', seen as struggling for self-determination and autonomy in the face of monopoly capitalism and the depredations of neoliberal markets (Guzmán and Martinez-Alier, 2006). The resources mobilized have been significant, less in financial terms although there are important backers, but in terms of the intellectual, organizational and mobilization capacities of movement participants and their allies in other movements, among radical academics, and in some cases within government agencies, in international organizations and among some political leaders.

This building of the movement over 20 years has nevertheless faced challenges, not least in the uncomfortable relationship between local concerns and political action on a global stage. The 'ideal type' peasant deployed in global campaigns very often does not exist. A strategically deployed essentialism in wider movement discourse may sit uneasily with the lived realities of people on the ground. Many people juggle different livelihoods – in town, in the rural areas, across occupations – and rarely follow the autonomous peasant route. Equally, by attempting to encompass consumers, workers and others in the overall frame, the potential class and political differences may disrupt a seeming consensus. Consumers may not be aligned with producers, and workers not with their farmer employers, so the coherence of a struggle against capital may sometimes fray at the edges.

Equally, the edicts about how to farm in an 'agroecological' way are resisted by those keen to use more modern technologies, arguing that these too can create positive environmental and livelihood impacts if used sensitively. A technological fundamentalism sometimes undermines the credibility of the argument in certain contexts, especially when the struggle to provide food and livelihoods is especially pressing. Such ideals, it is argued, may be all well and good in a richer context, where people are prepared to pay for the privilege of 'green' agroecological products, but when poverty and hunger stalks, such rich-world luxuries may not be possible.[3]

That said, La Via Campesina and the food sovereignty movement more broadly, with its building of networks and its increasing institutionalization, is making inroads into mainstream global debates. Once dismissed as the radical fringe, now food sovereignty and smallholder rights are being debated in international fora, with the UN announcing that 2014 is the Year of Family Farming, while on the ground and in the more local struggles, the radical edge and activist momentum is being maintained.

Genetically modified (GM) crops

A similar and overlapping set of mobilizations has occurred especially from the mid-1990s around genetically modified (GM) crops in different parts of the world. These have revolved variously around environmental concerns with crop genetic diversity and 'superweeds', human health issues, as well as a wider debate about corporate control of seeds and farming futures (Schurman, 2004). Alliances have formed between diverse groups, each framing the issue in a different way. A hybrid network of different actors has created something akin to a movement, but with hugely varied characteristics. Contrary to the claims of some that this was all an orchestrated conspiracy by powerful European environmentalists, the evidence shows a variegated response, all rooted in local concerns and contexts. By and large, the lead actors have been relatively rich, educated and middle class, claiming support in different forms from farmers' organizations and movements, including La Via Campesina. However, perhaps in contrast to the bottom-up peasants' movements of food sovereignty, the anti-GM campaigns have been characterized by a set of relatively elite alliances, with transnational characteristics, yet local roots.

Taking what Marc Edelman calls a 'messy, close up view of collective action' (Edelman, 2001, p286) we can get an insight into the texture of such a movement, its tactics and strategies, successes and failures, and draw out some broader lessons for mobilizing for green transformations more generally. In a comparative study of anti-GM activism in Brazil, India and South Africa, Scoones (2008, p339) concludes:

> They galvanize selective and strategic alliances among different and diverse groups around a variety of issues. Some would dismiss these as incoherent and poorly substantiated, but together they often add up to an alternative perspective on agrarian futures to the standard neoliberal line, even if sometimes poorly articulated and partially contradictory. Such positions are the result of complex, hybrid coalitions of interests and ideas, and, as discussed, do not represent a particular, defined set of (class) interests. With their global connections and elite, educated, urban leaderships, they can be seen as often very detached from rural realities and agrarian struggles. But the resonances and connections are definitely there . . . and the strength of their appeal, and the political force that they potentially have, lies in the way such connections – between local, national and global issues; rural and urban; producer and consumer; elite and poor – are constructed and mobilized.

Comparing countries and regions where GM activism has emerged highlights the importance of contrasting political cultures (Jasanoff, 2005). Such cultures suggest different options and open up different spaces for debate. Thus, in some settings close alliances between movements and political parties were possible, allowing for a penetration of political and bureaucratic structures to effect change. In other contexts the legal system created space for protest. The media is also an important space for raising questions and has been used very effectively by GM movements, even if the storylines are excessively dramatic. Thus, in Europe the spectre of 'Frankenstein foods' or 'Terminator' genes, even if strictly unscientific, allowed an otherwise constrained debate to enter the public sphere. Wider, more direct-action style protests have also characterized anti-GM campaigns, including consumer boycotts and 'trolley dumping', or crop burning and the destruction of field trials. Other campaigners have taken a more positive stance, demonstrating alternatives that are sustainable and based on local seed systems, and open access research and development. Demonstration projects have proliferated, under a variety of banners, showing that 'other worlds' are indeed possible (Levidow and Carr, 2007).

Different campaigns at different moments in different regions have focused on different elements of the debate, whether on consumer health, farmers' rights or environmental impacts. This has resulted in some tensions. As Scoones (2008, p340) notes: 'Holding a broad front often means engineering strategic silences about some tough issues, with contradictions and tensions held in abeyance. But avoiding some of these deeper issues may also mean the unravelling of coalitions and alliances'. Not everyone in the movement has agreed with all these tactics, and intense debates have emerged about the pros and cons of each.

Two decades since the start of the movement, has there been progress towards a greener, more sustainable form of agricultural technology? Success has been patchy. There has been retreat and roll-back over time, not least because controlling the distribution of seeds is nigh on impossible. Thus in India, GM crops were distributed 'by stealth' by entrepreneurs with the quiet acceptance of the property rights holding companies (Herring, 2005) and in Brazil the flood of GM seeds across the border from Argentina was unstoppable. In the context of a rapidly liberalizing agriculture seeking external investment in a neoliberal market economy where government capacity for regulation was weak or non-existent, the opportunies of sustained opposition were, of course, limited. Corporate messaging has also shifted in response. Having dramatically lost the public relations war at the outset, GM is now marketed as an environmentally sound alternative to agrochemicals, and in some quarters as a technological response to climate change. Others argue that GM per se is not the problem but the corporate control of agri-food systems, and that publicly funded and regulated alternatives – from China and beyond – offer sustainable alternatives.

Much as the rearguard responses of the techno-optimists aiming to tackle environmental problems more generally exclude politics, so have these responses from corporate agriculture and their backers. Yet many of the anti-GM campaigns have got trapped in the terms of this discourse, often as regulatory systems and legal cases require it, and have not articulated effectively the larger political critique. The limits to green transformations in this case thus concern less a disarticulation of local and global concerns as networks build and become institutionalized, and more a depoliticization of the debate. Drawing lessons from the case makes clear that fundamental transformations cannot occur through changing a technology, but only the wider sociopolitical system within which it is embedded.

Urban sustainability

A third area where mobilization offers potential to contribute to the processes of green transformation concerns urban sustainability. In both the global North and South, movements have articulated approaches to addressing both specific sustainability challenges associated with urban living and growth, and roles for towns and cities in broader green transformations (Mapes and Wolch, 2011).

For example, the Transition movement aims to mobilize community action and foster public empowerment and engagement around climate change, with the objective of catalyzing a transition to a low-carbon economy (www.transitiontowns. org). The idea originated in 2005 in Northern Ireland when a permaculture teacher, Rob Hopkins, initiated a community-designed 'Energy Descent Action Plan' for the town of Kinsale, with practical steps geared to reducing carbon emissions and preparing for a future post-cheap oil (Seyfang and Haxeltine, 2012). Described by their founder as 'an emerging and evolving approach to community-level sustainability' (Hopkins, 2008, p134), local Transition initiatives have multiplied and by 2013 there were 1,130 registered in 43 countries – largely in Europe, North America, Australia and New Zealand (www.transitionnetwork.org/initiatives). Some unite towns, while others are constituted in parts of larger cities.

Transition initiatives typically combine a range of practical activities, from local energy generation, food production, farmers' markets, community gardening, composting and seed exchanges, through to local currencies, designing and building eco-housing, recycling and repair schemes, car-sharing, skills-sharing and self-help groups. Each initiative develops its own series of plans and activities through a community-led process. Yet uniting these are a set of common framings. These include the development of alternative lifestyles and systems of provisioning that reject consumerism and enable a low-carbon existence. The aim is to demonstrate practical, positive solutions in the here and now, and so encourage people to shift their consumption patterns towards this 'post-oil' model.

Such initiatives emphasize collective action and capabilities at the community level. Yet there are major contrasts in terms of identity and culture. Far from being a movement of (and advocating inclusion of) the poor, participation in Transition Town initiatives tends to be strongly middle class (Seyfang and Haxeltine, 2012). Transition Town initiatives largely eschew political engagement. Rather than campaign for political changes that might bring about transformations towards low-carbon futures, challenge dominant regimes or engage in oppositional politics with powerful political or business players, the emphasis remains on positive, community-level demonstration of a 'niche' that can replace dominant patterns when, as is assumed, they wither away. While some see this as a valuable way of doing politics, fostering 'critical emancipation' (Scott-Cato and Hillier, 2010) and penetrating 'under the radar' of existing political conflicts (Hopkins, 2008), others critique it as naive, limited and leaving the movement vulnerable to co-option (Chatterton and Cutler, 2008; Connors and McDonald, 2011).

'Transitioners' share ideas and reproduce their sense of common identity through open-access wiki websites and blogs (Scott-Cato and Hillier, 2010). However, tensions are emerging between such standardization, and the diversity and flexibility needed for local initiatives to flourish in their particular settings. Some local initiatives find the hierarchical relationship with network organizers overly restrictive and controlling. Connors and McDonald (2011) suggest that a 'cultish, top-down culture' may be developing that will restrict the ability to attract new adherents and spread as a democratic, bottom-up movement. While successful in replicating itself, the movement is struggling to increase its impact through building wider alliances (Seyfang and Haxeltine, 2012). In this respect, it can be argued that the Transition Network might be undermining its own avowed aims to attract as many people as possible to share its vision and values, towards green transformation from below. Again, then, we see potential for green transformations, but emergent tensions between vibrant local agendas and the wider institution-building required to scale up globally.

Where there is no green movement

The cases we have discussed so far have had their origins in very particular social–political–cultural moments and milieux. Are green transformations generated from below through forms of collective action possible where there are no green movements, modelled in the style familiar in western Europe, North America and parts of Latin America and Asia? In places that do not have these traditions emerging from struggles against colonialism or dictatorship or in democratic societies as responses to an overbearing state or extractive corporate capitalism, what happens? Is it necessary to create new movements that can take up the struggle, or are other forms of quieter, more hidden, less confrontational mobilizations possible, resulting in similar effects?

Here we can turn to eastern Europe and the countries making up the former Soviet Union and China for examples. While hugely different, they all have notable agroecological and sustainable food-growing and provisioning activities ongoing, often on a large scale. Very often not visible as movements, although sometimes supported by projects from NGOs or the state, they may involve the changing practices of millions of people towards more sustainable production and consumption. Smith and Jehlička (2013) term this, in the context of Poland and the Czechia, 'quiet sustainability', which they define as 'widespread practices that result in beneficial environmental or social outcomes and that do not relate directly or indirectly to market transactions, but are not represented by their practitioners as relating directly to environmental or sustainability goals' (2013, p1). This is based on sharing, mutual aid, reciprocity and solidarity within communities, but not necessarily with an explicitly 'green' or 'alternative' framing. It is just what people do, and is valued as such for its intangible, non-market and social benefits. Reflecting on the people involved, they comment:

Theirs is not a fulfilment of environmental obligations, an attempt to achieve 'resilience', or a response to limits, but the daily practice of a satisfying life. In other words: it is not just that the journey to sustainability is less difficult than is sometimes presented – large sections of humanity may already be on it without feeling the need to proclaim the fact loudly.

(Smith and Jehlička 2013, p34)

In other instances – for example, in China – mobilizations around agroecological farming have emerged in some areas, often supported by environmental NGOs, but all approved and in some cases directly supported by the state. In such a political setting, mobilization separate from the state is not feasible or would be risky, so a strategic alliance is struck with the state, through negotiation with officials, that accommodates, and may even later support, such efforts. As the Chinese state increasingly recognizes the environmental challenges wrought by its rapid economic transition, such small-scale, very localized forms of organization may be seen as a useful route to influence (Geall, 2013).

A similar argument for 'quiet sustainability' could be made for small-scale producers, forest dwellers, informal shack dwellers and many others in the global South who often live outside the reaches of formal institutions and policy. Yet through diverse forms of solidarity – again often not constructed as movements – they carve out livelihoods that very often have positive environmental benefits. Whether this is the management of trees for the harvesting of non-timber forest projects, complex home gardening and multifunctional agricultural practices, the recycling of urban waste and the building of homes, or indeed the numerous daily practices of millions of people worldwide, many might represent a form of 'quiet sustainability'. Hidden from view, not appreciated as part of policy, these are pathways towards sustainability that are less visible and more difficult to institutionalize, yet are nevertheless highly significant. Some might dismiss such activities as simply environmentalism through poverty. But just as the Polish and Czech plot holders should not be seen as 'urban peasants' (Smith and Jehlička, 2013), such everyday environmentally oriented practices, rooted in the cultures of sharing, guardianship, repairing and responsibility, should not be dismissed lightly.

It is this practised behaviour, repeated and institutionalized in particular sociocultural contexts, which may represent the 'quiet' revolution to sustainability. It involves mobilization in that people are enlisted, relations of solidarity and exchange are established and motivations are articulated, but its political implications are different. By not confronting the state or even not engaging with it all, although sometimes strategically allying with it, important strides are made towards green transformations that take a different form, and with a different politics compared to the classic mobilizations and movements described in the cases of La Via Campesina and the anti-GM movement. The urban Transition initiative case perhaps lies somewhere in between; less noisy and confrontational than these others, yet deploying particular, calculated political strategies of negotiation and the demonstration of alternatives.

Tensions and contradictions

Across these cases, then, green transformations are emerging from diverse spaces, grounded in citizen concerns and mobilization but involving diverse political strategies. In some cases spaces have been opened up by direct protest and lobbying. This has often been complemented by increasingly sophisticated media, and particularly new social media, and activism. Political cycles have an important effect in some places, as green agendas rise and fall with political parties sometimes linking their agenda to green issues, and social movements pushing them to comply. The law and regulatory institutions have been important sites for debate about green transformations in certain places where opportunities for legal activism are present. In other instances changes in behaviours and practices have become embedded in either explicitly 'alternative' activities or through quieter, less explicit but often large-scale shifts in practice. Some such changes may be facilitated and encouraged by sites of experimentation and demonstration organized by movements (perhaps identified as 'niches') explicitly to show and share alternatives, or alternatively as part of local practices that others observe, copy and share in a much more informal way. Whatever combinations of tactics, strategies are used which will depend, as the cases show, on the social, political, cultural and economic context. There is no standard script for green mobilizations and there is enormous diversity, much of it hidden from view, as we have noted.

In effecting often radical change that challenges incumbent institutions and confronts powerful interests, there are no easy or predictable forms of mobilization. Each must be attuned to the circumstance and moment. Inevitably there are often intense debates, within and between movements, about what is the best approach. Multiple tensions and sometimes deep contradictions exist, as hinted at in some of the cases discussed earlier. Debates around framing are often significant: What is green? What is agroecological farming? What is appropriate technology? These are not easy to resolve and, depending on one's position, class, identity, location and aspiration, the answers may be quite different. As discussed earlier, drawing different people from diverse backgrounds into a movement may be challenging. Networks may be quite fragile in some instances, held together by a common opposition to a loosely defined enemy, but with real differences in outlook and perspective among participants. This often becomes especially apparent when identities and identifications clash: between being an environmentalist, a feminist and indigenous person, for example. While multiple subject positions, and associated frames and stances may be able to be held together, this may be more challenging when tensions over strategy and tactics arise.

Within the environment movement more generally, tensions have often arisen when once loose, fragmented activities as part of movements and networks become institutionalized and 'mainstreamed'. Contradictions then often arise between the radical foundations of a movement and reformist green agendas that see success being generated through collaboration with governments, businesses and others, as space is opened up by environmental awareness and activism. New frames are adopted that are appealing to such allies, such as 'green economy' or 'sustainable intensification', 'ecological modernization' or 'responsible innovation'. Reformists will argue that staying on the sidelines is not an option and that the world has changed over the last 40 years, with new opportunities arising for alliance-building under new configurations.

Others, of course, argue that such moves inevitably result in co-optation, or at the minimum a lowest common denominator debate that rarely confronts power, and indeed too often reinforces interests, allowing a type of 'greenwash' under the guise of corporate or governmental 'responsibility' initiatives. Such 'ecological modernization' may reduce the environmental footprint of industry, but it may not change the power structures that created environmental and social justice problems in the first instance. By not naming and confronting power and entrenched interests, true transformation does not happen, and the green agenda thus gets captured by neoliberal, conservative interests as incumbent forces reconfigure to accommodate and absorb, rather than fundamentally change.

Much of this, of course, comes down to a conflict over the understanding of what is transformation. Is the challenge, for example, simply reducing carbon emissions or is it a more fundamental structural change in ownership, production and consumption that delivers a lower carbon future for the long term, but also meets other objectives of justice, distribution and a wider conception of sustainability? Is transformation simply reducing deforestation, planting more trees or changing the chemical impacts of modern agriculture, or is it again a more fundamental shift in the structure, power relations, ownership patterns and resource access of the global agri-food system?

As neoliberal and ecological modernization agendas, allied to various complexions of corporate social and environmental responsibilities, have gained purchase and have indeed influenced government and business behaviour and practice, they have proved difficult to reconcile with a more radical vision of societal economic and social transformation. As 'green' reformist agendas become more mainstream, with the rhetoric around the 'green economy' increasing in recent years, this has pushed more radical visions of transformation to the fringes. The environmental 'movement' (or more accurately diverse movements) has become increasingly fragmented, making coordinated action more difficult, and the productive relationship between movements, networks and institutions more challenging to uphold.

This has perhaps become especially so as environmental agendas have moved from multiple, local actions around particular issues to a much larger global frame. Tensions have thus intensified between particularism and what it means to effect wider green transformations. Climate change as a global phenomenon has in particular influenced this shift, supported by arguments that humanity is hitting 'green limits' around other 'planetary boundaries' (see Leach, this book). Of course, since the 1970s, as discussed earlier, environmental issues have been framed in global terms – 'spaceship earth', 'only one earth', 'blueprint for a small planet'. However, in recent times, the tensions between local mobilizations and global framings have become more stark. Do the multiple micro-initiatives initiated in particular places add up to a global transformation affecting planetary processes, or do actions now have to take place at a different scale, removing control and agency from local actors, the lifeblood of any movement? With mechanisms structured at international levels – through various commissions, committees, assessments, protocols or agreements – how do locally rooted but internationally networked movements fit in, and what space do they have to make a difference? Some have argued that the primary role of mobilizations is to protect local perspectives and priorities in the face of proliferating global initiatives and forms of thinking and action. As Esteva and Prakash (1997, p47) put it:

> [T]he solidarity of coalitions and alliances does not call for 'thinking globally'. In fact, what is needed is exactly the opposite: people thinking and acting locally, while forging solidarity with other local forces that share this opposition to the 'global thinking' and 'global forces' threatening local spaces.

In contrast, others suggest that the local and global can – and must – be meshed in powerful ways. Is such translocal networking a key to fostering green transformations that respond both to the particularity of grounded experience and to the needs for wider, global scale change?

Conclusion

Mobilizations have vital roles to play in the politics of green transformations. These transformations are certainly multiple, as our analysis of framings, identities, resource mobilization and networks across the cases suggests. We see mobilizations linked to a wide range of framings, subjectivities, values and identities. They have engaged with political processes in different ways, across a spectrum from overt contestation of structures of power through more subtle negotiations with the state and inter-national agencies, through to withdrawal from dominant regimes to demonstrate alternative ways of living. These differences depend partly on the issue and place, but political contexts also matter. As we have seen, political histories, cultures and styles of decision-making vary between nations, regions and localities, and around particular 'sectors' – from agriculture to climate change, urban design to forestry – shaping which political strategies and combinations are feasible and desirable. A diversity of strategies and styles, therefore, will almost inevitably be needed, and today these can draw on a wide variety of spaces and practices from face-to-face protest and legal and media action through to more practical, everyday forms of material life and community organizing.

Across these arguments and examples, we see processes of emergent social solidarity – forms of 'green citizenship' – but around diverse, rather than singular, notions of 'green', 'social justice' and 'transformation'. Just as a conceptual framework to understand these needs to draw together diverse strands of social movement theory, so it also requires an integrative perspective on citizenship (Leach and Scoones, 2005). Mobilizations must galvanize creative, knowledgeable citizens, and must operate in an increasingly interconnected knowledge society where forms of democratic politics are being reconstituted.

Yet how might such multiple, diverse, fragmented mobilizations add up to and contribute to the bigger challenges of green transformation? Scaling up and out through networking and alliance-building can be key but, as we have shown, there are dangers if this comes at the expense of the critical edge and locatedness in context that gave life to mobilization in the first place. Indeed, we have highlighted tensions along an axis from movement through network to institutionalization, interconnected with those from local particularism to wider, including global, concerns. The cases show how these tensions can be navigated in a variety of ways, depending not just on context but on varied analyses of power. Thus a structural political economy analysis, as adopted, for example, by strands of the food sovereignty and anti-GM movements, underlines a logic of alliance-building to confront capitalist corporate and state power. Yet a more 'capillary' notion that locates power in diffuse social relations, informs other efforts to reclaim democracy through micro-social practices and negotiations in multiple spaces. Even mobilizations that appear to withdraw from or ignore the centres of power can be viewed as transformatory in their potential to advance alternatives, and overturn stereotypes and traditions, and reframe ideas and practice into more participatory and negotiable models.

The potential of green movements to contribute to the politics of green transformations, then, lies in their analyses (whether overt or implicit), as well as their action. By embodying particular theories of power and deploying these in diverse political strategies, they contribute to a vital opening up of the politics of sustainability, which must increasingly be concerned not just with the allocation of material resources, ecological space, status and authority, but with who defines the future and what perspectives and experiences matter. This involves cultivating a wider breadth of knowledge and experience to define goals and appropriate ways of reaching them, enabling the diversity that is required to respect diverse ecological and social contexts, and to keep options open in the face of the unexpected. It is by continuously offering alternatives and maintaining a critically-aware position of the inevitable movement-institutionalization and local-global tensions that affect their operation, that green mobilizations offer their greatest potential to inspire the kind of thinking and action that green transformations require.

Notes

1 Available online at: www.theguardian.com/global-development/poverty-matters/2013/jun/17/la-via-campesina-food-sovereignty. Accessed 20 June 2014.
2 The Nyeleni declaration was produced in 2007 in Nyeleni, a village in Mali. Available online at: www.nyeleni.org/spip.php?article290. Accessed 20 June 2014.
3 Available online at: www.future-agricultures.org/blog/entry/missing-politics-and-food-sovereignty#.U4NI2E1OXIU. Accessed 20 June 2014.

9

THE GREEN ENTREPRENEURIAL STATE

Mariana Mazzucato

Introduction

Never more than today is it necessary to question the way in which we discuss the role of the State in the economy. This is because in most parts of the world we are witnessing a massive *withdrawal* of the State, one that has been justified in terms of debt reduction and – perhaps more systematically – in terms of rendering the economy more 'dynamic', 'competitive' and 'innovative'. Business is accepted as the innovative force, while the State is cast as inertial – necessary for the 'basics', but too large and heavy to be the dynamic engine.

This chapter is committed to dismantling this false image and in particular looks at 'green' technology and innovation. Unsurprisingly, we find that across the globe the countries that are leading in green transformations (solar and wind energy are the paradigmatic examples explored) are those where the State is playing an active role. And the public sector organizations involved, such as development banks[1] in Germany, Brazil and China, are not just providing countercyclical lending (as Keynes would have asked for), but are even 'directing' that lending towards the most innovative, risky and uncertain parts of the 'green' economy. Questions about whether such 'directionality' should raise the usual worries about the State's inability to 'pick winners' are confronted head on, demystifying old assumptions.

Green entrepreneurship – what every policy-maker today seems to want to encourage – is not (just) about start-ups, venture capital and 'garage tinkerers'. It is about the willingness and ability of economic agents to take on risk and uncertainty: what is genuinely unknown. Most of the radical, revolutionary innovations that have fuelled the dynamics of capitalism – from railroads to the Internet, to modern-day nanotechnology and pharmaceuticals – trace the most courageous, early and capital-intensive 'entrepreneurial' investments back to the State. Such radical innovations did not exist before the State envisaged and developed them, consequently, markets for these new products or services had also to be created and shaped by the 'visible hand' of the State.

Yet most economists talk simply of fixing 'market failures'. Standard economic theory justifies State intervention when markets fail to efficiently allocate resources and reach a 'Pareto equilibrium',[2] as when the social return on investment is higher than the private return, making it unlikely that a private business will invest. Classic cases include cleaning up pollution (a negative 'externality' not reflected in prices) and funding basic research (a 'public good' difficult to appropriate privately). However, State investment must be more than this. Visionary investments are exemplified today by confident State investment banks that are directing lending to new uncertain areas that private banks and venture capitalists (VCs) fear. The State can act as a force for innovation and change, not only 'derisking' the economic landscape for risk-averse private actors, but also boldly leading the way, with a clear and courageous vision – exactly the opposite image of the State that is usually sold.

In economics, the 'crowding-out' hypothesis is used to analyse the possibility that increased State spending reduces private business investment, since both compete for the same pool of savings (through borrowing). This in turn might result in higher interest rates which reduce the willingness of private firms to borrow, and hence invest. While Keynesian analysis has argued against this possibility during periods of underutilized capacity, the point is that even in the boom (when in theory there is full capacity utilization), there are in practice many parts of the risk landscape where private business fears treading and the State must lead the way. Therefore, if government is 'transforming' – creating and shaping markets, not only fixing them – then the crowding-out hypothesis would not apply here either.

Thus, to dismantle that false image, a proper defence of the State should argue that it not only 'crowds in' private investment (by increasing gross domestic product (GDP) through the multiplier effect) – a correct but limited point made by Keynesians – it does something more. It is necessary to build a theory of the State's role in shaping and creating markets, more in line with the work of Karl Polanyi (1980 [1944]) who emphasized how the capitalist 'market' has from the start been heavily shaped by State actions. In innovation, the State not only 'crowds in' business investment but also 'dynamizes it in', creating the vision, the mission and the plan. This chapter explains the process by which this happens as a central feature of green transformations.

The chapter in particular focuses on the role of the 'entrepreneurial' risk-taking State in launching specific 'green' technologies, in this case wind turbines and solar photovoltaic (PV) panels. It was State funding and the work of particular State agencies that provided the initial push, early stage high-risk funding and institutional environment that could establish these important technologies. Currently, it is also State funding, particularly through development banks, that is promoting the diffusion of those green energy technologies, which highlights that States have a role to play throughout the entire innovation chain and not just in public good areas such as research and development (R&D). The chapter emphasizes the role of countries like Germany, Denmark and China in directing green transformations. The chapter thus provides a fuller understanding of the public sector's centrality to risk-taking activities and radical technological change, essential to promote green transformations.

Transforming the energy sector

We cannot influence the emergence of innovative new 'green' companies, technologies or transform energy markets without policies directed at both the demand- and supply-side (Edler and Georghiou, 2007). Each influences either the structure and function of markets or the investment of firms attempting to grow or transition into green technology sectors. So, in the case of the energy sector, demand-side policies include environmental regulations, public procurement, support of private demand and other systemic policies that have an impact on energy consumption patterns. Supply-side policies are focused on how energy is generated and distributed, and influence the development of innovation in energy technologies through the provision of finance (e.g. grants, equity support, tax incentives) or through service support (e.g. information brokerage, networking, development of common visions). Examples of demand-side policies include Renewable Portfolio Standards, greenhouse gas (GHG) emission reduction targets, energy-intensity targets (a measure of energy use per unit of GDP), new building standards or even a 'carbon tax' that affect consumer preferences. Each targets energy consumption patterns and establishes a demand for reduced pollution, increased clean energy or better energy-system efficiency. State stimulus to green energy technologies is therefore indirect, via changes in consumer demand that stimulate the development of innovations. Supply-side policies could include tax credits, subsidies, loans, grants or other monetary benefits for specific energy technologies, favourable energy pricing schemes (such as 'feed-in tariffs'), R&D contracts and funding for discovery and development of innovations, and so on. Such policies directly support the development of technologies, complementing and providing a 'solution' to demand-side policies.

Understanding how businesses transform government support mechanisms into lower-cost, higher-performance products through the innovation process is typically the 'missing link' in discussions of energy policy, and this missing link can undermine not just our desire to push an energy transition, but to do it with high-road investments in innovation. State support for clean technologies must continue until they overcome the sunk-cost advantage of incumbent technologies, and these sunk costs are a century long in some cases (Unruh, 2000). That is why much of this chapter focuses on supply-side support mechanisms. In the current policy environment, many countries have been aggressively deploying public finance with the aim of promoting green industry, and this is the most direct support possible for business development.

Funding a 'green' industrial revolution

Advanced clean technologies, like all radical technologies, have many hurdles to clear. Some hurdles may relate to technical development (such as improving or inventing production techniques), others are due to market conditions or competition. In the case of renewable energy sources, like wind or solar power, broad social acceptance or the need to provide energy at a price lower than possible by other firms and technologies are also major hurdles (Hopkins and Lazonick, 2012). Given these challenges, the financial risk of supporting a firm until it can mass produce, capture market share and reach economies of scale, driving down unit costs, is too great for most VC funds (Hopkins and Lazonick, 2012).

In the innovation game, it is therefore crucial that finance be 'patient' and be able to accept the fact that innovation is highly uncertain and takes a long time (Mazzucato, 2013a). Patient capital can come in different forms. The German feed-in tariff (FIT) policy is a good form of public 'patient capital' supporting the long-term growth of renewable energy markets (Lauber and Mez, 2006). By contrast, the availability but also frequent uncertainty surrounding tax credits in the US and the UK are a form of 'impatient capital' – which indeed has not helped industry take-off (Porritt, 2011; Cowell, 2012). The most visible patient capital made available to renewable technology manufacturers and developers has been delivered through State-funded investment or 'development banks'. According to the Global Wind Energy Council (GWEC):

> The main factor that distinguishes development banks from private sector lending institutions is the ability of development banks to take more risk associated with political, economic and locational aspects. Further, since they are not required to pay dividends to private stakeholders, the development banks take higher risks than commercial banks to meet various national or international 'public good' objectives. Additionally, long-term finance from the private sector for more than a ten year maturity period is not available.
> (Fried *et al.*, 2012, p6)

The role and scope of development banks is more diverse than simply financing projects (Griffith-Jones and Tyson, 2013; Mazzucato and Penna, forthcoming 2014). Development banks can set conditions for access to their capital, in an effort to maximize economic or social value to their home country. Most development banks deliberately seek to invest in areas that have high social value and are willing to make risky loans that the commercial sector would shy away from. Additionally, while these banks support consumption of renewable energy, they can also support manufacturing. Development banks are flexible financiers and can provide significant capital to renewable energy projects, which can represent as great an investment risk as the development of new technologies. Given the amount of financial resources in their possession, their investment decisions play an important role in economic development trajectories. In this sense, it came as good news

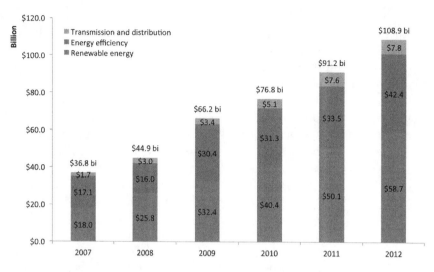

FIGURE 9.1 Development bank broad clean energy investment by sector (US$, billions)

Source: Based on data from Louw (2013).

that in 2013 some development banks (such the World Bank and the European Investment Bank) decided to curtail funding for coal power (FS-UNEP/BNEF, 2014). And in recent years, development banks have been a key source of funding for 'clean energy' projects, committing more than US$100 billion in 2012 (Figure 9.1).[3]

In 2012, China announced its plan to produce 1,000 GWs of wind power by 2050, which would be approximately equal to replacing the entire existing US electric infrastructure with wind turbines (Liu, 2012). Are the US and Europe still able to dream so big? It appears not. In many countries, the State is asked to take a back seat and simply 'subsidize' or incentivize investments for the private sector. We thus fail to build visions for the future similar to those that two decades ago resulted in the mass diffusion of the Internet.

What, then, is the role of 'patient' finance – for example, that supplied by State development banks – in creating the 'catalytic' early, and risky, investments necessary to make it happen? Clean energy is a paradigmatic example of technology that needs to be widely deployed in order for the green industrial revolution to succeed. In recent years, governments around the world have once again taken the lead in pumping up R&D of many clean technologies like wind and solar power, and efforts are being made to establish modernized energy grids. They also subsidize and support the growth of leading manufacturers that compete for domestic and global market leadership. And governments deploy both policy and finance to encourage stable development of competitive markets for renewable energy. As has been the case in the development of other industries such as biotech and IT, private businesses have entered the game only after successful government initiatives absorb most of the uncertainty and not a little risk of developing new energy technologies in the first place.

The 'green' energy industry is still in its early stages: even though development of wind and solar power technologies received a big push in the 1970s (due to the energy crisis), they are both still characterized by market and technological uncertainty.[4] It will not develop 'naturally' through market forces, in part because of embedded energy infrastructure, but also because of a failure of markets to value sustainability or to punish waste and pollution. In the face of such uncertainty, the business sector will not enter until the riskiest and most capital-intensive investments have been made, or until there are coherent and systematic policy signals in place. In a recent interview, Microsoft founder Bill Gates, one of the principals of the American Energy Innovation Council (AEIC) recognized that 'a key element to get an energy breakthrough is more basic research. And that requires the government to take the lead. Only when that research is pointing towards a product then we can expect the private sector to kick in.'[5]

As in the early stage of IT, biotech and nanotech industries, there is little indication that the business sector alone would enter the new 'green' sector and drive it forward in the absence of strong and active government policy. Indeed, the Climate Policy Initiative (2013) reports that institutional investors contributed with only US\$0.4 billion to climate change mitigation and adaptation projects (a minimal figure considering the US\$70 trillion in assets that they manage); venture capital, private equity and infrastructure funds invested another US\$1 billion only. Thus, while 'nudging' might incentivize a few entrepreneurs to act, most business actors will need stronger signals to justify their engagement in clean technology innovation. Only long-term policy decisions can reduce the uncertainty of transforming core business from legacy into clean technologies. In fact, no other high-tech industry has been created or transformed with a 'nudge' (Mazzucato, 2013b). Most likely, a strong 'push' is needed.

National approaches to green economic development

There are differences in how countries are reacting to the challenge of developing a green economy. Some countries have used the post-crisis stimulus spending as a way to direct government investments into global clean technology industries, with two goals: to provide economic growth, while mitigating climate change. While some countries lead, others are lagging behind. As investments in innovation are cumulative and the results are 'path dependent' (innovation today is dependent on innovation yesterday), it is likely that the leaders emerging from this race will remain leaders for years to come. In other words, those acting first or as a fast-follower will enjoy a early-mover advantage, as in the success case of Toyota, who pioneered hybrid vehicle technology and benefited from an early 'halo effect', which later resulted in it being the biggest winner of the US 'cash for clunkers' scheme[6] (Sperling and Gordon, 2009; USDOT, 2009).

Yet, failure of some governments to provide the vision and to 'push' clean technology is having an impact on the amount of investment occurring. Countries that pursue a patchy policy towards clean technology will not stimulate enough investment to alter their 'carbon footprints', nor should they expect to host the clean technology leaders of the future. An example of a country going for a 'big push' is China; Germany is also a first mover among European countries. The US has shown contradictory trends, with the State making early and substantive investments in green technologies. By proceeding without a clear vision and goal in mind, however, and without a long-term commitment to several key technologies, the US has failed to alter significantly its energy mix, despite the bigger push at the state level (notably in California, North Carolina and, surprisingly, Texas) (Carley, 2011; Prasad and Munch, 2012). The UK is also lagging behind.

In the US, the 2009 American Recovery and Reinvestment Act stimulus packages devoted 11.5 per cent of their budget to clean technology investments, lower than China (34.3 per cent), France (21 per cent) or South Korea (80.5 per cent), but higher than the UK (6.9 per cent). In July 2010, the South Korean government announced that it would double its spending on green research to the equivalent of US$2.9 billion by 2013 (almost 2 per cent of its annual GDP), which means that between 2009 and 2013 it will have spent US$59 billion on this type of research in total. Figure 9.2 shows that Europe, the US and China have dominated global new investment in renewable energy between 2004 and 2012, with other economies from Asia (such as South Korea and Japan) and Oceania catching up in 2013. In Europe, investments are led by Germany (FS-UNEP/ BNEF, 2014).

Other than R&D expenditures, State investment banks are taking a leading role in clean technology development and diffusion in some emerging countries.

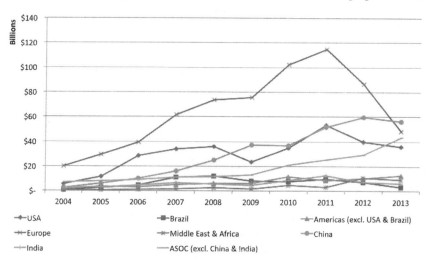

FIGURE 9.2 Global trend in renewable energy investment by region (US$, billions)

Source: Based on data from FS-UNEP/BNEF (2014).

In 2011, Germany's KfW bank announced that it would make available €100 billion (US$120–130 billion) over the following five years to promote renewable energies and contribute to Germany's *Energiewende* plan ('Energy Turnaround'), which will promote the complete decommissioning of the country's nuclear power plants by 2022 (OGFJ, 2011; Reuters, 2012). Indeed, in 2012 KfW was the top development bank in terms of clean energy investments, with its total commitments amounting to US$34 billion (Louw, 2013, p6). In China, investments by the China Development ment Bank (CDB) are a key source of its success in solar power. CDB funding to green energy projects in general is indeed generous: between 2007 and 2012, CDB committed US$78 billion to clean energy, US$26 billion in 2012 alone (Louw, 2013, p6). The CDB extended US$47 billion after 2010 to approximately 15 leading Chinese solar PV manufacturers to finance their current and future expansion needs, though firms had drawn on approximately US$866 million in 2011 (Bakewell, 2011). The rapid scaling of solar PV manufacturing firms made possible by public finance has quickly established Chinese solar technology manufacturers as major international players. As such, they are able to slash the cost of solar PV panels so quickly that much of the financial media argues that this access to credit is the reason behind bankruptcies of solar companies based in the United States and Europe (e.g. Forbes, 2011). The Brazilian Development Bank (BNDES) approved over US$4.23 billion in clean technology financing in 2011 (Fried *et al.*, 2012, p5). Today, state investment banks are spending over US$100 billion annually on energy efficiency and renewable projects (Louw, 2013), while clean energy project bond issuance reached just US$3.2 billion in 2013 (FS-UNEP/BNEF, 2014, p44). While precise figures comparing all public and private sources of finance for renewable energy projects are not available, the picture is likely to be similar to the 'Global Landscape of Climate Finance' (Climate Policy Initiative, 2013), which includes all types of climate change mitigation and adaptation projects (Figure 9.3).

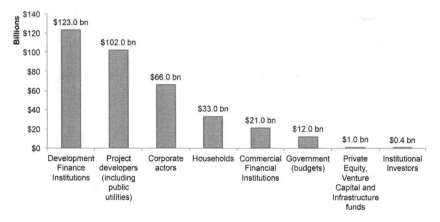

FIGURE 9.3 Sources of finance for climate change adaptation or mitigation projects in 2012 (US$, billions)

Source: Based on data from Climate Policy Initiative (2013).

China's 'green' five-year plan

Facing backlash in European and US markets (through trade war and tariffs backed by government and initiated by competing firms) against the success of its nascent solar industry in lowering prices, China opted to revise its domestic solar power development goal to 20 GWs by 2015, at a time when just three GWs existed in the country (Patton, 2012). Complementing these targets are regional feed-in tariffs that fix the price of energy produced by wind and solar projects on more favourable terms (Landberg, 2012). Other incentives for Chinese energy developers ensure that today's technologies can recover their costs in seven years, and generate returns for decades, while manufacturers continue to improve technologies (Liu, 2011). China's goal of 100 GWs of wind power by 2015 and 1000 GWs by 2050 is a second aggressive goal-promoting economic development and reduced carbon emissions (Liu, 2012). So far, China's targets have only been revised upwards, suggesting that ample opportunity for domestic industry will persist into China's foreseeable future.

What is more, China's green strategy is guided by an overarching vision encapsulated in its ongoing twelfth five-year plan (2011–2015). China's visionary and ambitious plan aims to invest US$1.5 trillion (or 5 per cent of GDP) across multiple industries: energy-saving and environmentally friendly technologies, biotechnology, new generation ITs, advanced manufacturing, new materials, alternative fuels and electric cars (Mathews *et al.*, 2011; Yuan and Zuo, 2011b). Overarching these investments are intentions to adopt a 'circular' approach to economic development that places sustainability first, a directive which defines pollution- and waste-control as forms of competitive advantage (Mathews *et al.*, 2011). Accompanying investment in industrial development are energy-intensity reduction targets, emission controls and renewable development goals – a combination of supply-side and demand-side policies.

Recognizing that the competitive advantage of the future depends on effective resource management as well as reduced waste and pollution, China's 'green development' strategy is reframing the notion of how 'optimal' economic development unfolds with aggressive demand- and supply-side measures. China's 'win–win' plans make 'profit' and 'environment' complementary pursuits rather than trade-offs, as they are often treated in many Western economies. As a result, China is poised not only to continue as a major manufacturer of solar PV panels, but also to become a major market for them.

In sum, China now prioritizes clean technologies as part of a strategic vision and long-term commitment to economic growth. While already providing billions of dollars for new renewable energy project finance, China is in fact just beginning its serious investment in solar and wind technology (Lim and Rabinovitch, 2010; Zhang *et al.*, 2014). Given the huge size of its economy, however, China's GHG emissions are still poised to grow in absolute terms, and it is still to be seen whether the country will be able to decouple economic growth from GHG emissions, which would represent an original development path, never before seen in the history of industrialization.

United States: an ambiguous approach to green technologies

A clue to what is required to accelerate green transformations is found in the US, where government-funded initiatives are busy building on their understanding of what has worked in previous technological revolutions. While the US has been good at connecting academia with industry, in its own push into clean technologies, its performance has been uneven. As one of the first countries to push into wind and solar power in the 1980s, the US failed to sustain support and watched as Europe, Japan and now China take the lead. Worse, the US failed to alter its energy mix significantly, setting up its position for decades as a world-leading CO_2 emitter. With world-class innovative capability, the world's largest economy and a massive energy grid, the US is ideally positioned to kick off a clean technology revolution, yet it has not.

A key reason for uneven US performance has been its heavy reliance on venture capital to 'nudge' the development of green technologies. The United States is the VC capital of the clean technology world, with US$7 billion invested in 2011 versus US$9 billion globally (Hopkins and Lazonick, 2012). However, VCs have shown themselves to be 'impatient capitalists': they are not interested in sustaining the risks and costs of technological development over a long-term period. Indeed, together, private equity, venture capital and infrastructure funds provided just US$1 billion for climate change mitigation/adaptation projects in 2012, much less than State development banks (US$123 billion) and even other governmental agencies (US$12 billion) that obtain their own funding from limited budgets (Climate Policy Initiative, 2013). VCs also have limits to the financial resources they can allocate to finance fully the growth of clean technology companies. Since some clean technologies are still in the very early stages when uncertainty is highest, VC funding is focused on some of the safer bets, rather than on the radical innovation that is required to allow the sector to transform society so as to meet the double objective of promoting economic growth and mitigating climate change. Ghosh and Nanda (2010) argue that it is virtually only public sector money that is currently funding the riskiest and the most capital-intensive projects in clean technology. Federal and state incentives provide billions to support the establishment and growth of a domestic solar PV market, ensuring that companies have an opportunity to capture market share and reap economies of scale.

Impatient capital can destroy firms promising to deliver government-financed technology to the masses, but critics often focus on the government as the source of failure, rather than examining the behaviour of the smart, profit-hungry business community in producing that failure by jumping ship, restricting their total commitments or demanding financial returns over all other considerations. If VCs are not interested in capital-intensive industries or in building factories, what exactly are they offering in terms of economic development? Their role should be seen for what it is: limited. More importantly, the difficulties faced by the growing clean technology industry should highlight the need for better policy support, not less, given that existing financing models favour investors and not the public interest.

'Nudging' economies is not conducive to igniting a real green transformation. Those nations that cling to the bogus idea that government investment has some sort of a natural balancing point with the business sector will miss their opportunity to seize on an historic energy transition or be forced to import it from elsewhere. In reality, government and business activities frequently overlap. Clean technology businesses, like most businesses, are apt to call for subsidy and government-led R&D. Venture capitalists and technology entrepreneurs respond to government support in choosing technologies to invest in, but are rarely focused on the long term.

Getting to much-needed green transformations presents a serious problem: given the risk aversion of businesses, states need to sustain funding for the search for radical ideas that push a green industrial revolution along. Governments thus have a leading role to play in supporting the development of clean technologies past their prototype stages through to their commercial viability.

Real courage exists in those countries that use State resources to give a serious 'push' to clean technologies, by committing to goals and funding levels that attempt seemingly impossible tasks. Courage is China's attempt to build a US and European electric grid-sized market for wind turbines by 2050 and to increase its solar PV market by 700 per cent in just three years. Courage is also development banks stepping in where commercial banks doubt, promoting development, growth of the firm and a return on investment to taxpayers that is easier to trace. It is important that tax money is traceable in its promotion of technologies and generation of returns. Success makes support for another round of risky investments more likely and creates better visibility for the positive role that government can play in fostering innovation (Lazonick and Mazzucato, 2013).

If some European countries have demonstrated the value of long-term policy support for R&D and market deployment, the United States has in contrast demonstrated how maintenance of a state of uncertainty can lead to missed opportunities. The US failed to adopt a long-term national energy plan that places renewables at the forefront, while also refusing to reduce or abandon support for other, more mature energy technologies, leaving the task of direction setting with its states.

Nurturing green technologies

Historically, different types of government policies have played important roles in the origins of many green technologies. This section looks at the history of two renewable energy technologies: wind turbines and solar PV modules.

As characteristically 'intermittent' and 'diffuse' sources of energy, wind and solar power have benefited from what Madrigal (2011, p263) describes as 'throwing software at the problem': increasing the productivity and reliability of wind and solar projects with advanced computer modelling, management of power production and remote monitoring. Investments in a 'smart grid' are meant to digitize modern energy systems to optimize the flexibility, performance and efficiency of clean technologies while providing advanced management options to grid operators and end users. Such flexibility and control are not unlike the sort that emerged with digitized communication networks. Given time and broad deployment, the smart grid could change the way we think about energy, create new commercial opportunities and improve the economics of renewable energy by establishing new tools for optimal energy supply management and demand response.

Were it not for the commitments of governments around the world to R&D and the diffusion of technologies like wind turbines and solar PV panels, the energy transformation taking off in the last decade would not have occurred. The 'push' has required major regulatory shifts, financial commitments and long-term support for emerging companies. It is not always clear how to connect the dots between dominant firms and their technologies and the efforts of governments around the world, but it is clear that no leading clean technology firm emerged from a pure 'market genesis' – that is, as if the State played no role at all.

The apparent willingness of the State to accept the risk of clean technology development has had a positive impact. In the last few decades, wind turbines and solar PV panels have been two of the most rapidly deployed renewable energy technologies on the planet, spawning growing industries that are emerging in many regions of the world. In 2008, US$194 billion was directed at emerging clean technologies in an effort to provide badly needed economic stimulus to counteract the global economic crisis (NSB, 2012, p62). An unofficial global 'agreement' was thus reached out of the economic crisis, and that agreement was that the time for clean technologies had come (again). A green energy revolution seemed to be within the realm of possibility – but such 'green transformation' is yet to be seen.

Widescale deployment of solar PV panels and wind turbines are two technological solutions for meeting future energy needs and mitigating climate change. The 'ecosystem' of innovation in clean technology is one in which the public sector has taken the leading role. Wind and solar power technologies have been the fruit of major government investments that catalyzed their historical development around the world.

While the US and China possesses the largest quantity of wind capacity deployed worldwide, Denmark produced the leading manufacturer of wind turbines decades ago: Vestas (Morales, 2014). In the US, leading manufacturers also emerged during the 1980s, but each was lost through acquisition or bankruptcy. Germany's solar resources are inferior to those of the United States, yet it remains the world leader of deployed solar PV power. China has emerged as the world's major solar PV manufacturing region, successfully out-competing US, Japanese and European rivals that led in prior decades (Zhang *et al.*, 2014, p904).

What must be explained is how a country like the US can become a leading market, but fail to produce a leading manufacturer, and conversely, how a country like China can produce a leading manufacturer in the absence (until recently) of a domestic market. What distinguishes these nations has nothing to do with their 'comparative advantages' as producers of wind turbines or solar PV panels, and it has nothing to do with a natural abundance of wind or sun. Historically, the development of wind and solar power has reflected differences in government policies meant to foster these power sources. For some countries, this is a process that has unfolded over many decades. For others, it is a process of 'catching up' – but no matter the case, it is the tools deployed by the State that have supported and attempted to drive outcomes. The international histories of wind-power technology development and of leading wind and solar companies provide examples of the extent to which those industries have benefited directly (and indirectly) from different kinds of public funding and support.

Wind

The importance of government support is seen most starkly through the consequences of its withdrawal: when the United States government abandoned subsidies for wind-power development in the mid-1980s and slashed the Department of Energy's (DOE) R&D budget in a backlash against attempts to promote energy innovation, the domestic market stagnated and momentum for the industry shifted to Europe or, more accurately, to Germany. Germany's federal Ministry for Research and Technology launched a programme to develop 100 MWs of wind power in 1989. Combined with a FIT programme, which provided above-market prices for wind power and a 70 per cent tax credit to small producers, Germany began its reign as the hottest market for wind-power development in the world (Lauber and Mez, 2006, p106).

Combined with GHG reduction targets and the intention of meeting renewable energy development goals with domestic manufacturing, in 2009 Germany also set aside national and state funding of approximately US$2.2 billion to support continued wind energy R&D. Germany's long-term approach to wind- energy development gained momentum in the 1990s and continues today, enabling the emergence of leading manufacturers while providing stable annual growth in deployed wind capacity. Since the Fukushima Daiichi nuclear disaster, Germany decided to phase out its nuclear installations and develop its Energy Transition (*Energiewende*) strategy, whereby renewable energies such as wind will receive further push from the State (Smith Stegen and Seel, 2013). The 20-year investment horizons provided by government incentives are twice as long as those in the US, reducing market uncertainty and boosting investor confidence. Furthermore, KfW has been enlisted as the key source of finance for the *Energiewende* initiative.

China was a relative latecomer to wind-power technology, despite having pushed investment in renewable energy in the 1980s as a technical solution for rural electric infrastructure development (Ma *et al.*, 2010). China's partially State-owned Goldwind, a major wind-turbine manufacturer, was established in 1998, and initially licensed German technology from Jacobs (a company later purchased by REpower) and Vensys Energiesysteme GmbH (Lewis, 2007). Goldwind turbines benefited from aggressive Chinese domestic content rules, which were enacted in 2003 to require 70 per cent local content in all wind turbines sold in China

(Martinot, 2010). This effectively shut the door on foreign capital in the country, while China's dominant wind manufacturers strengthened their domestic supply chain and presence.

Chinese wind power developers also received 25-year fixed price contracts that were set through a 'concession' programme (competitive bidding). Wind projects had access to low-cost financing and after 2005, China began to publicly fund R&D and projects with grants or favourable loan terms. China has also prioritized reducing its overall energy intensity (the relationship between energy consumption and GDP) and established goals for renewable energy development (Martinot, 2010).

Solar

Many examples of innovative emerging firms focusing on solar PV can be found in the US, where First Solar, Solyndra, Sunpower and Evergreen, for example, each developed state-of-the-art C-Si or thin-film solar technologies (Perlin, 1999). First Solar emerged out of the search for commercialized cadmium telluride (CdTe) thin-film solar PV panels and became a major US-based CdTe thin-film producer. First Solar dominates the US market for thin-film solar PV panels and has produced record-setting technology and low-cost manufacturing, which have enabled the company to generate over US$2 billion in revenue each year since 2009. First Solar's patents have extensive links to prior DOE research (Ruegg and Thomas, 2011). The success of companies like First Solar was built over several decades, during which VCs entered at a relatively late stage and exited soon after the IPO was completed. Much of the risk of investing in First Solar was taken on by the US government, which actively promoted their solar technology through to commercialization. Subsidies supporting a domestic market and a market in Europe, coupled to First Solar's position as a dominant thin-film producer make it hard to imagine how such a company could fail. Yet the value extraction provided, and even promoted, by equity-driven investment and compensation methods ensures that VCs, executives and top managers of firms can reap massive gains from stock performance, whether short lived or not. This perverse incentive not only redistributes the investment in innovation away from its other core stakeholders (governments, schools, workers), but it risks undermining firm performance. Rather than make the risky investment in future innovation, those in positions of strategic control squander resources in a search for financial returns (Hopkins and Lazonick, 2012).

The story of another solar power technology company – Solyndra – provides an important example of what happens if venture capital suddenly withdraws their financial support. In 2009, Solyndra received a US$527 million loan guarantee from the US DOE, as part of the American Recovery and Reinvestment Act, in order to develop copper indium gallium (di)selenide (CIGS) solar panels. With the price of raw silicon soaring (silicon is the primary ingredient of standard solar panels), investing in high-tech CIGS made economic sense. Yet, a couple of years later, the price of silicon collapsed, before Solyndra could capitalize on its investments.

Solyndra VC backers, who had invested US$1.1 billion in the company, were the first to jump ship. Even though all of Solyndra's (public and private) stakeholders were betting on the company's success – not failure – for the critics, the company has become the most recent symbol of government's inability to invest competently in risky technology and to 'pick winners'.

Yet nearly the same amount of money that was lent to Solyndra was lent to another company: Tesla Motors. Tesla received a US$465 million guaranteed loan for its S car. Unlike the Solyndra investment, this one fared very well and Elon Musk, its founder, is today treated as the new hero of Silicon Valley. As is the case with all innovations, for every success there are many more failures. The problem is that by not admitting that the State provided the high-risk investment and that it is subject to the same high failure rates as private venture capital, innovation policy ends up socializing only the risks and not the rewards (Mazzucato, 2013b; Lazonick and Mazzucato, 2013). Instead of worrying about picking winners or losers the real question should be why the 'entrepreneurial state' does not insist that a small per cent of Tesla's profit comes back to the state coffers that provided the high-risk finance so that the Solyndra loss could be shouldered not only by the taxpayers but the entire innovation 'ecosystem' that benefits from such public risk taking.

The role of an active private sector

There is nothing 'accidental' about clean technology development or the formation of markets for renewable energy. Rather, clean technology firms are leveraging technologies and cashing in on the prior investments of an active public sector, and responding to clear market signals proclaimed by progressive government policies about the desired change and to the availability of support for clean technology industrial growth. The hope is that innovation will produce economic wealth, employment opportunities, as well as a solution for climate change.

While the performance of countries has varied tremendously over the decades, it is obvious that Germany has provided a glimpse of the value of long-term support, China has demonstrated that a rapid scale-up of manufacturing and deployment is possible and the United States has shown the value of R&D, but also the folly of permitting uncertainty, shifting political priorities and speculative finance to set the clean technology development agenda. Governments leading the charge into clean technology do not have to allow themselves to be cheated when investments go sour. Nor should they expect that taxpayers will happily bear the full risks of investing in these technologies and establishing markets without a clear future reward to be gained.

The challenge is to create, maintain and fund a long-term policy framework which sustains momentum in the clean energy sector that has built up over the last decade. Without such long-term commitments, it is likely that clean technology will become a missed opportunity for many nations. Such a framework would include demand-side policies to promote increased consumption of solar and wind energy, as well as supply-side policies that promote manufacture of the technologies with 'patient' capital.

R&D contributing to clean technologies like wind and solar power has occurred on a global scale for decades, as a result of significant public investments and learning, and the leveraging of a broad community that has been inclusive of educational and business knowledge networks. The technology works as a result, and improvements in cost and efficiency have proceeded despite the unequal commitments of governments and businesses over time. The cost of energy they produce has also fallen over the long term, while fossil fuel prices continue to be volatile and rise over time.

Some firms may conduct important R&D for decades and remain money losers without a clear commercial prospect in the pipeline. As shown by the history of First Solar, the government's role in pushing innovations out of the lab and into markets does not end with R&D, but can include a role in overcoming commercialization barriers, such as a lack of production capabilities. Likewise, First Solar's VCs needed to endure challenges and an investment horizon that stretched their commitment.

How can firms of different scales interact in generating green transformations? We should not underestimate the role of small firms nor assume that only big firms have the right resources at their disposal. Small firms that grow into big firms are active promoters of their own business models, often to the frustration of 'legacy' industries that one could argue would never have taken the same technologies so far, so fast. The willingness to disrupt existing market models is needed in order to manifest a real green industrial revolution, and it is possible that start-ups, lacking the disadvantage of sunk costs, are the right actors for the job. Many large firms involved in clean technologies look to smaller start-ups and have themselves in the past relied on the State.

For example, General Electric (GE) 'inherited' the prior investments of the State and innovative firms in its rise as a major wind-turbine manufacturer. GE's own resources are vastly superior to those of small start-ups, which include billion dollar R&D budgets, billions in annual profit available to reinvest in core technologies, complementary assets such as a vast global network, and, as with the wind industry, significant rapport and reputation that reduce its 'risk' to investors. For renewable energy, scale matters and larger firms can more easily supply enormous energy grids spanning the continents. Perhaps most importantly, large firms like GE more easily win the confidence of investors and utilities, given their extensive operating history, financial resources, debt rating, experience with electricity infrastructure and vast social networks. It is not so coincidental that wind projects picked up to a feverish pace following GE's entry into the wind-energy business.

The political challenges of green transformations

The challenges faced by clean technologies are therefore seldom just technical; they are political (and social) and include a need for greater commitments of patient capital by governments and businesses around the world. R&D works, but it is not enough. Nurturing risky new industries requires support, subsidy and long-term commitments to manufacturing and markets as well. Governments must also confront the reality that for most developed nations, the deployment of clean technologies is occurring within a well-developed infrastructure. The clean slate approach is not possible, meaning that investment is intended to manage a transition to clean technology, a transition that threatens fossil and other energy industries that have the benefit of a longer development period and significant sunk costs. Not all in the business community are shy about calling for an active government role in clean technology. The time is overdue to begin discussing what the real role of business is in technological development beyond funding R&D. The clean technology revolution is at a crossroads. Contrary to conventional wisdom, R&D is not enough, VC is not so risk loving and small is not necessarily always beautiful. In order for the crossroads to be decided and green transformations to be generated, government policies must overcome these naive perspectives.

Innovation cannot be pushed without the efforts of many, and it cannot proceed without a long-term vision that sets the direction and clarifies objectives. When government policies fail, public dollars can be wasted and promising technologies may fail to meet their potential, because politicians or taxpayers refuse to commit more resources. When businesses fail, thousands of jobs can disappear, investors lose confidence and the reputations of the technologies are scarred. Uncertainty and stagnation can prevail, while the potential for promising new solutions vanishes. With government and business activities so intimately linked, it is often impossible to point blame accurately. At the root of it, there is only collective failure.

What should be clear is that the green energy revolution that has been experienced so far is a result of a complex, long-term, multi-decade-long technological development and diffusion process that unfolded on a global scale. The process has benefited from major government investments that encouraged the establishment of new firms and supported their growth by creating market opportunities. The variety of policies was meant to produce technological development, market efficiency, scale and efficient regulation. Overarching this process is a broad call to accelerate economic growth through innovation in clean technologies that mitigate climate change and promote energy diversity. The long-term vision is to transform our current productive system into a sustainable green industrial system. That is a mission set on producing long-lasting benefits to the public while delivering on a promise of superior economic performance. Key to future green transformations taking off will be the building of innovation ecosystems that result in symbiotic public–private partnerships rather than parasitic ones. That is, increased investments by the State in the ecosystem should not cause the private sector to invest less and focus its retained earnings on areas like boosting its stock prices, rather than on human capital formation and R&D.

The challenges of developing clean technologies go far beyond establishing risky public sector energy 'innovation hubs'. Governments must reduce the risk of commercializing energy innovations while establishing and managing the risks of competing in diversified and global energy markets. When difficulty has arisen in the past, such as when wind or solar markets faltered following retraction of US support for renewables in the late 1980s, the tendency has been to focus on how government investment is flawed, while the role of business in contributing to that failure is ignored or written off as part of the 'natural' behaviour of competitive markets. Worse, some interpret difficulties as proof that a technology 'can't compete' or will never compete with incumbent technology and should be shelved rather than exploited. This would go against the historical record, which suggests that all energy technologies have needed and benefited from lengthy development periods and long-term government support. What matters more is that the effort continues as if the future of the planet depended on it – because it does.

Conclusion

In seeking to promote innovation-led green transformations, it is fundamental to understand the important roles that both the public and private sector can play and the political dynamics involved. This requires not only understanding the importance of the innovation 'ecosystem' but especially what it is that each actor brings. The assumption that the public sector can at best incentivize private sector-led innovation (through subsidies, tax reductions, carbon pricing, technical standards, and so on) fails to account for the many examples in which the leading entrepreneurial force came from the State rather than from the private sector. Ignoring this role has had an impact on the types of public–private partnerships that are created and has wasted money on ineffective incentives that could have been spent more effectively.

To understand the fundamental role of the State in taking on the risks present in modern capitalism, it is important to recognize the 'collective' character of innovation. Different types of firms (large and small), different types of finance and different types of State policies, institutions and departments interact sometimes in unpredictable ways, but surely in ways we can help shape to meet the desired ends. For years we have known that innovation is not just a result of R&D spending, but about the set of institutions that allow new knowledge to diffuse throughout the economy.

What distinguishes the State is, of course, not only its mission but also the different tools and means that it has to deploy the mission. Polanyi argued that the State created – pushing, not only nudging – the most 'capitalist' of all markets, the 'national market', while local and international ones have predated capitalism. The capitalist economy will always be embedded in social, cultural and political institutions and therefore subordinate to the State and subject to its changes (Evans, 1995). Such embeddedness in fact renders meaningless the usual static state vs. market juxtaposition, because, as Polanyi (2001 [1944], p144) has demonstrated, the State *shapes* and *creates*: '[t]he road to the free market was opened and kept open by an enormous increase in continuous, centrally organized and controlled interventionism'.

Thus, rather than relying on the false dream that 'markets' will run the world optimally for us 'if only we just leave them alone', policy-makers must better learn how to use efficiently the tools and means to shape and create markets, making things happen that otherwise would not, and making sure those things are things we need. Increasingly, this requires growth to be not only 'smart' but also 'inclusive' and 'sustainable'.

It is, of course, important not to romanticize the State's capacity. The State can leverage a massive national social network of knowledge and business acumen, but we must make sure its power is controlled and directed through a variety of account-ability measures and diverse democratic processes. However, when organized effectively, the State's visible hand is firm but not heavy, providing the vision and the dynamic push (as well as some 'nudges') to make things happen that otherwise would not have. Such actions are meant to increase the courage of private business. This requires understanding the State as neither a 'meddler' nor a simple 'facilitator' of economic growth. It is a key partner of the private sector – and often a more daring one, willing to take the risks that business won't. The State cannot and should not bow down easily to interest groups who approach it to seek handouts, rents and unnecessary privileges like tax cuts. It should seek instead for those interest groups to work dynamically with it in its search for green growth and technological change.

Notes

1　'Development banks' and 'State investment banks' are used as synonyms throughout this chapter.
2　In a Pareto equilibrium, no person can be become better off without another person being made worse off.
3　Data on development bank investment in clean energy for 2013 was not available as of the time of writing this chapter (May 2014), but they 'are likely to have increased their investment in clean energy in 2013' (FS-UNEP/BNEF, 2014), despite a 14 per cent decrease in the overall clean energy investments (i.e. including all sources of funding) between 2012 and 2013.
4　Some green energy subsectors, such as on-shore wind power, are more technologically mature than others, such as offshore wind power.
5　Online interview, available at: www.youtube.com/watch?v=x54bVuduggU. Accessed 24 June 2014.
6　The 2009 'Cash for Clunkers' scheme – officially the Car Allowance Rebate System (CARS) – was a US$3 billion car-scrappage programme that offered consumers a credit of US$3500–US$4500 towards the purchase of a new, more fuel-efficient vehicles. Throughout the programme, 700,000 cars had been traded in, with Toyota being the biggest 'winner', as it accounted for 19.4 per cent of all trade-in sales (USDOT, 2009).

10

FINANCING GREEN TRANSFORMATIONS

Stephen Spratt

Introduction

Finance is not neutral: different forms influence the activities that they fund. Most obviously, the return required on investment determines the minimum return that must be generated, precluding many activities and encouraging others. Maturity operates in a similar way; if money needs to be repaid over a short period, activities that would come to fruition over longer time scales will not be financed.

Many forms of 'green transformation' are conceivable. Some focus on economic structures, particularly energy, while the broadest envisage a full transformation of economic, social and political systems. They may be local, national or global in scope. For some, transformation is desirable to achieve a particular end-state. Others argue that transformation is characterized by complexity and ultimate consequences cannot be known.

Different green transformations are more compatible with some types of finance than others, but not all forms of finance are equally abundant. Building on these two facts, this chapter examines the relationship between the financial systems and the types of transformation that might emerge.

While recognizing the emergence of different financing models, particularly in large emerging economies such as China, the main focus is on the major financial centres that have evolved in developed countries. There are three main reasons. First, despite the ravages of the global financial crisis, these remain the most likely sources of finance for achieving a global 'green transformation', as well as the main risks to international financial stability. Second, financial sector policy advice for developing countries has largely been drawn from practices in these centres. The impact of reforms would therefore be expected to have implications far beyond their national jurisdictions. Finally, we have a rich body of literature on the political economy of these financial systems: understanding how they have been shaped is a starting point for how they might be reformed.

The chapter is structured as follows. The first section examines the different types of 'green transformation' that have been proposed. The following section develops a complementary 'typology of finance'. Then follows an examination of the financing needs of different types of 'green transformation' and a comparison with the forms of finance that exist. To better understand why we have the configuration of finance we do, there is a review of some of the literature on the economics of regulation and political economy of finance. In the light of this analysis and research the chapter concludes with some thoughts on how financial systems might be reformed to facilitate a plurality of 'green transformations'.

A typology of transformations

Conceptions of transformation that are purely environmental still vary in scope. Climate change-focused perspectives, for example, focus on the need to decarbonize economies. The assumption is that, once placed on a carbon-neutral footing, economic systems can carry on much as before.[1] Widening the lens somewhat, the reduction of other air- and water-borne pollutants to sustainable levels is a component of most environmental models of transformation.

Expanding the focus again brings in the sustainable use of natural resources. The science of maintaining renewable resources such as fish stocks at sustainable levels is well established, though the practicalities of achieving this are certainly not (Hilborn, 2008). For forests, the issue is complicated by their role as carbon sinks, but we have a reasonable understanding of what is needed (Nabuurs et al., 2007). The supply of non-renewable resources is finite. Beyond a certain point, therefore, limits to use can only be avoided by recycling materials within a 'circular economy' (Andersen, 2007). Again, the assumption is that economic 'life' can continue broadly as now.

For many, restructuring to decarbonize economies, protect ecosystems and ensure the sustainable use of natural resources is what a full 'green transformation' would look like. Indeed, this might be thought of as the mainstream view (e.g. UNEP's 'Green Economy').[2] If this is the 'destination', the consensus on how to get there is through prices and market mechanisms. For climate change, this means a carbon price high enough to incentivize a switch to renewable energy (Bowen, 2011). For other emissions, the 'polluter pays' principle would see green taxes applied to reduce emissions to desirable levels.[3] Fiscal instruments are also central to incentivising zero-waste resource use in a circular economy (Stahel, 2010).

For others, the phrase 'green growth' is an oxymoron. The idea of there being 'limits to growth' has a long history (Leach, this book). From Malthus (1798) to Meadows et al. (1972), and more recently Tim Jackson (2009), there are two parts to the argument. First, the capacities of the natural environment are finite. Population growth combined with rising living standards will inevitably run up against these limits; the only question is when. Second, assuming that growth can be made compatible with these limits is unrealistic. From a climate change perspective, for example, economic output would need to be completely 'decoupled' from carbon emissions, which is seen as impossible.[4] The answer is not to make growth 'green', therefore, but to restrict it, or even to reduce economic activity.[5]

While calls for limits to growth can be made on purely environmental grounds, they are more commonly linked to social justice. In a world of limits to global growth, a more equitable distribution of income and wealth requires redistribution – it cannot be achieved by 'trickle-down', even in principle. Tim Jackson (2009) shows how much harder it would be to reduce carbon emission to sustainable levels while also addressing global inequality. To reach sustainable emissions levels by 2050, while raising global income levels to the EU 2007 average level, requires a 55-fold reduction in carbon intensity, compared with a 21-fold reduction if patterns of inequality remain unchanged.

Arguments in favour of redistribution are not restricted to the more radical views of green transformation. To address climate change at the global level, many argue for the creation of a global carbon market, where countries trade their carbon emission rights, potentially creating a mechanism to transfer finance from rich to poor countries. The level of transfers, however, would be determined by the way national emission rights are allocated. At one extreme, some propose 'grand-fathering', with rights allocated in line with the current pattern of emissions (Bovens, 2011). At the other end of the spectrum, others suggest that emissions are allocated on an equal per capita basis, or progressively moved towards this.[6] Under this framework, low-income countries would generally receive more permits than they needed, allowing them to sell these to richer countries, creating large annual cash transfers, or a mechanism for global redistribution.

Broadly, green transformations can vary across two broad dimensions: how 'green' they are, and the extent to which they take account of 'social justice'. For this dimension I take inequalities of income and wealth as a proxy for social justice, recognizing that there are many other important elements that this does not cover.

Table 10.1 organizes these distinctions into four forms of green transformation. In quadrant 1 we would find those that take a relatively 'light-green'[7] view on the environment, focus on restructuring economic systems, particularly the energy sector, and do not question existing patterns of inequality. The World Bank would broadly fit into this camp.[8] Quadrant 2 combines a relative lack of interest in social issues, with a 'precautionary' approach to the environment, emphasizing the fragile

TABLE 10.1 Forms of greenhouse transformation

	⟵ 'Green' ⟶	
↑ 'Social' ↓	1	2
	4	3

interdependence of complex ecosystems and opposing anthropocentric views that privilege human interests over those of other forms of life. We might call these 'dark-green' transformations.

Denizens of quadrant 3 would also be sceptical about the possibility of 'dematerializing growth', but combine this with concerns over the distribution of income and wealth. We might call this a 'dark-green and red' transformation, where we would find academics such as Tim Jackson, think-tanks like the New Economics Foundation,[9] and networks such as Research & Degrowth.[10]

Quadrant 4 is where much of the international development community would be found, where traditional emphasis on poverty and inequality are combined with environmental concern. Within this framework, the dominant approach to 'sustainable development' has generally been more 'light' than 'dark' green. As a result, we might call this type of transformation 'light green and red'.

These different types of transformation are not equally compatible with different modes of finance. Before examining these interactions the next section sketches out a 'typology of finance'.

A typology of finance

Modern financial systems contain a dizzying range of instruments, employed by a diverse set of institutions. Despite large ostensible differences, however, the core characteristics of these instruments fall into a relatively small number of groups: equity, debt or derivatives, or some combination of these.[11] Equity is an ownership stake, which may be publicly traded or privately held, and debt is the loaning of a specified amount of money for a given time period at a rate of interest.

Originally used for hedging risk, but increasingly traded for speculative gain, derivatives are financial instruments whose value is 'derived' from that of an underlying financial asset. The main forms are forwards, futures, options and swaps. While some are traded on formal exchanges (and the proportion is increasing due to post-crisis regulatory pressure), the bulk of contracts are still agreed between counterparties directly or 'over-the-counter' (OTC).

The main private financial institutions, the instruments they use and the approximate size of their assets are described in Table 10.2. These institutions aim to maximize their returns for a given level of risk – broadly, the higher the level of risk, the greater the return required. Different institutions are prepared to accept different levels of risk and so target different levels of returns. In Table 10.2, for example, pension funds are quite risk averse, reflecting their need to be able to meet liabilities for many decades. In contrast, private equity funds, most hedge funds and investment banks, have a relatively high-risk tolerance. Public equity and bond funds have varying degrees of risk appetite, as do commercial banks.

Similar differences exist between institutions with respect to maturities. Pension funds have a relatively long-term approach to investment, while equity and bond fund managers have a range of outlooks. Some 'buy and hold' based on long-term value; other funds trade frequently in response to changes in macro indicators, politics

TABLE 10.2 Commercial financial institutions and financial instruments

Institution/ Instruments originated (or purchased directly or in primary market)	Instruments traded	Estimated loans assets[*]
Commercial banks Personal (including mortgages), corporate loans and securitization instruments	Hedging products for credit exposures.	US$35 trillion[†]
Investment banks Corporate and sovereign bonds; private equity stakes	All financial instruments.	~US$500 billion[‡]
Portfolio equity investors Public equities	Secondary market equities	US$23.5 trillion
Portfolio bond investors Corporate and sovereign bonds	Secondary market bonds	
Pension funds Public equities and bonds	Public equities and bonds (plus 'non-traditional instruments': commodities, private equity and hedge funds, securitized products)	£33.9 trillion
Insurance funds As pension funds	As pension funds	US$25.8 trillion
Private equity investors (including venture capital) Private equity stakes	Private equity stakes	US$2.3 trillion
Hedge funds Any financial instrument	Any financial instrument	US$2.1 trillion
TOTAL		~US$123 trillion

Sources: [*] The CityUK (2013) (minus estimated SRI and impact investment). [†] Outstanding international (i.e. cross-border) bank loans 2012 (BIS). [‡] Annual revenues of ten largest investment banks (*Financial Times*).

or movements in 'market sentiment'. The rate at which portfolios have been turned over has been rising, as investors have held stocks for shorter periods.[12] At the extreme, high-frequency investors use automated strategies to buy and sell in fractions of seconds and now account for three-quarters of trading on the New York Stock Exchange.[13]

Increasing short-termism can be seen in banking, where the incentives facing senior managers of banks encourage the maximization of short-term profits (Dallas, 2012). In the 1970s, the overwhelming majority of banks' revenues came from lending. By the 1990s, 35 per cent of US banks revenues came from trading activities and by 2007 this had risen to 50 per cent (Boot and Ratnovski, 2012).

TABLE 10.3 Non-commercial financial institutions and financial instruments

Institution	Instruments originated (or purchased directly or in primary market)	Total assets
Microfinance institutions (MFIs)	Personal and small business loans	US$38 billion[*]
Community and co-operative banks	Personal and small business loans	US$1.69 trillion[†]
National public development banks	Corporate and sovereign loans and bonds; private and public equity stakes	US$2 trillion[‡]
Multilateral development banks and development finance institutions (DFIs)	Corporate and sovereign loans and bonds; private and public equity stakes	~US$500 billion[§]
Sovereign Wealth Funds (SWFs)	Any financial instrument	US$5.2 trillion[¶]
Socially Responsible Investors (SRIs) and Impact Investors	Public and private equity	~US$3 trillion[¶]
TOTAL		US$12.8 trillion

Sources: [*] Outstanding loans: MIX (2009). [†] Credit unions: World Council of Credit Unions (2013). [‡] Various sources; de Luna-Martínez and Vicente (2012). [§] The CityUK (2013). [¶] Various sources.

Table 10.3 lists financial institutions that are not purely commercial. While it is not possible to get accurate figures for all these sectors, it is clear that their combined assets are only a fraction – around 10 per cent – of those controlled by commercial institutions. Although these institutions are not *purely* commercially oriented, many do seek a market-level return: Socially Responsible Investment (SRI) funds and Sovereign Wealth Funds (SWFs) seek good returns, for example, but may also have ethical or strategic objectives, respectively. For the other institutions, the main aim is to maximize development impacts, with financial sustainability being necessary to ensure that they can continue to do this. To varying degrees, all the institutions in Table 10.3 are likely to take a relatively long-term view.

Table 10.4 differentiates forms of finance by maturity and expected returns. Cell 1 contains institutions that aim for high returns, take high levels of risk and have very short time horizons. Here we would find high frequency traders (HFTs), many hedge funds and the trading arms of investment banks. In cell 2 similarly high returns are targeted, but over a slightly longer time-frame – up to a year. Equity and bond investors with high-risk strategies would be found here. Cell 3 combines high-return expectations with time horizons beyond a year, and would include aggressive private equity and venture capital funds, and some high-risk/high-return commercial lending.

TABLE 10.4 Forms of finance

	← Maturities →		
	1	2	3
Financial returns	4	5	6
	7	8	9

Institutions located in cell 4 have lower return expectations but with very short time horizons. Here we would find similar institutions, but employing less risky investment strategies than those in cell 1. Similarly, cell 5 would again contain equity and bond funds, but now with less risky portfolios, perhaps based on diversified exposure to mainstream indices. SRI funds would also be located here. Institutions in cell 6 would take a longer term view. As well as pension, insurance and SWFs, much commercial bank lending would be found here, as would most microfinance funds and DFIs aiming to create a 'demonstration effect'.[14]

Due to the low financial return expectations, the bottom row of Table 10.4 contains only non-commercial institutions. As described above, these investors also tend to take a relatively long-term view, so little would be found in Cell 7. Cell 8 would contain lending by community banks, as well as some development bank loans and impact investors. The bulk of activities would be of maturities beyond a year, however, and so be found in cell 9, as would most equity investment by DFIs.

To summarize, most commercial finance would be found in cells 1, 3, 5 and 6, while non-commercial finance is mainly in cell 9. In the next section we consider how this pattern of finance might affect the types of green transformation that might emerge.

Why different transformations need different types of finance

Earlier I sketched out a typology of different transformations, which varied according to how 'green' and 'socially inclusive' they aimed to be. This is illustrated in Table 10.5.

Finance for 'light-green' transformations would have three functions. The first is investments in non-fossil fuel-based energy. The International Energy Agency (IEA) estimates that 85 per cent of the required US$500bn per year will need to come from private sources. This type of finance should be long term (15–25 years) and would yield relatively low returns. Typically, debt/equity ratios in renewable energy projects are 70/30.[15] Returns are generally dependent on support through mechanisms such as feed-in tariffs, so public finance must be sufficient to fund these over the longer term.

TABLE 10.5 Forms of green transformation

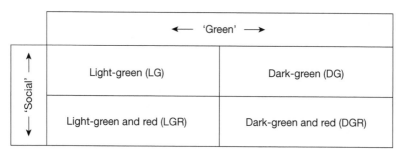

	← 'Green' →	
'Social' ↑	Light-green (LG)	Dark-green (DG)
↓	Light-green and red (LGR)	Dark-green and red (DGR)

The second function is to fund energy efficiency. Again, the sums are very large. Farrell and Remes (2009) estimate that US$90 billion of energy efficiency investment is needed per year in developing countries alone. Energy efficiency projects range from 'low-hanging fruit' yielding good returns in short periods of time, to longer term measures generating lower returns. Investors with different maturity (i.e. 2–10 years) and return expectations would thus be needed. Longer term, 'patient capital' fits well with the requirements of 'deeper' forms of energy efficiency, while providers of debt finance with shorter time horizons could provide the capital to finance 'quick wins' (Spratt *et al.*, 2013).

The third function is to finance the transition to a circular economy. These are higher risk (and potentially higher return) investments suited, in principle, to venture capital and private equity. Given the record of such institutions, however, there are good reasons to doubt this will happen (Mazzucato, this book). There are two alternative sources of finance. First, products could be developed by current producers of related products. Second, the public sector could invest directly in innovation through public development banks, and/or incentivize the private sector to do so (Mazzucato, 2013b).

Returning to our typology, we see plenty of finance that matches these requirements. Pension and insurance funds control huge assets, have a naturally long-term perspective, and a cautious approach to risk and return. They are thus well suited to renewable energy investments in principle. For energy efficiency, there are numerous debt financiers with time horizons and returns expectations compatible with those described above. For new product development for a circular economy, venture capital and private equity funds should have the right characteristics, and public development banks are well suited to invest and intervene in this area. If there is already a reasonable match with existing forms of finance, however, why are we not seeing the emergence of well-funded 'light-green transformations' already?

There are four main reasons. First, financial institutions do not always act as they might be expected: despite their long-term liabilities, pension funds have not been immune to the increasing short-termism in finance. Second, vehicles that make it easy for large, financial institutions to invest are often missing. Energy efficiency is a good example: most projects are too small to be investable on an individual basis, but mechanisms to reduce information asymmetries and enable diversified access to such investments do not exist in the form needed. Third, as described above, financial institutions aim to maximize *risk-adjusted* returns. Renewable energy investments that generate modest returns will therefore only be attractive if risks are also low. For many investors, the fact that returns are dependent on continuing public subsidy creates significant risk. This brings us to the fourth reason: the long-term commitment to a 'green transformation' of many governments is not sufficiently trusted, making the risks of investing high.[16]

How would the financing needs of the other transformation in Table 10.5 differ? Proponents of 'light-green and red' (LGR) transformations have similar environmental goals, but also seek a more equitable distribution of income and wealth, both between and within countries. One way of improving intercountry inequality would be through a global carbon market based on equal per capita emission rights. There is nothing incompatible with this and the financial system we have. Indeed, some of the strongest advocates for a global carbon market have been large financial institutions. This is unsurprising, as the creation of such a market would represent a new financial asset class that financial institutions could manage and trade.

Reducing intracountry inequality would require deep changes. As well as mechanisms such as a wealth taxes,[17] reducing inequalities of income and wealth would require a relative reduction of 'returns to capital'[18] and a more equal distribution of wages. From a financing perspective, lower returns to capital would be likely to reduce financial returns as private sector profitability fell. More equality in terms of wages, perhaps achieved through higher marginal tax rates on top incomes, would impact directly on financial market actors, of course.

Although 'light-green' transformations with a social element would most likely be opposed by financial actors, this is still evolution rather than revolution: a financial system compatible with this form of transformation would still be recognizable to what we have today. What happens when our transformations turn a darker shade of green?

The most fundamental difference between light- and dark-green visions of transformation is their attitude to growth. From a light-green perspective, 'green growth' is the solution. Proponents of dark-green transformations consider consumerism to be the issue, whatever its colour, and argue for limits to growth or 'degrowth'. While 'light-green' transformations are broadly compatible with the financial system we have, this is not so for 'dark-green' versions, which see finance, particularly debt-finance, as at the heart of the problem.

In mainstream finance, capital should be invested where the greatest increases in output and productivity can be achieved. Proponents of 'dark-green' transformation would fundamentally disagree. The need for investments to produce a return greater than the cost of finance (i.e. the rate of interest) leads to an expansion in economic output and productivity. This is the problem, and the principal reason why economic systems based on interest-bearing debt must continue to grow, and therefore cannot be made compatible with environmental sustainability. Historically, this impulse was limited as the supply of money was fixed to gold (i.e. the gold standard). The supply of credit would rise and fall in line with government's gold stocks. The last constraint was broken in 1971 when the link between the dollar and gold was broken and there ceased to be an external constraint on the money supply. Countries moved to a 'fiat system', with money created by commercial banks in the form of credit.[19] Combined with the expansionary impulse of interest-bearing debt, the removal of limits on credit creation is a primary driver of (unsustainable) growth.

What about 'dark-green and red' transformations? If the global economy cannot grow, then the unequal distribution of wealth within it either becomes fixed or needs to be changed through radical redistributive mechanisms. The same is true for inequality within countries, for which various mechanisms have been proposed. Proposals on wealth include but go beyond the standard wealth tax arguments. Many of these are grassroots, or community-led in nature.[20] 'Dark-green and red' transformations thus have similar financial implications to their dark-green cousins, though with additional features.

Generally speaking, the more change required, the harder it will be to achieve. If this is the case, then transformations that are compatible with the financial system we currently have will be more attainable than those which are not. This suggests that a 'light-green' transformation will be easier to achieve than one that is 'light-green and red', and that both will be easier than either of the dark-green varieties. This is not so say that these are impossible, just more difficult. In order to change a system, however, it is first necessary to understand the forces that created it. The next section reviews the literature on this subject, with a focus on political economy.

How did we end up here?

In developed countries at least, the financial systems we have do not appear to be 'fit for purpose' with respect to green transformations, particularly of the more radical variety. More generally, finance does not appear to flow to those parts of economies that would yield the greatest benefits. The shortfall in finance for infrastructure in developing countries, for example, has been estimated at more than US$1 trillion per year (Bhattacharya et al., 2012), with Africa alone requiring US$93 billion (Foster and Briceño-Garmendia, 2010). A third of small and medium enterprises (SMEs) in developing countries cite lack of access to finance as a major constraint on growth (Beck, 2007). This is not simply the result of immature financial systems. Many SMEs in developed countries are also unable to access sufficient, affordable finance,[21] and infrastructure funding gaps remain large.

If the financial system does not serve the interests of society as well as it might, whose interests does it serve? On this question, the most plausible answer is the interests of financiers themselves. As described above, lending to the 'real economy' has been a declining part of banks' activities for decades. Between 1996 and 2008, for example, lending to businesses in the productive parts of the UK economy fell from 30 per cent to 10 per cent of the total, while lending to property and other financial institutions rose sharply (CRESC, 2009). Lending has become increasingly short term.

This is not just a matter of banks preferring to lend short term. The 'financial instability hypothesis' describes how the maturity structure of finance in the economy becomes increasingly short term during periods of stability. Short-term loans are cheap. Assuming the 'good times' will continue, borrowers have an incentive to increasingly rely on (cheap) short-term borrowing, which they can 'roll-over' to mimic a longer term loan. This works fine until loans can no longer be rolled over, defaults multiply and crises engulf unstable financial systems (Minsky, 1992).[22] Banks are borrowers too, of course. A striking feature of the 2007–2008 crisis was the extent to which banks came to fund their activities through short-term borrowing in the wholesale market. When a 'Minsky moment' caused credit to freeze in the interbank market, the whole edifice came crashing down.[23]

Banks' have also become more leveraged: between 2003 and 2007, average leverage ratios of the major US investment banks doubled from 15 to 30. UK banks were no different. By 2006, the Royal Bank of Scotland had assets of £848 billion, equivalent to 64 per cent of UK gross domestic product (GDP). Its capital (equity) was only £38 billion, or 4.5 per cent of these assets. The attraction is straightforward: a 10 per cent return on these assets yields a profit of £85 billion, more than 200 per cent of total equity. The higher the leverage ratio, the greater the return on equity, but the more vulnerable the bank (MacKensie, 2013).

As banks became larger, more short term and leveraged, trading in financial markets exploded, fuelled by the creation of ever-more complex derivative products. The notional value of outstanding over-the-counter (OTC) derivatives rose from around US$50 trillion in 1998 to more than US$600 trillion by 2013 (BIS, 2013), or from roughly equal to almost six times global GDP.

Similar to increased leverage in the banking system, the purpose of much financial innovation is to increase the profits of financial institutions. As we saw all too clearly in 2007–2008, however, and is true even in the absence of financial crises, 'what's good for Wall Street' is not necessarily 'good for Main Street'. This begs the question as to how financiers have been able to influence events such that the financial system serves their interests rather than those of wider society.

One explanation comes from the economics of regulation. The theory of regulatory capture describes how regulators come to serve the interests of those they regulate. To a greater or lesser extent, the history of financial regulation since the 1970s has been one of steady liberalization, as restrictions on financial actors – or 'financial repression' (Stigler, 1971) – were removed. Some of these restrictions – such as the Glass–Steagall Act[24] that separated investment from commercial banking in the US – had been in place since the 1930s. Others were implemented soon after the Second World War.

It is easy to see why financial market actors would want restrictions on their activities removed, but why did regulators come to share this view? Pagliari (2012) describes four reasons why financial regulators are particularly prone to capture. First, financiers devote a huge amount of time and resources in the attempt to influence policy: financial lobbyists in the US spent US$2.7 billion on lobbying between 1999 and 2008 (ibid.). The complexity of financial regulation also gives sector insiders an advantage compared to other actors when regulators are considering policy change: less than 10 per cent of the stakeholders who participate in official consultations on regulation are from trade unions, consumer groups, NGOs or independent research institutions (Pagliari and Young, 2012).

Second, outside official consultations, the financial industry retains preferential access to regulators, mostly behind closed doors (Pagliari, 2012). In some cases, the explanation is that regulatory agencies are not independent in the first place. Part of the UK's Financial Services Authority mandate, for example, was to support the interests of the City of London. The powerful Office of the Comptroller of the Currency is required to promote the interests of US banks (Pagliari, 2012).

Third, and perhaps most importantly, even where regulators are formally independent, the last 30 years saw an increasing convergence of mindset with those they are charged with regulating. This 'intellectual' or 'cultural capture' went way beyond regulation of finance to incorporate a distrust of the state and blind faith in markets (Kwak, 2013).

A final element supporting capture is the 'revolving door' between policy-makers and financial institutions. This has long been a feature of US regulation and politics. A surprising number of Treasury Secretaries in recent years have worked for Goldman Sachs, for example, but this is not confined to the US: the current Governor of the Bank of England, Mark Carney, and President of the European Central Bank, Mario Draghi, for example, also held senior positions at Goldman Sachs.

As well as 'captured' regulators, another source of influence is the politicians who appoint them. Pagliari (2012, p12) summarizes the factors identified in the literature:

> [T]he financial industry [in the US] remains one of the major contributors to politicians' electoral campaigns across the political spectrum; consequently it is able to exercise a significant influence over the voting behaviour of Congress on certain regulatory issues. Second . . . politicians may interfere in the actions of regulators in order to achieve key political objectives such as economic growth, employment, social and economic stability . . . [or] pressure regulators in order to achieve short-term political objectives by pleasing powerful electoral constituencies or special interest groups . . . during boom times regulatory agencies are likely to face pressures to be accommodating in the implementation of financial rules, thus hindering their capacity to 'remove the punchbowl from the party'.

Further insights can be gained from other branches of the literature. The 'fiscal sociology' of the 1970s and 1980s remains relevant. Maxfield (1991, p422) argues that:

> the ability of financiers to influence public policy results from the strategic interaction between revenue-raising states and private holders of relatively liquid assets ... To the extent that capital is mobile, and government depends on financial contributions from holders of mobile assets, we will always find financiers shaping government policy.[25]

Given the huge growth of financial sectors and the removal of restrictions on international capital mobility, it seems highly likely that the 'structural power' of finance (Winters, 1994) has increased.

As well as explaining how national regulations became increasingly liberalized, particularly in jurisdictions with major financial centres, it is important to understand how these norms are transmitted to other countries, particularly poorer countries with immature financial sectors.

On this question, a rich and varied literature on the international diffusion of ideas has developed. Simmons *et al.* (2008) identify four strands of this literature that may have encouraged liberalization: coercion, competition, learning and emulation. On the first of these, Simmons *et al.* (2008, p11) suggests:

> The diffusion of economic liberalization is thought by many to be the outcome largely of coercive pressures ... The logic is straightforward. Developing countries need financial assistance from the strong either to ward off crises or to make infrastructural investments that are hard to fund through private markets. Lenders, however, then condition their financial support on domestic economic reforms they deem desirable – macroeconomic stabilization, free trade and cross-border capital movements, privatization and deregulation.

'Coercion' need not be overt, but may result from the spread of 'hegemonic ideas'. Here, the idea of liberalization is increasingly accepted, not least because of the powerful actors promoting these views.[26] As well as more formal channels, an important transmission mechanism may be the 'epistemic community' (Haas, 1980) of economists. Chwieroth (2007), for example, shows how US-trained economists played a prominent role in capital account liberalization in developing countries.

Other strands of the diffusion literature stress the role of choice, albeit heavily constrained 'choice'. The mobility of international capital, for example, encourages *competition* between countries to implement 'market-friendly' policies, particularly financial liberalization, and the reduction of tax rates (Jenson, 2003, cited in Simmons *et al.*, 2008). A third mechanism is where governments *learn* from the experience of other countries which policies are likely to work (Simmons *et al.*, 2008).

While the relative economic success of the United States appears to have been important in this respect, the global financial crisis may have changed perceptions about finance in particular. Similarly, the rapid and sustained growth of China, achieved in a far from laissez-faire way, may also be provoking a reassessment of the merits of different development trajectories.

The final mechanism in the literature is *emulation*. This constructivist strand explores why some policies become accepted while others do not, based on the subjective understanding of policy-makers. The question is why they come to think the way they do:

> Policymakers are constrained by bounded rationality, meaning that they are unable to envision the full range of policy alternatives and unable to assess the costs and benefits of each. In consequence it is often the rhetorical power of a new policy approach, rather than hard evidence . . . that matters.
>
> (Simmons *et al.*, 2008, p33)

As with the coercion, powerful countries and institutions are often those with the greatest 'rhetorical power'. A key difference in the emulation literature, however, is that policy-makers 'choose' to adopt the policies they *genuinely* believe will be most effective.

While it is undeniable that private financiers have a disproportionate influence, they are not the only influence. Borrowers may prefer short-term finance in some cases, and politicians have strong incentives to foster economic booms. The power of industrial interests is also important. In developing countries, we would expect different patterns of influential groups. The 'new political economy' school has undertaken empirical work on how the balance of power between different interest groups affects the regulation of the financial system, and its resultant structure.[27]

While there may have been too much financial sector development (FSD) in some developed countries,[28] this is not true in most of the developing world. In many countries, financial systems are dominated by a few large banks, which provide too little (expensive) credit to the private sector. Financial exclusion is also the norm in many countries: only 24 per cent of adults in sub-Saharan Africa have a bank account.[29] For Rajan and Zingales (2003) low FSD in developing countries results from collusion between government and incumbent financial institutions, both of whom are incentivized to restrict competition: incumbent institutions because this allows them to maintain market share and monopolistic profits; governments because they can use the financial sector for their own ends.

A related school attributes the growth of financial systems to the emergence of political institutions to check the power of government. Without such institutions, governments face strong incentives to use the financial system to support their own survival, rather than develop into an effective mechanism for financing broad-based economic activity (Haber *et al.*, 2008).

We thus have a rich and varied set of literatures that can help us understand why we have the financial systems we do. There are two main elements: first, there are the forces which shape finance at the national level; second, there is the spread of policy between countries, generally from developed countries (with major financial centres) to developing countries. Thus, while domestic finance is often quite weak in developing countries, governments may still adopt liberalizing policies because of the international diffusion of these ideas.

Some concluding thoughts on achieving transformations

Reforming finance to support light-green transformations seems possible. If the right incentives were put in place – most importantly that environmental costs were priced into investment decisions – the financial sector might even become a force driving transformation globally (Newell, this book). As mentioned previously, the financial lobby is broadly supportive of environmental change – as long as new financial asset classes are integral to this process. With 'light-green transformations', therefore, the obstacle is not finance, but the incumbents who benefit from the status quo, as well as collective action problems operating at the international level. It is possible to envisage alliances of public, private and civic groups becoming strong enough to overcome these incumbents (Schmitz, this book). Were the financial lobby, with all its power and influence, to be part of such alliances, the chances of success would be greatly increased.

The situation is more complex with the other forms of transformation identified. Each would require reforms that would be opposed by financial actors, vehemently in some cases. It is reasonable to assume that financial actors will try to protect their own interests. History suggests these are equated with profit maximization through financial 'innovation' and leverage, and that this requires minimal restrictions on financial institutions. Achieving reductions in inter- and intracountry inequalities would require measures likely to reduce the freedoms and profitability of the financial sector, and so be strongly opposed.

As a result, alliances working to achieve transformations of this kind would need to be different, not least as the financial lobby would be found in the opposing camp. This does not mean they could not succeed, however. The attention captured by Thomas Piketty's (2014) work on capitalism and inequality suggests a strong appetite for change. Moreover, the interests of the 'real economy' are often ill-served by finance. Reforms that reoriented finance towards the real economy, and which encourage transformations to more equitable societies, could potentially garner support from a range of actors.

While the international mobility of capital suggests that these alliances would need to be transnational, the international spread of finance-friendly policies from particular countries points towards an initial focus on reform in the major financial centres. This is difficult. The authorities with power to reform these centres – i.e. the governments of the jurisdictions in which they operate – are those which are most likely to be 'captured' by the financial lobby. Understanding what forms of alliance would have the most influence, and analysing how they could be mobilized and maintained, seems a precondition for achieving substantive reform, and an important area of future research.

Reforming finance to achieve 'dark-green' transformations implies the need for a different form of alliance. As such transformations tend to be antithetical to economic growth, they are incompatible with the financial systems we have, particularly with respect to debt. They would also require a broader transformation of capitalism, however, and so be likely to be opposed by much of the 'real economy' as well as the financial sector and mainstream politicians. Alliances would thus need to be built from the grassroots up. Given the global nature of the 'opposition', such alliances would also need to be international in scope. This is an inherently long game, which does not mean that it is not worth playing, of course.

Understanding how financial systems can influence environmental and social change in different countries may be a necessary precondition for achieving 'green transformation'. This is not sufficient, however. Actually achieving change requires a nuanced understanding of the political economy of finance. While this chapter has sketched some of the issues, addressing these two questions – particularly the intersection between them – remains a crucial area for future research.

Notes

1 The Stern Review (2006) is perhaps the most representative of this perspective.
2 Available online at: www.unep.org/greeneconomy/. Accessed 24 June 2014.
3 See Spratt (2012) for a discussion of environmental taxes.
4 There is some evidence of relative decoupling (i.e. where the carbon intensity of output falls) at the global level, but none at all of absolute decoupling. To put this into perspective, the global carbon intensity of growth in 2007 was 760 grams of CO_2 per US$. To be compatible with a 2-degree threshold, this would have to fall to 36 grams by 2050, a 21-fold reduction, which equates to a 7 per cent reduction every year. Between 1990 and 2007, the average annual reduction was 0.7 per cent (Jackson, 2009).
5 Available online at: www.degrowth.org/. Accessed 24 June 2014.
6 For details on the 'contraction and convergence' framework, see: www.gci.org.uk/index.html. Accessed 24 June 2014.
7 These could be thought of as a 'weak sustainability' position that takes a relatively sanguine view of the substitutability of natural capital (Neumeyer, 2010).
8 When the bank mentions 'inclusive green growth', for example, this is conceived of as something that poor people benefit from in an absolute rather than relative sense. As a result, there is no need for inequalities to fall for green growth to be 'inclusive'. For a discussion, see Spratt et al. (2013).
9 Available online at: www.neweconomics.org/. Accessed 24 June 2014.
10 Available online at: www.degrowth.org/. Accessed 24 June 2014.
11 I have not included foreign exchange in this set, as it is not a financial asset per se, but a denomination or unit of account.
12 In the 1990s, 97 per cent of the average portfolio of large growth funds in the US turned over each year. By the 2000s, this had risen to 162 per cent. See: www.morningstar.com/. Accessed 24 June 2014.

13 See Lewis (2014) for a fascinating account of the rise of high-frequency trading in the US.

14 Many DFIs aim to attract private investment into countries and sectors with high potential impact by demonstrating that profitable investments can be made, with acceptable levels of risk.

15 Projects in developing countries are generally assumed to be riskier, such that debt investors demand a higher proportion of equity, which is essentially a form of collateral from their perspective. Debt/equity ratios are thus more like 60/40 (IRENA, 2012).

16 For a flavour of investors' perceptions on these issues, see Parhelion and Standard & Poor's (2010).

17 See Piketty (2014) for a rationale and detailed suggestions for wealth taxes.

18 In most countries, as well as globally, the 'factor' shares going to labour have steadily declined since the 1960s at least (Glyn, 2009). Recent debates on stagnating or falling real wages are thus only the most recent manifestations of this longer term trend.

19 It is estimated that 97 per cent of money in circulation in the UK today has been created in this way (Greenham et al., 2012).

20 See NEF (2010) for a comprehensive 'manifesto' along these lines.

21 In a 2013 survey in the European Union access to finance was cited as the most pressing problem by 40 per cent of SMEs in Cyprus, 32 per cent in Greece, 23 per cent in Spain and Croatia, and 20 per cent in Italy, Ireland and the Netherlands. It was mentioned least in Germany (8 per cent), Austria (7 per cent) and Luxembourg (6 per cent) (European Commission, 2013).

22 As well as the global financial crisis of 2007–2008, the financial instability hypothesis describes very well the Asian financial crisis of 1997, where international bank lending became increasingly short term.

23 This process led to the demise of Northern Rock, the first UK bank failure in 150 years.

24 The Glass–Steagall Act was passed in 1933 and finally repealed in 1999 after decades of lobbying by the financial sector. See Crawford (2011) for a history and account of the impact of the repeal of Glass–Steagall on the global financial crisis of 2007–2008.

25 Maxfield (1991) argues that the interests of finance are more likely to be reflected in policy where an effective 'bankers alliance' of private financiers and central bankers has developed. Where this is the case, monetary policy will remain tight – with negative impacts on the real economy – and government intervention in the financial system will be minimized.

26 See Femia (1983) or Hirschman (1989), for example. See Pagano and Volpin (2001) for a review.

27 Other perspectives on financial structure stress the role of legal origins (La Porta et al., 1998). From this perspective, countries with an English common law, rather than a French civil code tradition are more likely to have stronger protection for creditors and minority shareholder rights. As a result, financial sector development, particularly with respect to capital markets, will tend to be more advanced. Another school of thought sees differences in financial structures in developed countries – particularly 'arm's-length' Anglo-Saxon models with large capital markets, versus systems based on 'relationship banking' in Germany and Japan – as more a matter of cultural and deep-rooted political differences between countries (Roe, 2003).

28 Arcand et al. (2012) show that the impact of the financial sector on growth becomes negative when private sector credit exceeds 110 per cent of GDP. In 2012, the figure was 176 per cent for the UK and 184 per cent in the US (WDI).

29 World Bank's World Development Indicators.

11

GREEN TRANSFORMATION

Is there a fast track?

Hubert Schmitz

Introduction

The green transformation is different from previous transformations in one critical respect: urgency. This is the first transformation in history to be achieved against a deadline. Hence the question in the title: is there a fast track? This chapter seeks answers by addressing five subquestions: what, why, how, who and when?[1]

The following section asks *what* the problem is. Then follows the question *why* this problem needs urgent attention and a reflection on how robust the call for urgent action is. *How* transformations occur, *who* can be expected to drive the transformation forward and *when* the green transformation is most likely to occur are the questions asked in the sections that follow. The concluding section returns to the overall question posed in the title of this chapter. Since this is the final chapter of the book, it also draws together elements of preceding chapters.

What?

The green agenda encompasses many issues. If asked *what* the most fundamental problem is, most scientists studying our planet would probably say 'climate change'. 'Each of the last three decades has been successively warmer at the Earth's surface than any preceding decade since 1850' (IPCC, 2013, p3). A continuation of this trend would make human life very difficult in many parts of our planet. This is the first part of the climate and earth scientists' message. The second part is that humans have brought about the problem, by increasing carbon emissions. 'It is *extremely likely* that human influence has been the dominant cause of the observed warming since the mid-20th century' (IPCC, 2013, p12). 'Extremely likely' means that these scientists are '95–100 per cent' certain (ibid., p2).

However, both parts of the message remain contested. One of the leading climate scientists, Mike Hulme, has provided an in-depth analysis of the reasons 'Why we disagree about climate change' (Hulme, 2009). There are hard and soft disagreements. Hard disagreements come from the powerful vested interests who question the existence and human causes of climate change (Newell and Paterson, 2010; Blasberg and Kohlenberg, 2012). Trying to defend its assets, the fossil fuel lobby has fought hard to discredit the scientific case for connecting climate change with carbon emissions. Soft disagreements arise over concerns that the discourse on green economy and growth depoliticizes the transformational change required (Wanner, 2014). These hard and soft disagreements are discussed in Chapter 2 by Melissa Leach and in Chapter 5 by Peter Newell.

This chapter raises a different concern over the climate change debate: the narrative of the earth and climate scientists does not connect with the experience of ordinary citizens. The climate change paradigm is a result of research carried out by many groups of scientists in different parts of world, using different approaches, different data sets and often focused on different parts of the planet. The collective confidence of these scientists in their analyses and predictions comes from the convergence of their findings with regard to some key variables, notably changes in land and ocean surface temperatures. Scientists have focused in particular on the globally averaged temperatures and shown that small rises in these global *averages* have huge consequences. The discourse of global warming has centred on the need to limit the temperature rise to two degrees (over the 1990 level) and to do this by bringing carbon emissions down. While scientifically robust, it has been politically ineffective.

I would argue that language and discourse have a lot to do with it. Small rises in average temperature are of little concern to ordinary citizens; in countries such as the UK small temperature rises seem even desirable to most people. Shifting the discourse from climate change to *climate chaos* (Sachs, 2007) would help to connect the findings of scientists with the observations of citizens. Climate chaos is precisely what they experience – extreme weather events have become more frequent in most parts of the world.

My main argument in this chapter is that clarity is needed with regard to what the problem is. While scientific clarity is necessary, it is not sufficient. Shifting the focus from climate change to climate chaos would be more effective politically. This is not to suggest that this in itself would accelerate action. An action-oriented approach needs to concentrate on the transformation that is needed to tackle the problem. This is precisely what we do this in this book. We call it the *green transformation*. 'Transformation' signals structural change, 'green' gives the direction of travel and the two together invite questions about the drivers of change. In this chapter, I suggest a parsimonious definition: the green transformation is the process of restructuring that brings the economy within the planetary boundaries.

Previous chapters of this book prefer the plural 'green transformations'. I agree that problem constellations and actor constellations can differ over time, between sectors and between places, and ways forward may therefore differ. So as to acknowledge this diversity, this chapter will henceforth also use the plural. Where the singular appears it is not meant to deny diversity. There is a parallel in the term 'industrial revolution' which consisted of interdependent transformations in different sectors and places.

Why?

Earth and climate scientists tell us that the transformations required for sustainability need to be achieved *quickly*. A key feature of their message is *urgency*. Continuing on the current path would mean soon reaching tipping points beyond which life on earth would suffer *irreversible damage*. Such ideas on the depth and speed of the required transformations are increasingly influenced by the concept of 'planetary boundaries' (Rockström *et al.*, 2009). These boundaries define 'a safe operating space for humanity'. A breach of these 'planetary guard rails' (WBGU, 2011) would give rise to intolerable consequences so significant that even major advances in other fields could not compensate for the damage.

Rockström *et al.* (2009) identify nine planetary boundaries that human-induced changes threaten to breed: climate change, ocean acidification, stratospheric ozone depletion, global phosphorus and nitrogen cycles, biodiversity loss, global freshwater scarcity, land-system change, atmospheric aerosol loading and chemical pollution. Seven of the nine boundaries are quantified, but these seven cannot therefore be considered firm thresholds. The indicators of change and their exact values chosen by Rockström *et al.* are for the most part arbitrary. Moreover, boundaries do not always apply globally. Local circumstances can ultimately determine how soon water shortages or biodiversity loss reach a critical threshold (Editorial of *Nature*, 2009). In short, the claimed *urgency* does not apply equally to all planetary boundaries and locations.

Melissa Leach in this book goes a step further and expresses concern that the planetary boundaries discourse invites top-down approaches and technocratic fixes. I agree that there is a danger that the search for solutions is depoliticized, but there is also the danger of undermining a collective scientific undertaking and playing into the hands of those who deny the underlying problem. While uncertainties remain, the concept of planetary boundaries seems a constructive attempt to define the limits to economic growth. And for some boundaries the evidence is fairly robust – notably, the one concerning climate change due to increasing carbon emissions. The scientific and policy debate on mitigating climate change has exploded partly because there is a deadline for achieving the transformation from a high to low-carbon economy. Climate scientists have produced a timetable for reducing these carbon emissions (IPCC, 2007, 2013): the most common reference point is that global emissions must fall by an average of 50 per cent below 1990 levels by 2050, in order to avoid more than two degrees of global warming. Intermediate carbon reduction targets have been set for 2020 and 2030. While the precise dates and figures can be questioned, there is increasing scientific consensus that with each passing year of continued high emissions, the prospect of avoiding climate chaos sinks and the cost of dealing with the consequences rises (Stern, 2007).

The problem is that this has not led to international joint action and that global carbon emissions keep rising (Latin, 2012; Helm, 2012). A participant at the Oslo conference 'Transformations in a changing climate' (June 2012) put it very succinctly: 'Hell does not sell'.[2] This prompts the questions for the next two sections: what do we know about *how* the green transformation can be brought about and *who* can accelerate the process?

How?

There is no established transformation theory, but there are various lines of work that can provide useful insights on how transformations occur. The most fundamental point is that there is no single line of causation: transformation results from a concurrence of multiple changes. This is the conclusion of Osterhammel's (2014) history of the nineteenth century, Leggewie and Messner's (2012b) review of theory and history of transformations, and of Geels and Schot's (2007) analysis of big 'Technological Transitions'. This emphasis on the concurrence and interaction of multiple changes immediately raises the question of how to deal with complexity.

This is where the Multi-Level Perspective (Geels, 2002, 2011) is relevant as a way of categorizing these changes. It distinguishes three analytical levels: niches which are the locus of radical innovations, sociotechnical regimes and landscapes which are exogenous. Transformations are regime shifts brought about through interactions between these levels. Radical innovations taking place in niches can destabilize existing regimes and break through more widely if changes in the external landscape – for example, the global financial crisis or the Fukushima disaster – create pressures on the regime that lead to cracks and windows of opportunity. As a result, the existing regime might be replaced, or it might be strengthened if it can adapt. This is very useful but it is not (yet) clear what it tells us on our central question: whether and how transformations can be managed and accelerated in a purposeful way.

Therefore, it seems worth asking what we can learn from the work on Transition Management (Rotmans *et al.*, 2001). Central to Transition Management is involving stakeholders in developing shared visions, conducting experiments to explore concrete ways forward as well as putting the existing regime under pressure. As stressed by Kern (2013, p21), 'its long term sustainability orientation, its focus on learning and innovation, its elaborate process architecture, its theoretical underpinnings in a sophisticated understanding of processes of sociotechnical change all contributed to the appeal of the Transition Management model'. However, the implementation experience in the Netherlands and Belgium revealed that it was too technocratic, focused too much on the early stage of the policy cycle (design and formulation), shied away from conflict and therefore failed to change structures (Kern and Smith, 2008; Paredis, 2013). It lacked what this book is centrally concerned with: an understanding of the politics of transformation.

Recognizing the enormity of the ambition of managing the transition, innovation scholars have put energies into a more focused agenda: finding ways of piercing through the prevailing sociotechnical regime by promoting specific niches (Schot and Geels, 2008; Smith and Raven, 2012). The niche concept presumes that green technologies are often disadvantaged and require strategic support to protect them against premature rejection by investors and users. In evolutionary terms, novel environmentally friendly varieties struggle to develop under unfavourable selection pressures (Nill and Kemp, 2009).

Smith and Raven (2012) suggest a framework conceptualizing the construction of protective space as consisting of three processes: shielding, nurturing and empowering. Screening the literature, they find that innovation scholars have a lot to say on shielding and nurturing but little on empowering. Of particular relevance for this book is their notion of 'stretch-and-transform empowerment', which seeks to reframe the rules of the game and reform institutions that influence prevailing performance criteria. In their most recent work (Raven et al., 2014, p26), they highlight 'the importance of narratives as key devices in undertaking this socio-political work'. They argue that 'to successfully secure resources for niche development, advocates need to link socio-technical narratives to socio-political agendas, and enrol powerful actors into their networks' (Raven et al., 2014, p8). Significantly, their conclusion stresses the need for 'analysis of the wider political economy beyond those directly involved in and targeted by sustainable technology advocacy, i.e. to fully include analysis of the political economy of fossil fuel energy systems as well' (Raven et al., 2014, p27). This is also the conclusion of Geels (2014) who suggests that the destabilization of existing regimes requires equal attention. Referring to Schumpeter's notion of 'creative destruction' he stresses the need to better understand the 'destruction' part. To conclude, innovation scholars are making big contributions to the 'How?' debate. What is missing are insights on accelerating the pace of the transformation – given the central question of this chapter: is there a fast track?

Perhaps a more promising way of throwing new light on to the speed question is to ask what can be learnt from experiences where rapid transformations occurred. Both China and Vietnam have undergone transformations which were managed and very rapid, involving major economic reforms, big sectoral shifts, build-up of new production capabilities and massive job creation. The speed and depth of changes were unprecedented in economic history. Assessments and explanations of this experience are contested, not least because the environmental consequences are horrendous. However, for our concern – is there a fast track? – there are useful insights. Both China and Vietnam progressed by using *transitional institutions* and *transitional arrangements* (Qian, 2003). Note that 'transitional' here means temporary, appropriate for the next stage in a longer process. Experimentation was also a key feature, sometimes organized purposefully from above, sometimes pushed on the agenda from below – called 'fence breaking' in Vietnam (Malesky, 2008; Heilmann, 2008).

Such insights seem highly relevant for this book and are therefore worth elaborating. The key feature of China's development strategy and that of other East Asian countries is that they did not follow models from elsewhere. Mike

Hobday (2003), in a review of the rapid Asian industrial development, concludes that it is diversity rather than uniformity in the institutional arrangements and development policy that characterizes the innovation experience of the Asian Tigers. In 'Institutions and Economic Growth', Stephan Haggard (2004) emphasized how East Asia succeeded through a process that was highly experimental in nature.

The importance of step-by-step experimentation comes out most strongly in the Chinese experience. Qian shows this convincingly in his article 'How reform worked in China' (2003). 'Transitional institutions' rather than 'best practice institutions' were the key. He stresses that the adopted institutions need to take account of the conditions at each stage of the reform process. For example, a market was created through a dual-track approach to liberalization, enterprises were created through the non-conventional ownership of township–village enterprises and government was reformed through a particular type of fiscal federalism. These institutional innovations worked for a while and then had to be replaced. Not all of them succeeded but there was a common thread to those that did: 'pragmatic innovation' and aligning the interests of the newly enabled decentralized actors with those of the reformers in central government.

The Communist Party failed to give this transformation a green direction but it was a transformation that was deep and fast. Attributing this depth and speed to a big push from the Centre along a predetermined path would be misleading. Distributed entrepreneurship, trial and error, diversity and transitional arrangements are key features of the Chinese, and indeed East Asian, fast track. The picture that emerges is one of making progress by swinging from one branch to another (in spite of the occasional fall) rather than sticking to one strategy. Each stage brings new obstacles – and new opportunities. If this is a useful way of thinking about the dynamics, we still need to figure out *who* moves the process forward – or holds it back.

Who?

In order to discuss *who* can drive green transformations forward, it helps to start with a distinction between *transformation from above* and *from below* and then unpack the different actors and approaches (see Table 11.1). Over the last decade, most attention has been given to the left side of the table. The ambition was to bring economic development within the planetary boundaries by pursuing an approach which was *top-down*, had a *global* scale, was (supposed to be) led by the *North*, and driven forward by *public actors* that recognized the need to mitigate *climate change*. This global governance approach has failed, as shown by successive climate conferences of parties (COPs) and the sustainability conferences in Rio de Janeiro (Latin, 2012). In the meantime, however, progress was made on the right side of the table: using *bottom-up* approaches and relying on *local* initiatives in which *civic actors* play a major role. Chapter 7 by Smith and Ely and Chapter 8 by Leach and Scoones discuss the significance of civil society organizations and movements in these bottom-up approaches. Local government also plays an important role in many cases, as shown by case material from both West and East (OECD, 2010; Harrison and Kostka, 2012).

Similarly, at the *national* level, substantial progress was made in some countries, with governments implementing green industrial policies and the private sector making big investments in renewable energy and other low-carbon technologies. Such progress made at the national level, however, risks running out of steam in the countries expected to lead the green transformation: most of Western Europe and North America is politically paralysed and financially constrained. The *rising powers* have become the default movers and shakers in the green transformation, in both the negative and positive sense. While responsible for the continuing growth of carbon emissions, they are also the biggest investors in mitigation. Seen globally, China is No. 1 investor in renewable energy and India has recorded high recent growth rates in 2011 (BNEF, 2012).

To elaborate on the *national* level, the two Western countries with the biggest progress are Denmark (wind energy) and Germany (solar and wind energy). In the German case, renewable energy accounts for 24 per cent of electricity (2013 level) and 206,000 jobs were created in wind and solar power (2012 level), but investment is slowing down (Luetkenhorst and Pegels, 2014). While most of the investment comes from the private sector, public subsidies are essential in this early stage of the low-carbon transformation. This public support has come under attack with arguments that, in times of austerity, the public sector cannot prioritize investments in energy infrastructure and consumers cannot afford increases in energy bills needed to pay for these subsidies. Arguments that fostering new green industries helps to promote growth, jobs and public revenue are drowned out by opposing forces in much of Europe and the US.

In contrast, China continues to storm ahead with big investments in renewable energy (BNEF, 2013).[3] Its government is not encumbered by national or foreign debt; it has the ability to act fast. A good example of its 'entrepreneurial state' (see Mazzucato, this book) is the support for the solar energy industry. When European demand for Chinese photovoltaic panels declined in 2009, the Chinese government launched a programme to speed up the deployment of such panels within the country (Fischer, 2012) in order to ensure that the build-up of this new industry could continue.

TABLE 11.1 Accelerating green transformation

Approach	Top-down			Bottom-up
Level	Global	National		Local
Location	North	Rising powers		South
Actor	Public	Private		Civic
Motive	Climate change	Energy security	Competitive green sectors	Green jobs

Table 11.1 helps to categorize existing approaches and actors. On their own, none of them will achieve the green transformation. Most observers would agree that the bottom-up and top-down approaches need to be combined and that multilevel governance is needed (Bulkeley and Newell, 2010, p3). But which force can bring this about? Recall that this is the first transformation in history that has to be achieved purposefully and against a deadline. In other words, the task of accelerating the process takes centre stage.

Where can this acceleration come from? Here we turn again to Table 11.1, in particular the last two lines, which focus on the range of relevant actors and the motives of these actors. Analysis of these actors and motives then needs to take four critical steps: first, recognize that no single actor has the resources to bring about the green transformation; second, recognize that within government, civil society and business there are actors seeking to block or slow down the green transformation. Third, attention needs to focus on supportive alliances across these categories. Fourth, including actors with different motives helps to understand and accelerate the green transformation. The transformative alliance becomes the central concept. Let us elaborate.

Bringing about green transformations requires resources of different types: expertise, money, organizational capacity, legitimacy and leadership. These resources tend to be distributed over a range of public, private and civic actors. It is therefore useful to concentrate on alliances between actors in government, business and civil society.

Who, then, can be considered a member of such an alliance? Is the deciding criterion motivation or action? While it is tempting to let motivation count and opt for an alliance of the like-minded, this is a limiting step to take. There is a range of actors that can support the green transformation through their action (such as investing, providing expertise, lobbying) but their motive need not be to mitigate climate change; the main motive might be to secure energy, to build competitive green industries or to foster green jobs, with climate change mitigation at best a 'co-benefit'. In other words, there is a potential for alliances that include actors whose priority is not environmental sustainability. This can be a 'game changer' in the dynamics of the transformation. It is supported by historical research which shows actor groups with differing intentions advancing the change in a specific direction (WBGU, 2011, p85, drawing on research by Osterhammel, 2014).

Such alliances seem to have been important in both China and Europe. In Denmark, for example, the experimentation with wind energy received substantial support from politicians and business leaders concerned with energy security, in the wake of various oil crises. Actors with environmental motivations played a role at the start and increased in importance over time, but they were never sufficient. Actors motivated by the chance to build a globally competitive hub (for providing wind-energy solutions and creating highly paid jobs) have played a big role. In China, such alliances were equally if not more relevant. China's massive investment in renewable energy was not driven primarily by concerns with global climate change but by concerns to secure energy and ambitions to build new competitive sectors. These were major concerns in both Chinese government and industry. Add to this the more recent concern in urban society to reduce pollution, now openly acknowledged in the Chinese media.

Recent research in China (Dai, 2014) shows that such alignments of interest matter in both policy formulation and implementation. In China, policy formulation tends to take place at central level and implementation at local level. Dai (2014) stresses that the local take-up of centrally designed policies varies enormously within China. 'Dynamic' localities which implement central policies for solar and wind energy are driven forward by local government and business joining forces, motivated not by concerns with the climate but by ambitions to promote local economic development, create jobs, increase tax revenue (local government) and generate profit (business).

The relevance of alliances is confirmed by the research of Harrison and Kostka (2012) on the local politics of climate change in China and India:

> In both countries the ability to build and sustain coalitions is central to the effectiveness and sustainability of climate change policy. For various reasons, state strategies in China and India have focused on the need to bring different parties with otherwise divergent interests on board to build a coalition in favour of climate mitigation measures.
>
> (Harrison and Kostka, 2012, p5)

Recent research in India (Chaudhary et al., 2014) shows that such coalitions have played a critical role also at the national level, but that the combinations of interests varied between sectors. The solar industry was supported for reasons of both securing energy and building competitive low- carbon industries. The 'National Solar Mission' is the most visible symbol of an industrial policy for this sector. The most vigorous implementation of this policy occurred in the state of Gujarat where Chief Minister Narendra Modi (now Prime Minister of India) spearheaded an alliance of government and business interests determined to accelerate economic development. There is no equivalent 'national wind mission' in India, indicating that concerns with building a competitive wind-turbine industry played less of a role in policies supporting this sector (Chaudhary et al., 2014). Energy security was the main driver – on the part of government. Climate change mitigation was only a 'co-benefit' (Dubash et al., 2013).

To summarize, the composition of transformational alliances varies, depending on the specific policy or project or sector in question. Actors in these alliances might see climate change mitigation as a co-benefit but tend to have other priorities, such as securing energy, building new competitive industries, creating new jobs in their region, raising public revenue or generating private profit. While not surprising in itself, it questions the discourse which pitches economic growth against environmental sustainability, so popular in many parts of the world. Policies which foster structural transformation promote rather than hinder economic growth.

This is not to suggest that there are only winners. Far from it. Some stand to lose from the transformation. In the early stages of green transformations, the losers might even outnumber the winners. Whatever the numbers, they are agents of resistance and they need to be analysed in the same way as the agents of change. The opponents also seek alliances. The opposing forces are not necessarily against decarbonization as such but they are fighting for their jobs and/or protecting their assets which are tied to fossil fuel and related sectors.

To return to our overall argument, focusing on alliances is essential for understanding and fostering green transformations. Such alliances are best seen as vehicles for bundling diverse interests for a particular purpose, such as influencing legislation, policies or projects. In order to be effective, analytical and political work needs to deal with both agents of change (prospective winners) and agents of resistance (prospective losers).

Putting such alliances centre stage is a critical step for addressing the central question of this chapter: is there a fast track? It is not sufficient, however. Two further steps are needed: first, we need to be able to distinguish between alliances of different types. At one end there is the *strategic alliance* based on joint action. At the other end there is the mere *alignment of interest* without coordination between the parties. Both can be transitional (short term) or enduring (long term). All types can be instrumental in bringing about collective action or blocking it.

Second, we need to ask where these alliances come from. They are not given but are in themselves a product of history. Here we go back to the previous section which suggested that we conceive of transformations as a process in which countries swing or scramble forward – and sometimes drop back – but in which each stage provides a political and economic platform for the next stage. As shown in Chapter 6, the policies adopted in one stage have knock-on effects for subsequent stages and influence the momentum of green transformations. Depending on how these policies are designed and implemented, they give rise to new stakeholders such as business and workers who invested their money or careers in the deployment of green technologies, or create a backlash from those who pay for the subsidized investments.

When?

The understanding of these political processes (drivers, policies, knock-on effects) remains limited. While the researchers draw boundaries around their analyses so as to not drown in complexity, actors in the real world do not have this privilege; they need to keep an eye on the whole picture. In most countries of Europe and North America, this picture was darkened by the financial crisis. This issue needs to be raised here because it seems to have major repercussions for our central question: is there a fast track? The answer is more likely to be negative when a financial crisis affects public and private investment decisions – at least this is what the contrast between renewable energy investment before and after the financial crisis suggests (BNEF, 2012 and Stephen Spratt, this book).

However, this is not necessarily so, as stressed by Carlota Perez (2013). She sees the current crisis as a recurrent historical event midway along a technological revolution. Historical research (Perez, 2002) leads her to suggest that the capitalist economy has lived through four previous situations equivalent to the current crisis and that these have occurred midway along each of four technological transformations (the early Industrial Revolution; the age of steam and railways; the age of electricity and heavy engineering; the age of oil, automobile and mass production). The installation period of these technological transformations has led each time to a major bubble, followed by a financial crash and then a 'golden age' of prosperity. Currently, we are midway through the information and communication technology transformation and, in line with previous experience, we have experienced a major bubble and a financial crash. What is not yet clear is whether this time it is followed by a new golden age. Perez (2013) argues that there is no automaticity but suggests that the stage is set for a new age of prosperity that could be channelled in a green direction. Grasping this opportunity requires an active state that shifts the balance of power from finance to production and changes the incentives from resource wasting to resource saving. On this point, the views of Perez converge with those of Mazzucato who stresses the key role of the *entrepreneurial state* in fostering innovation and restructuring – see Chapter 9 of this book. Further reinforcement comes from various strands of 'Green Keynesianism'; they have in common the idea that tackling the economic crisis is helped by tackling the environmental crisis. It requires that the state makes big public investments in green infrastructure and provides strong incentives for private green investment (Zenghelis, 2012; Jacobs, 2013).

The arguments that the financial crisis can be turned into an opportunity for green investment have been examined in a recent article by Geels (2013). In 'The impact of the financial-economic crisis on sustainability transitions', he concludes that the early crisis years (2008–2010) created a window of opportunity for positive solutions. However, since 2011 this window has shrunk and political support for green policies has weakened. In the UK, Germany and other countries, public debate began to concentrate on the cost of shifting to renewable energy. The effect has been to slow down rather than fast-track the green transformations. Such slowdown has not, however, occurred in the rising powers of Asia. As a result of the financial crisis, the global power shift from West to East accelerated (Jacques, 2012, pp585–636). The transformative capacity of China in particular increased, whereas that of Western Europe and North America declined. This is beginning to affect the cost of green transformations in the sense that green technologies from China are cheaper. Whether this makes their diffusion faster is not yet clear because price is just one of several determinants (Schmitz, forthcoming 2014).

What are we to do with these observations? They do not provide clear answers to the 'When?' question which drives this section. They do, however, highlight the importance of keeping an eye on the political windows needed to accelerate green transformations.

Conclusion: riding the green tiger

Is there a fast track? This is the question driving this chapter. Posing it is somewhat cheeky without asking the prior question: is the green transformation possible? The German Advisory Council for Global Change (WBGU) and its research staff have addressed this very question in some depth and gives a categorical answer:

> the technological potential for comprehensive decarbonisation is available . . . and the policy instruments needed for a climate-friendly transformation are widely known. *Now it is foremost a political task to overcome the barriers of such a transformation, and to accelerate the change.*
>
> (WBGU, 2011, p1; emphasis added)

This is precisely the starting point for this concluding chapter and indeed the entire book.

In this chapter I have tried to decompose the fast-track question and distil some of the insights that can be derived from the literature and experiences on the ground. What I have not done is ask what it means to investigate the politics of acceleration and at what level of abstraction? One approach would be to test the reality of those insights for those countries that have made the biggest progress. Take the case of Germany. There is a transformative alliance, but who has the convening power? Is Angela Merkel riding the green tiger? This is very relevant for the fast-track issue and a cartoonist's dream, but how real is it?

The answer is that Angela Merkel is far too clever to pose as the queen of low-carbon prosperity. As a former research scientist (physics and chemistry) she understands and accepts the arguments of climate and earth scientists. As a politician, however, she knows that accelerating the pace may require working – at particular moments – with those who do not accept that case (recall transitional arrangements). And it requires taking advantage of opportunities when they arise. Within days of the Fukushima disaster she put her foot on the accelerator (recall Geels's windows of opportunity due to change in the landscape). And acceleration happened because the legislation was in place and because thousands of small investors and hundreds of municipalities responded to a policy designed for them (recall Lockwood's argument on the knock-on effects of policies – see Chapter 6). More recently, Merkel found that she had to put the brake on because too much renewable energy is being generated and the cost to consumer and taxpayer is very transparent – while the cost of fossil-fuel energy is not (Luetkenhorst and Pegels, 2014).[4] Her new economics and energy minister (leader of the Social Democratic party) is now in charge of administering the slow-down. The green tiger is in a cage – for now. The battle is on for when it will be let out again and in what shape. Leaner and meaner? The key point is that this battle is now taking place on an economic and political platform which is more advanced and very different from five or even three years ago (recall the earlier point which emphasizes trial and error, and uses the metaphor of climbing a tree by swinging upwards from branch to branch – with the occasional fall).

Is this what is needed to understand the politics of green transformations? In a way, yes. Of course, the above is at best a condensed sketch and a more detailed account is needed. My key point is that testing our insights more systematically for those countries which have made the greatest strides forward (Denmark, Germany and China) is essential for answering the fast-track question. If this question has a clear answer, one would expect to find it here.

In the meantime, we need to continue at a more abstract level. And this is what the German Council for Global Change does when it stresses that the transformation is above all a political task. Central to this political task, according to the Council, is the forging of *World in Transition: A Social Contract for Sustainability* (WBGU, 2011). What is meant here is a contract between the state and citizens. 'The contract has to bring two important new protagonists into the equation: the self-organized civil society and the community of scientific experts' (WBGU, 2011, p8). I agree with this political turn of the Council but suggest that the state–civic nexus is not sufficient. Business needs to be included explicitly, thus turning attention to the role of state–business–civic alliances. The earlier 'Who?' section of this chapter stressed the role of such alliances. Since it is central to the fast-track issue, it deserves further elaboration.

Focusing on alliances and including business in such alliances is critical according to recent political science analysis which shows that alliances (or coalitions) can be effective in overcoming complex collective action problems (Leftwich, 2009; Peiffer, 2012). Including business in the analysis and formation of alliances makes a significant difference. Maxfield (1991, p421) stressed long ago the critical role of policy coalitions which cut across state and society and include business. More recently, Abdel-Latif and Schmitz (2010) have shown why and how state-business alliances matter for overcoming bottlenecks in industrial development. When it comes to green transformations, the inclusion of business seems particularly important. As stressed by Newell and Paterson, 'many capitalists and state elites, for a range of different reasons, now have a political and financial stake in the project of decarbonisation' (2011, p41) . . . 'short or medium term transitions to a low carbon economy will have to be supported (financially and politically) by powerful fractions of capital with a stake in the success of such a project' (p23).

This is a key point. There are parts of the business community which are keen to support green transformations but are, in fact, driven by ambitions in other fields – notably, securing energy or building a competitive new industry. Understanding the political dynamics needs to include also those interests which are not green in themselves but support the green cause. Effective cooperation between public and private actors does not require that the players support renewables for the same reasons. On the contrary, the chance of effective cooperation increases dramatically if players with different motivations are brought into the picture.

Accepting this is not easy for those who have argued that capitalism is destroying our planet. It feels like a call to sleep with the enemy. The point made here is not that their analysis is entirely wrong but that it is incomplete. Preventing the destruction of human life on earth requires working with those parts of industry and finance that are willing and keen to make green investments. The division between high- and low-carbon investors runs right through industry and finance, as stressed in Chapter 5 by Peter Newell. In some cases it runs right through individual corporations in which some departments continue to be tied to the fossil fuel sectors, while others are pioneering new low-carbon technologies. Investments in the latter can be counted in billions of dollars, euros or pounds. The problem is that investments in fossil fuel and related industries amount to trillions. Changing this balance and achieving it rapidly is – in economic terms – the hard core of the green transformation.[5]

Such emphasis on working with business is also worrisome to those concerned with the distributional consequences of the green transformation. History tells us that big transformations can entail big increases in inequality. However, history also tells us that some big transformations happened when the interests of business and large sections of society coincided (Perez, 2002, 2013). So which is it? As always, the answer is: it depends. The determinants are politically constructed.

A comparison of China and Vietnam is illuminating. As mentioned earlier, no two economies have averaged more rapid growth in the nineties and noughties – and have transformed faster – than China and Vietnam. The point to be added here is that the Vietnamese system has generated lower inequality than the Chinese system. Abrami *et al.* (2008) suggest that this is because of the difference in party organization. Compared with China, Vietnam's institutions empower a larger group of insiders and place more constraints on party leadership, both through vertical checks and semi-competitive elections. As a result, Vietnam spends a larger proportion of its revenue on transfers and has been able to achieve more equalization between provinces and individuals.

A comparison of Germany and the UK is also illuminating and directly relevant for green transformations. In Chapter 6 of this book, Lockwood shows that different designs of green industrial policy have different consequences. The key insights are first, that some policy designs have more inclusive outcomes than others and second, that the more inclusive design in Germany contributed in a decisive way to the greater momentum of the transformation in that country. The proposition emerging from this comparison is that transformation and inclusion reinforce each other. To what extent and how needs further examination.

To conclude, there is no motorway into the green future. Embarking on the fast track is not about the big push from the centre along a predetermined path. It is about joining forces to dismantle the old and joining forces to achieve the new. But joining forces with whom? Stephen Spratt in Chapter 10 of this book distinguishes between the deep and light green. I would add those who are not green at all in conviction but can nevertheless support the green cause through their investments and expertise. Including them in our alliances provides much needed hope that green transformations can be accelerated, and it provides an analytical grip on where, when and why accelerations occur – or not.

Notes

1 Helpful comments on a previous draft were provided by Melissa Leach, Wilfried Lütkenhorst, Anna Pegels and Carlota Perez.
2 Or is it that the hell scenario does not look so hellish? As suggested earlier, shifting the narrative from climate *change* to climate *chaos* would make the scientific discourse more real for most citizens.
3 For an overview of China's high carbon legacies and low-carbon initiatives, see Slusarska (2013).
4 The green burden to consumers is higher than expected partly because the amount of renewable energy produced is higher than expected and partly because there are more exceptions for industry than expected. The burden sharing is lop-sided.
5 Sovereign wealth funds are likely to play a role in changing this balance, for instance, the Norwegian oil fund, which collects taxes from oil profits and invests the money in stocks, is reassessing its investment portfolio.

REFERENCES

Abdel-Latif, A. and Schmitz, H. (2010) 'Growth alliances: Insights from Egypt', *Business and Politics*, vol 12, no 4, pp1–27.

Abraham, J. (2008) 'Sociology of pharmaceuticals development and regulation: A realist empirical research programme', *Sociology of Health & Illness*, vol 30, no 6, pp869–885.

Abrami, R., Malesky, E. and Zheng, Y. (2008) *Accountability and Inequality in Single-Party Regimes: A Comparative Analysis of Vietnam and China*, HBS Working Paper 08–099, Harvard Business School, Cambridge, MA.

Abrol, D. (2005) 'Embedding technology in community-based production systems through people's technology initiatives: Lessons from the Indian experience', *International Journal of Technology Management and Sustainable Development*, vol 4, no 1, pp3–20.

Adams, W. M. (2003) *Green Development: Environment and Sustainability in the Third World*, Routledge, London.

Adams, W. M. (2009) *Green Development: Environment and Sustainability in a Developing World* (3rd edn), Routledge, London.

Agamben, G., Badiou, A., Bensaid, D., Brown, W., Nancy, J-L., Ranciere, J., Ross, K. and Žižek, S. (2011) *Democracy in What State?*, Columbia University Press, New York.

Aglietta, M. (2000) *A Theory of Capitalist Regulation: The US Experience*, Verso, London.

Agyeman, J., Bullard, R. D. and Evans, B. (eds) (2003) *Just Sustainabilities: Development in an Unequal World*, MIT Press, Cambridge, MA.

ALAI & TNI (2012) *Transnational Capital versus People's Resistance*, Quito, Ecuador, http://alainet.org/publica/alai476w-en.pdf, accessed 2 June 2014.

Aldrich, H. E. and Pfeffer, J. (1976) 'Environments of organizations', *Annual Review of Sociology*, vol 2, pp79–105.

Allen, R. (2012) 'Backward into the future: The shift from coal and implications for the next energy transition', *Energy Policy*, vol 50, pp17–23.

Altieri, M. A. (2009) 'Agroecology, small farms, and food sovereignty', *Monthly Review*, vol 61, no 3, pp102–113.

Altvater, E. (2006) 'The social and natural environment of fossil capitalism', in L. Panitch and C. Leys (eds) *Coming to Terms with Nature: Socialist Register 2007*, Merlin Press, London, pp37–60.

Andersen, M. (2007) 'An introductory note on the environmental economics of the circular economy', *Sustainability Science*, vol 2, no 1, pp133–140.

Anon. (2013a) 'Genetically modified crops needed to "feed the world", says Government's chief scientific advisors Mark Walport', *The Independent*, 18 April 2013, available at: www.independent.co.uk/news/science/genetically-modified-crops-needed-to-feed-the-world-says-governments-chief-scientific-advisor-mark-walport-8578952.html, accessed 20 April 2013.

Anon. (2013b) Oxford English Dictionary, Oxford University Press, www.oed.com/view/Entry/, accessed 19 February 2014.

Anon. (n.d.) 'The story of Silent Spring', www.nrdc.org/health/pesticides/hcarson.asp, accessed 10 June 2014.

Arcand, J. L., Berkes, E. and Panizza, U. (2012) 'Too much finance?', *IMF Working Paper*, 12/161.

Arendt, H. (1963) *On Revolution*, Penguin Books, London.

Arrighi, G. (2010) *The Long Twentieth Century: Money, Power and the Origins of Our Times*, 2nd edn, Verso, London.

Arthur, W. B. (1989) 'Competing technologies, increasing returns and lock-in by historical events', *Economic Journal*, vol 99, pp116–131.

Bäckstrand K. (2006) 'Multi-stakeholder partnerships for sustainable development: Re-thinking legitimacy, accountability and effectiveness', *European Environment*, vol 16, no 5, pp290–306.

Bacon, F. (1597) *Meditationes Sacrae and Human Philosophy*, Kessinger, Whitefish, MT.

Baer, P., Athanasiou, T., Kartha, S. and Kemp-Benedict, E. (2008) *The Greenhouse Development Rights Framework: The Right to Development in a Climate Constrained World*, Publication Series on Ecology, vol 1, Heinrich Böll Foundation, Christian Aid, EcoEquity and the Stockholm Environment Institute.

Baker, L., Newell, P. and Phillips, J. (2014) 'The political economy of energy transitions: The case of South Africa', *New Political Economy*, vol 19, no 6, pp791–818.

Bakewell, S. (2011) 'Chinese renewable companies slow to tap $47 billion credit', *Bloomberg Business Week*, 16 November, www.bloomberg.com/news/2011–11–16/chinese-renewable-companies-slow-to-tap-47-billion-credit-line.html, accessed 24 June 2014.

Bakker, K. (2010) *Privatising Water: Governance Failure and the World's Urban Water Crisis*, Cornell University Press, Ithaca, NY.

Bandyopadhyay, S. (2013) *Tax Exemptions in India: Issues and Challenges*, Centre for Budget and Governance Accountability, Delhi.

Beck, S., Borie, M., Chilvers, J., Esguerra, A., Heubach, K., Hulme, M., Lidskog, R., Lövbrand, E., Marquard, E., Miller, C., Nadim, T., Neßhöver, C., Settele, J., Turnhout, E., Vasileiadou, E. and Görg, C. 2014) 'Towards a reflexive turn in the governance of global environmental expertise: The cases of the IPCC and the IPBES', *GAIA*, vol 23, no 2, pp80–87.

Beck, T. (2007) *Financing Constraints of SMEs in Developing Countries: Evidence, Determinants and Solutions*, Tilburg University, Tilburg.

Béland, D. (2010) 'Reconsidering policy feedback: How policies affect politics', *Administration and Society*, vol 42, pp568–590.

Bell, M. (1979) 'The exploitation of indigenous knowledge, or the indigenous exploitation of knowledge: What use of what for what?', *IDS Bulletin*, vol 10, no 2, pp44–50.

Benecke, E. (2011) 'Networking for climate change: Agency in the context of renewable energy governance in India', *International Environmental Agreements*, vol 11, pp23–42.

Benton, T. (ed.) (1996) *The Greening of Marxism*, Guilford, New York.

Berkhout, F., Leach, M. and Scoones, I. (eds) (2003) *Negotiating Environmental Change: New Perspectives from Social Science*, Edgar Elgar, Cheltenham.

Bhattacharya, A., Romani, M., and Stern, N. (2012) *Infrastructure for Development: Meeting the Challenge*, G-24 Policy Paper, Centre for Climate Change Economics and Policy, Leeds and London, www.cccep.ac.uk/Publications/Policy/docs/PP-infrastructure-for-development-meeting-the-challenge.pdf, accessed 24 June 2014.

Biermann, F. (2007) '"Earth system governance" as a crosscutting theme of global change research', *Global Environmental Change*, vol 17, no 3–4, pp326–337.

Biermann, F., Abbott, K., Andresen, S., Bäckstrand, K., Bernstein, S., Betsill, M. M., Bulkeley, H., Cashore, B., Clapp, J., Folke, C., Gupta, A., Gupta, J., Haas, P. M., Jordan, A., Kanie, N., Kluvánková-Oravská, T., Lebel, L., Liverman, D., Meadowcroft, J., Mitchell, R. B., Newell, P., Oberthür, S., Olsson, L., Pattberg, P., Sánchez-Rodríguez, R., Schroeder, H., Underdal, A., Vieira, S. C., Vogel, C., Young, O. R., Brock, A. and Zondervan, R. (2012a) 'Navigating the Anthropocene: Improving earth system governance', *Science*, vol 335, no 6074, pp1306–1307.

Biermann, F., Abbott, K., Andresen, S., Bäckstrand, K., Bernstein, S., Betsill, M. M., Bulkeley, H., Cashore, B., Clapp, J., Folke, C., Gupta, A., Gupta, J., Haas, P. M., Jordan, A., Kanie, N., Kluvánková-Oravská, T., Lebel, L., Liverman, D., Meadowcroft, J., Mitchell, R. B., Newell, P., Oberthür, S., Olsson, L.,Pattberg, P., Sánchez-Rodríguez, R., Schroeder, H., Underdal, A., Camargo Vieira, S., Vogel, C., Young, O. R., Brock, A. and Zondervan, R. (2012b) 'Transforming governance and institutions for global sustainability: Key insights from the Earth System Governance Project', *Current Opinion in Environmental Sustainability*, vol 4, no 1, pp51–60.

BIS (Bank for International Settlements) (2013) *OTC Derivatives Statistics at end-June 2013*, Monetary and Economics Department, Bank for International Settlements, www.bis.org/publ/otc_hy1311.pdf, accessed 24 June 2014.

Blasberg, A. and Kohlenberg, K. (2012) 'Die Klima Krieger', *Die Zeit*, vol 48, pp17–19.

BNEF (Bloomberg New Energy Finance) (2012) *Global Trends in New Energy Investment 2012*, Frankfurt School of Finance and Management, Frankfurt.

BNEF (2013) *Global Trends in New Energy Investment 2013*, Frankfurt School of Finance and Management, Frankfurt.

Böhm, S. and Dabhi, S. (eds) (2009) *Upsetting the Offset: The Political Economy of Carbon Markets*, Mayfly Books, Colchester.

Bond, P. (2012) *Politics of Climate Justice: Paralysis Above, Movement Below*, University of KwaZulu-Natal Press, Scottsville, KY.

Boot, A. and Ratnovski, L. (2012) 'Banking and trading', *IMF Working Paper*, 12/238, International Monetary Fund, Washington, DC.

Borlaug N. E. (2000) 'Ending world hunger: The promise of biotechnology and the threat of antiscience zealotry', *Plant Physiology*, vol 124, no 2, pp487–490.

Borras Jr., S. M., Edelman, M. and Kay, C. (2008) *Transnational Agrarian Movements Confronting Globalization*, Wiley-Blackwell, Oxford.

Borras Jr., S. M., McMichael, P. and Scoones, I. (2010) 'The politics of biofuels, land and agrarian change: Editors' introduction', *Journal of Peasant Studies*, vol 37, no 4, pp575–592.

Bouwman, H., Bornman, R., van den Berg, H. and Kylin, H. (2013) 'DDT: Fifty years since Silent Spring', in *Late Lessons From Early Warnings: Science, Precaution, Innovation*, vol 2, European Environment Agency, Report 1/2013, Copenhagen, Chapter 11.

Bovens, L. (2011) 'A Lockean defense of grandfathering emission rights', in D. Arnold (ed.) *The Ethics of Global Climate Change*, Cambridge University Press, Cambridge, pp124–144.

Bowden, P. (1997) *Caring: Gender-Sensitive Ethics*, Routledge, London.

Bowen, A. (2011) *The Case for Carbon Pricing*, Grantham Research Institute on Climate Change and the Environment, London.

Bracmort, K. and Lattanzio, R. K. (2013) *Geoengineering: Governance and Technology Policy*, Congressional Research Service Report, Washington, DC.

Brand, U. (2012a) *Beautiful Green World: On the Myths of a Green Economy*, Rosa Luxemburg Foundation, Berlin.

Brand, U. (2012b) 'Green economy and green capitalism: Some theoretical considerations', *Journal fur Entwicklungspolitik*, special issue on 'socio-ecological transformations', vol XXVIII, no 3, pp118–137.

Braudel, F. (1982) *The Wheels of Commerce*, Harper & Row, New York.

Brown, K., O'Neill, S. and Fabricius, C. (2013) 'Social science understandings of transformation', in *Changing Global Environments. World Science Report*, ISSC/UNESCO, Paris.

Brundtland, G. H. (1987) *Our Common Future: Report of the World Commission on Environment and Development*, Oxford University Press, Oxford

Bryne, R., Smith, A., Watson, J. and Ockwell, D. (2011) 'Energy pathways in low-carbon development: From technology-transfer to socio-ecological transformation', *STEPS Working Paper* 46, STEPS Centre, Brighton.

Buck, D. (2006) The ecological question: Can capitalism prevail? in L. Panitch and C. Leys (eds) *Coming to Terms with Nature: Socialist Register 2007*, The Merlin Press, London, pp60–72.

Bulkeley, H. and Newell, P. (2010), *Governing Climate Change*, Routledge, London and New York.

Bulkeley, H., Jordan, A., Perkins, R. and Selin, H. (2013) 'Governing sustainability: Rio+20 and the road beyond', *Environment and Planning C: Government and Policy*, vol 31, no 6, pp958–970.

Bulkeley, H., Andonova, L., Backstrand, K., Betsill, M., Compagnon, D., Duffy, R., Kolk, A., Hoffman, M., Levy, D., Newell, P., Milledge, T., Paterson, M., Pattberg, P. and VanDeveer, S. (2012) 'Governing climate change transnationally: Assessing the evidence from a database of sixty initiatives', *Environment and Planning C: Government and Policy*, vol 30, no 4, pp591–612.

Burchell, P., Gordon, C. and Miller, P. (eds) (1991) *The Foucault Effect: Studies in Governmentality*, University of Chicago Press, Chicago/Harvester Wheatsheaf, Hemel Hempstead, UK.

Büscher, B., Sullivan, S., Neves, K., Igoe, J. and Brockington, D. (2012) 'Towards a synthesized critique of neoliberal biodiversity conservation', *Capitalism Nature Socialism*, vol 23, no 2, pp4–30.

Çalışkan, K. and Callon, M. (2009) 'Economization, part 1: Shifting attention from the economy towards processes of economization', *Economy and Society*, vol 38, no 3, pp369–398.

Carbon Tracker (2013) www.carbontracker.org, accessed 12 June 2013.

Carley, S. (2011) 'The era of state energy policy innovation: A review of policy instruments', *Review of Policy Research*, vol 28, no 3, pp265–294.,

Carney, M., Gedajlovic, E. and Yang, X. (2009) 'Varieties of Asian capitalism: Toward an institutional theory of Asian enterprise', *Asia Pacific Journal of Management*, vol 26, pp361–380.

Carson, R. (1962) *Silent Spring*, Houghton Mifflin, Boston, MA.

CEC (Commission of the European Communities) (1977) 'Report of the Scientific Committee for Food on saccharin', *Reports of the Scientific Committee for Food*, Fourth Series, Commission of the European Communities, Luxembourg, pp7–23.

CEC (1985) 'Report of the Scientific Committee for Food on sweeteners', *Reports of the Scientific Committee for Food*, Sixteenth Series, Commission of the European Communities, Luxembourg, pp1–20.

Chang, H. J. (2002) 'Breaking the mould: An institutionalist political economy alternative to the neo-liberal theory of the market and the state', *Cambridge Journal of Economics*, vol 26, no 5, pp539–559.

Chapin, III, F. S., Power, M. E., Pickett, S. T. A., Freitag, A., Reynolds, J. A., Jackson, R. B., Lodge, D. M., Duke, C., Collins, S. L., Power, A. G. and Bartuska, A. (2011) 'Earth stewardship: Science for action to sustain the human-earth system', *Ecosphere*, vol 2, no 8, art 89.

Chatterton, P. and Cutler, A. (2008) *The Rocky Road to a Real Transition: The Transition Towns Movement and What it Means for Social Change*, http://trapese.clearerchannel.org/resources/rocky-road-a5-web.pdf, accessed 20 June 2014.

Chaudhary, A., Narain, A., Krishnan, C. and Sagar, A. (2014) *Who Shapes Climate Action in India? Insights from the Wind and Solar Energy Sectors*, IDS Evidence Report 46, Institute of Development Studies, Brighton.

Cho, A. and Dubash, N. (2005) 'Will investment rules shrink policy space for sustainable development? Evidence from the electricity sector', in K. Gallagher (ed.) *Putting Development First: The Importance of Policy Space in the WTO and IFIs*, Zed Books, London, pp146–179.

Chwieroth, J. (2007) 'Neoliberal economists and capital account liberalization in emerging markets', *International Organization*, vol 61, no 2, pp443–463.

CityUK, The (2013) www.thecityuk.com/research/our-work/reports-list'fund-management-2013/, accessed 18 September 2014.

Clapp, J. and P. Dauvergne (2011) *Paths to a Green World: The Political Economy of the Global Environment*, 2nd edn, MIT Press, Cambridge, MA.

Clark, B. and York, R. (2005) 'Carbon metabolism: Global capitalism, climate change and the biospheric rift', *Theory and Society*, vol 34, no 4, pp391–428.

Clarke, S. (1978) 'Capital, fractions of capital and the state: Neo-Marxist analysis of the South African state', *Capital and Class*, vol 2, no 2, pp312–377.

Climate Policy Initiative (2013) *The Global Landscape of Climate Finance 2013*, CPI Report, http://climatepolicyinitiative.org/wp-content/uploads/2013/10/The-Global-Landscape-of-Climate-Finance-2013.pdf, accessed 24 June 2014.

Cluff, L. E. and Binstock, R. H. (eds) (2001) *The Lost Art of Caring: A Challenge to Health Professionals, Families, Communities, and Society*, Johns Hopkins University Press, Baltimore, MD.

Cole, H. S. D., Freeman, C., Jahoda, M. and Pavitt, K. L. R. (eds) (1973) *Models of Doom: A Critique of the Limits to Growth*, Chatto & Windus, Sussex.

Connors, P. and McDonald, P. (2011) 'Transitioning communities: Community, participation and the transition town movement', *Community Development Journal*, vol 46, no 4, pp558–572.

Corbera, E. and Brown, K. (2010) 'Offsetting benefits? Analysing access to forest carbon', *Environment and Planning A*, vol 42, no 7, pp1739–1761.

Correlje, A. and Verbong, G. (2004) 'The transition from coal to gas: Radical change of the Dutch gas system', in B. Elzen, F. Geels and K. Green (eds) *System Innovation and the Transition to Sustainability: Theory, Evidence and Policy*, Edward Elgar, Cheltenham, pp114–136.

Costanza, R., de Groot, R., Sutton, P., van der Ploeg, S., Anderson, S. J., Kubiszewski, I., Farber, S. and Turner, R. K. (2014) 'Changes in the global value of ecosystem services', *Global Environmental Change*, vol 26, pp152–158.

Cowell, R. (2012) 'The greenest government ever? Planning and sustainability in England after the May 2010 elections', *Planning Practice & Research*, vol 28, no 1, pp27–44.

Cox, R. (1987) *Production, Power and World Order*, Columbia University Press, New York.

Cox, R. (1994) 'Global restructuring: Making sense of the changing international political economy', in R. Stubbs and G. Underhill (eds) *Political Economy and the Changing Global Order*, Macmillan, Basingstoke, pp5–60.

Cozzens, S. and Sutz, J. (2014) 'Innovation in informal settings: Reflections and proposals for a research agenda', *Innovation and Development*, vol 4, no 1, pp5–31.

Crane, A., Matten, D. and Moon, J. (2008) 'The emergence of corporate citizenship: historical development and alternative perspectives', in A. Scherer and G. Palazzo (eds) *Handbook of Research on Global Corporate Citizenship*, Edward Elgar, Cheltenham, pp25–49.

Crate, S. A. and Nuttall, M. (eds) (2009) *Anthropology and Climate Change: From Encounters to Actions*, Left Coast Press, Walnut Creek, CA.

Crawford, C. (2011) 'The repeal of the Glass–Steagall Act and the current financial crisis', *Journal of Business & Economics Research*, vol 9, no 1, pp127–133.

Crepaz, M. (1998) 'Inclusion versus exclusion: Political institutions and welfare expenditures', *Comparative Politics*, vol 31, no 1, pp61–80.

CRESC (Centre for Research on Socio-Cultural Change) (2009) *An Alternative Report on UK Banking Reform*, Centre for Research on Socio-Cultural Change, University of Manchester, Manchester.

Crouch, C. (2004) *Post-democracy*, Polity, Cambridge.

Crouch, C. (2005a) 'Models of capitalism', *New Political Economy*, vol 10, no 4, pp439–456.

Crouch, C. (2005b) *Capitalist Diversity and Change: Recombinant Governance and Institutional Entrepreneurs*, Oxford University Press, Oxford.

Crouch, C. (2011) *The Strange Non-Death of Neo-Liberalism*, Polity, Cambridge.

Crouch, C. and Streeck, W. (1997) *Political Economy of Modern Capitalism: Mapping Convergence and Diversity*, London, Sage.

Crouch, C. and Streeck, W. (eds) (2006) *The Diversity of Democracy: Corporatism, Social Order and Political Conflict*, Edward Elgar, Cheltenham.

Crutzen, P. and Steffen, W. (2003) 'How long have we been in the anthropocene?', *Climatic Change*, vol 61, pp251–257.

Crutzen, P. and Schwägerl, C. (2011) 'Living in the Anthropocene: Toward a new global ethos', *Yale Environment 360* (24 January), pp6–11.

Cunha, M. P. E., Cunha, J. V. da and Correia, M. F. (1999) 'Scenarios for improvisation: Long range planning redeemed', paper presented to 15th EGOS Colloquium, Warwick, 4–6 July.

Dai, Y. (2014) *Who Drives Climate-Relevant Policies in China?* mimeo, School of Public Policy and Management, Tsinghua University, Beijing.

Dale, G. (2010) *Karl Polanyi: The Limits of the Market*, Polity, Cambridge.

Dale, G. (2012) 'The growth paradigm: A critique', *International Socialism*, no 134, pp1–26.

Dallas, L. (2012) 'Short-termism, the financial crisis, and corporate governance', *Journal of Corporation Law*, vol 37, no 2, p264.

Dauvergne, P. (2008) *The Shadows of Consumption: Consequences for the Global Environment*, MIT Press, Cambridge, MA.

Davidson, M. (2013) 'Transforming China's grid: Sustaining the renewable energy push', http://theenergycollective.com/michael-davidson/279091/transforming-china-s-grid-sustaining-renewable-energy-push, accessed 12 February 2014.

Davis, D. L. (2007) *The Secret History of the War on Cancer*, Basic Books, New York.

de Alcántara, C. H. (ed.) (1993) *Real Markets: Social and Political Issues of Food Policy Reform*, Frank Cass, London.

de Luna-Martínez, J. and Vicente, C. L. (2012) 'Global survey of development banks', *Policy Research Working Paper 5969*, World Bank, Washington, DC.

DEFRA (Department for Environment, Food and Rural Affairs) (2014) 'Natural capital committee', www.defra.gov.uk/naturalcapitalcommittee/, accessed 2 February 2014.

Della Porta, D. and Diani, M. (2006) *Social Movements: An Introduction*, Wiley-Blackwell, Malden, MA.

Deshmukh, R., Gambhir, A. and Sant, G. (2011) 'India's solar mission: Procurement and auctions', *Economic and Political Weekly*, vol XLVI, no 28, pp22–26.

Desmarais, A. A. (2007) 'La Vía Campesina', *Wiley-Blackwell Encyclopedia of Globalization*, Wiley-Blackwell, Malden, MA.

Dobson, A. (1998) *Justice and the Environment: Conceptions of Environmental Sustainability and Dimensions of Social Justice*, Oxford University Press, Oxford, pp125–142.

Dobson, A. (2000) *Green Political Thought*, 3rd edn, Routledge, Psychology Press, London.

Dobson, A. (2009) 'Citizens, citizenship and governance for sustainability', in W. Neil Adger and A. Jordan (eds) *Governance for Sustainability*, Cambridge University Press, Cambridge.

Dorfman, P. (ed.) (2008) *Nuclear Consultation: Public Trust in Government*, Nuclear Consultation Working Group, University of Warwick.

Douthwaite, R. (1996) *Short Circuit: Strengthening Local Economies for Security in an Unstable World*, Green Books, Totnes, Devon, UK.

Dubash, N. K., Raghunandan, D., Sant, G. and Sreenivas, A. (2013) 'Indian climate change policy: Exploring a co-benefits based approach', *Economic & Political Weekly*, vol XLVIII, no 22, pp47–61.

EarthLife (2013) 'Renewable energy is peoples' power', www.earthlife.org.za/?page_id=193, accessed 15 January 2013.

Eckersley, R. (1992) *Environmentalism and Political Theory: Toward an Ecocentric Approach*, State University of New York Press, New York.

Eckersley, R. (2004) *The Green State*, MIT Press, Cambridge, MA.

Ecowatch (2014) 'Divestment goes mainstream as major funds kick the fossil fuel habit', http://ecowatch.com/2014/02/03/divestment-mainstream-kick-fossil-fuel-habit/, accessed 14 February 2014.

Edelman, M. (2001) 'Social movements: Changing paradigms and forms of politics', *Annual Review of Anthropology*, vol 30, pp285–317.

Edenhofer, O., Wallacher, J., Lotze-Campen, H., Reder, M., Knopf, B. and Müller, J. (eds) (2012) *Climate Change, Justice and Sustainability: Linking Climate and Development Policy*, Springer, Dordrecht.

Editorial (2009) 'Earth's boundaries?', *Nature*, vol 461, no 7263, pp447–448.

Edler, J. and Georghiou, L. (2007) 'Public procurement and innovation: Resurrecting the demand side', *Research Policy*, vol 36, no 7, pp949–963.

EEA (European Environment Agency) (2013a) *Science and the Precautionary Principle Lessons for Preventing Harm*, European Environment Agency, Copenhagen, www.eea.europa.eu/publications/late-lessons-2, accessed 10 June 2014.

EEA (2013b) *Late Lessons from Early Warnings: Science, Precaution, Innovation*, D. Gee, P. Grandjean, S. Foss Hansen, S. van den Hove, M. MacGarvin, J. Martin, G. Nielsen, D. Quist and D. Stanners (eds), European Environment Agency Report No1/2013, EEA, Copenhagen.

Ehlers, E. and Krafft, T. (eds) (2006) *Earth System Science in the Anthropocene*, Springer, Berlin.

Elkington, J. (2012) *The Zeronauts: Breaking the Sustainability Barrier*, Earthscan, London.

Ellison, N. (1997) 'Towards a new social politics: Citizenship and reflexivity in late modernity', *Sociology*, vol 31, no 4, pp697–717.

Elster, J. (1995) 'Strategic uses of argument', in K. Arrow, R. Mnookin, L. Ross, A. Tversky and R. Wilson (eds) *Barriers to Conflict Resolution*, Norton, New York, pp237–257.

Ely, A., Smith, A., Stirling, A., Leach, M. and Scoones, I. (2013) 'Innovation politics post-Rio+20: Hybrid pathways to sustainability?', *Environment and Planning C: Government and Policy*, vol 31, no 6, pp1063–1081.

ENSSR (European Network of Scientists for Social and Environmental Responsibility) (2013) *No Scientific Consensus on GMO Safety*, www.ensser.org/increasing-public-information/no-scientific-consensus-on-gmo-safety/, accessed 10 June 2014 – the author of this chapter was a signatory.

Esteva, G. and Prakash, M. (1997) 'From global thinking to local thinking', in M. Rahnema and V. Tawtree (eds) *The Post-development Reader*, Zed Books, London and New Jersey, pp277–289.

Euractive (2010) '"Guilt card" to force green behaviour on consumers?', *Euractive*, pp1–2.

European Commission (2013) *2013 SMEs' Access to Finance Survey*, European Commission, Brussels.

Evans, G. (2010) *A Just Transition to Sustainability in a Climate Change Hot-Spot: From Carbon Valley to a Future Beyond Coal*, VDM, Saarbrücken.

Evans, P. B. (1995) *Embedded Autonomy: States and Industrial Transformation*, Princeton University Press, Princeton, NJ.

Fairhead, J. and Leach, M. (1996) *Misreading the African Landscape: Society and Ecology in a Forest-Savanna Mosaic*, Cambridge University Press, Cambridge.

Fairhead, J. and Leach, M. (1998) *Reframing Deforestation: Global Analysis and Local Realities: Studies in West Africa*, Routledge, London.

Fairhead, J. and Leach, M. (2003) *Science, Society and Power: Environmental Knowledge and Policy in West Africa and the Caribbean*, Cambridge University Press, Cambridge.

Fairhead, J., Leach, M. and Scoones, I. (2012) 'Green grabbing: A new appropriation of nature?' *Journal of Peasant Studies*, vol 39, no 2, pp285–307.

Faroult, E. (ed.) (2009) *The World in 2025: Contributions from an Expert Group*, European Commission, Brussels.

Farrell, D. and Remes, J. (2009) 'Promoting energy efficiency in the developing world', *The McKinsey Quarterly*, February.

Felt, U., Barben, D., Irwin, A., Joly, P-B., Rip, A., Stirling, A. and Stöckelová, T. (2013) *Science in Society: Caring for our Futures in Turbulent Times*, European Science Foundation, Strasbourg.

Femia, J. (1983) 'Gramsci's patrimony', *British Journal of Political Science*, vol 13, no 3, pp327–364.

Fine, B., Saraswati, J. and Tavasic, D. (2013) *Beyond the Developmental State: Industrial Policy into the 21st Century*, Pluto, London.

Fischer, D. (2012) 'Challenges of low carbon technology diffusion: Insights from shifts in China's photovoltaic industry development', *Innovation and Development*, vol 2, no 1, pp131–146.

Fleming, J. R. (2010) *Fixing The Sky: The Checkered History of Weather and Climate Control*, Columbia University Press, New York.

Folke, C., Carpenter, S., Elmqvist, T., Gunderson, L., Holling, C. S. and Walker, B. (2002) 'Resilience and sustainable development: Building adaptive capacity in a world of transformations', *AMBIO: A Journal of the Human Environment*, vol 31, no 5, pp437–440.

Folke, C., Jansson, Å., Rockström, J., Olsson, P., Carpenter, S. R., Chapin, F. S., Crepín, A.-S., Daily, G., Danell, K., Ebbesson, J., Elmqvist, T., Galaz, V., Moberg, F., Nilsson, M., Österblom, H., Ostrom, E., Persson, Å., Peterson, G., Polasky, S., Steffen, W., Walker, B. and Westley, F. (2011) 'Reconnecting to the biosphere', *Ambio*, vol 40. pp719–738.

Forbes (2011) 'What Solyndra's bankruptcy means for Silicon Valley solar startups', *Forbes*, 31 August, www.forbes.com/sites/toddwoody/2011/08/31/what-solyndras-bankruptcy-means-for-silicon-valley-solar-startups/, accessed 3 July 2014.

Foster, J. B. (2002) 'Ecology against capitalism', *Monthly Review Press*, vol 53, no 5, http://monthlyreview.org/2001/10/01/ecology-against-capitalism, accessed 11 July 2014.

Foster, V. and Briceño-Garmendia, C. (eds) (2010) *Africa's Infrastructure: A Time for Transformation*, World Bank, Washington, DC.

Fouquet, R. and Pearson, P. (2012) 'Past and prospective energy transitions: Insights from history', *Energy Policy*, vol 50, pp1–7.

Frankfurt, H. G. (2004) *The Reasons of Love*, Princeton University Press, Princeton, NJ.

Fraser, N. (2012) 'Can society be commodities all the way down? Polanyian reflections on capitalist crisis', FMSHWP-2012, no 18, August, Fondation Maison des sciences de l'homme, Paris.

Freeman, C. (1973) 'Introduction: Malthus with a Computer', in H. S. D. Cole, C. Freeman, M. Jahoda, and K. Pavitt (eds) *Thinking About the Future: A Critique of Limits to Growth*, University of Sussex Press and Chatto & Windus, London and Brighton, pp1–10.

Fressoli, M., Around, E., Abrol, D., Smith, A., Ely, A. and Dias, R. (2014) 'When grassroots innovation movements encounter mainstream institutions: Implications for models of inclusive innovation', *Innovation and Development, Revised-Paper-rh-MF-x-STEPS.pdf*, http://steps-centre.org/wp-content/uploads/FressoliEtAl-Second, accessed 20 June 2014.

Fried, L., Shukla, S. and Sawyer, S. (eds) (2012) *Global Wind Report: Annual Market Update 2011*, Global Wind Energy Council, http://gwec.net/wp-content/uploads/2012/06/Annual_report_2011_lowres.pdf, accessed 24 June 2014.

FS-UNEP/BNEF (2014) *Global Trends in Renewable Energy Investment 2014*, Frankfurt am Main, Frankfurt School.

Galaz, V. (2012) 'Environment: Planetary boundaries concept is valuable', *Nature*, vol 486, no 7402, p191.

Galaz, V., Biermann, F., Crona, B., Loorbach, D., Folke, C., Olsson, P., Nilsson, M., Allouche, J., Persson, Å. and Reischl, G. (2012) 'Planetary boundaries: Exploring the challenges for global environmental governance', *Current Opinion in Environmental Sustainability*, vol 4, no 1, pp80–87.

Gallagher, K. (ed.) (2005) *Putting Development First: The Importance of Policy Space in the WTO and International Financial Institutions*, Zed Books, London.

GCI (Global Commons Institute) (2014) 'Contraction and convergence: Climate truth and reconciliation', www.gci.org.uk/, accessed 1 July 2014.

GEA (Global Environmental Assessment) (2012) *Global Energy Assessment Toward a Sustainable Future*, G. Davis and J. Goldemberg (eds), Cambridge University Press, Cambridge.

Geall, S. (2013) *China and the Environment: The Green Revolution (Asian Arguments)*, Zed Books, London.

Gee, D., Vaz, S. G., Harremoës, P., MacGarvin, M., Stirling, A., Keys, J. and Wynne, B. (eds) (2001) *Late Lessons from Early Warnings: The Precautionary Principle 1896–2000*, European Environment Agency Report No22/2001, EEA, Copenhagen.

Geels, F. W. (2002) 'Technological transitions as evolutionary reconfiguration processes: A multi-level perspective and a case study', *Research Policy*, vol 31, no 8/9, pp1257–1274.

Geels, F. W. (2005a) *Technological Transitions and System Innovations: A Co-Evolutionary and Socio-Technical Analysis*, Edward Elgar, Cheltenham.

Geels, F. W. (2005b) 'The dynamics of transitions in socio-technical systems: A multilevel analysis of the transition pathway from horse-drawn carriages to automobiles (1860–1930)', *Technology Analysis and Strategic Management*, vol 17, no 4, pp445–476.

Geels, F. W. (2006) 'Co-evolutionary and multi-level dynamics in transitions: The transformation of aviation systems and the shift from propeller to turbojet (1930–1970)', *Technovation*, vol 26, no 9, pp999–1016.

Geels, F. W. (2011) 'The multi-level perspective on sustainability transitions: Responses to seven criticisms', *Environmental Innovation and Societal Transitions*, vol 1, pp24–40.

Geels, F. W. (2013) 'The impact of the financial-economic crisis on sustainability transitions: Financial investment, governance and public discourse', *Environmental Innovation and Societal Transition*, vol 6, pp67–95.

Geels, F. W. (2014) 'Regime resistance against low-carbon transitions: Introducing politics and power into the multi-level perspectives', *Theory, Culture & Society*, 27 June, http://tcs.sagepub.com/content/early/2014/06/27/0263276414531627.full, accessed 11 July 2014.

Geels, F. W. and Schot, J. (2007) 'Typology of sociotechnical transition pathways', *Research Policy*, vol 36, no 3, pp399–417.

Ghosh, S. and Nanda, R. (2010) 'Venture capital investment in the clean energy sector', *Harvard Business School Working Papers*, no 11–020, Harvard Business School, Massachusetts, PA.

Gill, S. (1995) 'Globalisation, market civilisation and disciplinary neoliberalism', *Millennium: Journal of International Studies*, vol 24, no 3, pp399–423.

Gillespie, B., Eva, D. and Johnson, R. (1979) 'Carcinogenic risk assessment in the United States and Great Britain', *Social Studies of Science*, vol 9, pp265–301.

Gilligan, C. and Richards, D. A. J. (2009) *The Deepening Darkness: Patriarchy, Resistance and Democracy's Future*, Cambridge University Press, Cambridge.

Glyn, A. (2009) 'Functional distribution and inequality', in W. Salverda, B. Nolan and T. M. Smeeding (eds) *The Oxford Handbook of Economic Inequality*, Oxford University Press, New York, pp101–26.

Gottlieb, R. and Joshi, A. (2010) *Food Justice*, MIT Press, Cambridge, MA.

Gramsci, A. (1971) *Selections from the Prison Notebooks*, ed. and trans. by Q. Hoare and G. Nowell Smith, International Publishers, New York.

Green Economy Coalition (2014) www.greeneconomycoalition.org/, accessed 20 January 2014.

Greenham, T., Ryan-Collins, J., Werner, R. and Jackson, A. (2012) *Where Does Money Come From? A Guide to the UK Monetary and Banking System*, New Economics Foundation, London.

Greenpeace International (2013) *Point of No Return: The Massive Climate Threats We Must Avoid*, Greenpeace International, Amsterdam.

Griffin, K. (1974) *The Political Economy of Agrarian Change*, Macmillan, London.

Griffith-Jones, S. and Tyson, J. (2013) 'The European Investment Bank: Lessons for developing countries', *WIDER Working Paper*, no 2013–19, UNU-WIDER, Helsinki.

Griggs, D., Stafford-Smith, M., Gaffney, O., Rockström, J., öhman, M. C., Shyamsundar, P., Steffen, W., Glaser, G., Kanie, N. and Noble, I. (2012) 'Sustainable development goals for people and planet', *Nature*, vol 495, pp305–7.

Grin, J., Rotmans, J., and Schot, J. (2010) *Transitions to Sustainable Development: New Directions in the Study of Long Term Transformative Change*, Routledge, London.

Grove, R. (1996) *Green Imperialism: Colonial Expansion, Tropical Island Edens and the Origins of Environmentalism*, Cambridge University Press, Cambridge.

Grubler, A. (2012) 'Energy transitions research: Insights and cautionary tales', *Energy Policy*, vol 50, pp8–16.

Guha, R. and Martinez-Alier, J. (1997) *Varieties of Environmentalism: Essays North and South*, Earthscan, London.

Gupta, A. K. (2013) 'Tapping the entrepreneurial potential of grassroots innovation', *Stanford Social Innovation Review*, Summer 2013 Suppl., pp18–20.

Gupta, A. K., Sinha, R., Koradia, D., Patel, R., Parmar, M., Rohit, P., Vivekanandan, P. (2003) 'Mobilizing grassroots' technological innovations and traditional knowledge, values and institutions: Articulating social and ethical capital', *Futures*, vol 35, no 9, pp975–987.

Guzmán, E. S. and Martinez-Alier, J. (2006) 'New rural social movements and agroecology', in P. Cloke, T. Marsden and P. Mooney (eds) *Handbook of Rural Studies*, Sage, London, pp472–484.

Haan, J. de and Sierman, C. L. J. (1996) 'New evidence on the relationship between democracy and economic growth', *Public Voice*, vol 86, no 1/2, pp175–198.

Haas, E. B. (1980) 'Why collaborate? Issue-linkage and international regimes', *World Politics*, vol 32, no 3, pp357–405.

Haber, S., North, D. C. and Weingast, B. R. (eds) (2008) *Political Institutions and Financial Development*, Stanford University Press, Stanford, CA.

Hackmann, H. and Clair, A. L. S. (2012) *Transformative Cornerstones of Social Science Research for Global Change*, International Social Science Council, Paris.

Hagedorn, S. (2013) 'The politics of caring: The role of activism in primary care', *Advances in Nursing Science*, vol 17, no 4, pp1–11.

Haggard, S. (2004) 'Institutions and growth in East Asia', *Studies in Comparative International Development*, vol 38, no 4, pp53–81.

Hajer, M. (1995) *The Politics of Environmental Discourse: Ecological Modernization and the Policy Process*, Clarendon Press, Oxford.

Hajer, M. and Wagenaar, H. (eds) (2003) *Deliberative Policy Analysis*, Cambridge University Press, Cambridge.

Hall, P. (1993) 'Policy paradigms, social learning and the state: The case of economic policymaking in Britain', *Comparative Politics*, vol 25, no 3, pp275–296.

Hall, P. and Soskice, D. (2001) *Varieties of Capitalism: The Institutional Foundations of Comparative Advantage*, Oxford University Press, Oxford.

Hamilton, K. (2009) *Unlocking Finance for Clean Energy: The Need for 'Investment Grade' Policy*, Energy, Environment and Development Programme Paper 09/04, December, Chatham House, London.

Hancké, B., Rhodes, M. and Thatcher, M. (2007) 'Beyond varieties of capitalism', in B. Hancké, M. Rhodes and M. Thatcher (eds) *Beyond Varieties of Capitalism: Conflict, Contradictions and Complementarities in the European Economy*, Oxford University Press, Oxford.

Hansard (2014) House of Commons, 26 February, Column 256, www.publications. parliament.uk/pa/cm201314/cmhansrd/cm140226/debtext/140226–0001.htm#1402267 7000005, accessed 20 June 2014.

Hansen, J., Sato, M., Ruedy, R., Kharecha, P., Lacis, A., Miller, R., Nazarenko, L., Lo, K., Schmidt, G. A., Russell, G., Aleinov, I., Bauer, S., Baum, E., Cairns, B., Canuto, V., Chandler, M., Cheng, Y., Cohen, A., Del Genio, A., Falufegi, G., Fleming, E., Friend, A., Hall, T., Jackman, C., Jonas, J., Kelley, M., Kinag, N. Y., Koch, D., Labow, G., Lerner, J., Menon, S., Novakov, T., Oinas, V., Perlwitz, J., Perlwitz, Ju, Rind, D., Romanou, A., Schmunk, R., Shindell, D., Stone, P., Sun, S., Streets, D., Tausnev, N., Thresher, D., Unger, N., Yao, M. and Zhang, S. (2007) 'Dangerous human-made interference with climate: A GISS model study', *Atmospheric Chemistry and Physics*, vol 7, pp2287–2312.

Harrison, K. and Sundstrom, L. M. (2010) *Global Commons, Domestic Decisions: The Comparative Politics of Climate Change*, MIT Press, Cambridge, MA.

Harrison, T. and Kostka, G. (2012) *Manoeuvres for a Low Carbon State – The Local Politics of Climate Change in China and India*, Research Paper 22, retrieved from Developmental Leadership Program, www.dlprog.org, accessed 25 June 2014.

Harvey, D. (2005) *A Brief History of Neoliberalism*, Oxford University Press, Oxford.

Heilmann, S. (2008) 'From local experiments to national policy: The origins of China's policy process', *The China Journal*, vol 59, pp1–30.

Heinrich Böll Foundation (2013) 'Research for and on the "Great Transformation"', Heinrich Böll Foundation, Berlin.

Held, V. (2005) *The Ethics of Care: Personal, Political and Global*, Oxford University Press, Oxford.

Helm, D. (2012) *The Carbon Crunch*, Yale University Press, New Haven, CT and London.

Herring, R. (2005) 'Miracle seeds, suicide seeds, and the poor: Mobilizing around genetically modified organisms in India', in R. Ray and M. F. Katzenstein (eds) *Social Movements and Poverty in India*, Rowman & Littlefield, Lanham, MD, pp203–232.

Hess, D. J. (2007) *Alternative Pathways in Science and Industry: Activism, Innovation and the Environment in an Era of Globalization*, MIT Press, Cambridge, MA.

Hickman, L. (2010) 'James Lovelock: Humans are too stupid to prevent climate change', *The Guardian*, 29 March, pp2–5, www.theguardian.com/science/2010/mar/29/james-lovelock-climate-change, accessed 9 November 2014.

Hilborn, R. (2008) 'Knowledge on how to achieve sustainable fisheries', in K. Tsukamoto, T. Kawamura, T. Takeuchi, T. D. Beard, Jr and M. J. Kaiser (eds) *Fisheries for Global Welfare and Environment*, 5th World Fisheries Congress 2008, pp45–56.

Hildyard, N. (1993) 'Foxes in charge of the chickens', in W. Sachs (ed.) *Global Ecology: A New Arena of Political Conflict*, Zed Books, London, pp22–35.

Hirschman, A. O. (1989) 'How the Keynesian revolution was exported from the United States, and other comments', in P. Hall (ed.) *The Political Power of Economic Ideas: Keynesianism across Nations*, Princeton University Press, Princeton, NJ, pp347–60.

HMG (2009) 'The Road to 2010: Addressing the nuclear question in the twenty first century', Cm 7675, HM Government Cabinet Office, www.gov.uk/government/publications/cabinet-office-the-road-to-2010, accessed 20 June 2014.

Hobbes, T. (1651) *The Leviathan*.

Hobday, M. (2003) 'Innovation in Asian industrialization: A Gerschenkronian perspective', *Oxford Development Studies*, vol 31, no 3, pp293–314.

Hobsbawn, E. (1997) *The Age of Capital*, Abacus, London.

Hoff, M. and Rockström, J. (2013) 'Johan Rockstrom: Protecting the earth's systems from catastrophic failure', *Ensia*, pp1–5, http://ensia.com/interviews/johan-rockstrom-protecting-the-earths-systems-from-catastrophic-failure, accessed 19 February 2014.

Hoffman, M. (2011) *Climate Governance at the Cross-Roads: Experimenting with a Global Response After Kyoto*, Oxford University Press, Oxford.

Holloway, J. (2002) *Change the World without Taking Power: The Meaning of Revolution Today*, Pluto Press, London.

Hopkins, M. and Lazonick, W. (2012) 'Soaking up the sun and blowing in the wind: Renewable energy needs patient capital', Ford Foundation Conference on Finance, *Business Models, and Sustainable Prosperity*, Ford Foundation, New York.

Hopkins, R. (2008) *The Transition Handbook: From Oil Dependency to Local Resilience*, Green Books, Totnes, Devon., UK

Hopkins, R. (2013) *The Power of Just Doing Stuff: How Local Action can Change the World*, Green Books, Cambridge.

Hopwood, B., Mellor, M. and O'Brien, G. (2005) 'Sustainable development: Mapping different approaches', *Sustainable Development*, vol 13, no 1, pp38–52.

Howard, V. (2003) 'Anti-precautionary risk assessment', presentation to Lobby Watch Independent Science Panel Conference, 8 June, www.lobbywatch.org/archive2.asp?arcid=921, accessed 10 June 2014.

Huber, M. (2008) 'Energizing historical materialism: Fossil fuels, space and the capitalist mode of production', *Geoforum*, vol 40, pp105–115.

Hulme, M. (2009) *Why We Disagree About Climate Change: Understanding Controversy, Inaction and Opportunity*, Cambridge University Press, Cambridge.

Hulme, M. (2010) 'Cosmopolitan climates: Hybridity, foresight and meaning', *Theory, Culture & Society*, vol 27, no 2–3, pp267–276.

Hulme, M. (2012) 'On the "two degrees" climate policy target', in O. Edenhofer, J. Wallacher, H. Lotze-Campen, M. Reder, B. Knopf and J. Muller (eds) *Climate Change, Justice and Sustainability: Linking Climate and Development Policy*, Springer, Dordrecht, pp122–125.

Hulme, M. (2013) '"A safe operating space for humanity": Do people's beliefs need to change?' presentation at Global Change and Biosphere Interactions, York Environment and Sustainability Institute, University of York, 8–9 April.

IPCC (Intergovernmental Panel on Climate Change) (1990) *First Assessment Report (of the Intergovernmental Panel on Climate Change, Working Group I: Scientific Assessment of Climate Change)*, J. T. Houghton, G. J. Jenkins and J. J. Ephraums (eds), Cambridge University Press, Cambridge, www.ipcc.ch/publications_and_data/publications_ipcc_first_assessment_1990_wg1.shtml, accessed 10 June 2014.

IPCC (2007) *IPCC Fourth Assessment Report: Climate Change 2007*, Intergovernmental Panel on Climate Change, Geneva.

IPCC (2012) *Renewable Energy Sources and Climate Change Mitigation: Special Report of the Intergovernmental Panel on Climate Change*, Cambridge University Press, Cambridge.

IPCC (2013) *Climate Change 2013: The Physical Science Basis, Summary for Policymakers*, Working Group 1 Contribution to the IPCC Fifth Assessment Report: Changes to the underlying Scientific/Technical Assessment, IPCC, Geneva, www.ipcc.ch/report/ar5/wg1/docs/WGIAR5_SPM_brochure_en.pdf, accessed 12 July 2014.

IPCC (undated) Intergovernmental Panel on Climate Change, www.ipcc.ch/publications_and_data/publications_and_data.shtml#.Uw9qMYWZaSo, accessed 10 June 2014.

IRENA (International Renewable Energy Association) (2012) *Financial Mechanisms and Investment Frameworks for Renewables in Developing Countries*, International Renewable Energy Association.

Iversen, T. and Soskice, D. (2006) 'Electoral institutions and the politics of coalitions: Why some democracies redistribute more than others', *American Political Science Review*, vol 100, no 2, pp165–181.

Jackson, T. (2009) *Prosperity without Growth: Economics for a Finite Planet*, Earthscan, London.

Jackson, T. (2011) *Prosperity without Growth: Economics for a Finite Planet*, reprint edn, Earthscan, London.

Jacobs, M. (2012a) *Green Growth: Economic Theory and Political Discourse*, Centre for Climate Change Economics and Policy Working Paper, Grantham Institute, London.

Jacobs, M. (2012b) 'A low-carbon future is the one we must all fight for', *The Guardian*, 2 December, www.guardian.co.uk/commentisfree/2012/dec/02/climate-renewable-energy-carbon-emissions, accessed 16 June 2014.

Jacobs, M. (2013) 'Green Growth', in R. Falkner (ed.) *Handbook of Global Climate and Environmental Policy*, Wiley Blackwell, Oxford, pp197–215.

Jacobsson, S. and Lauber, V. (2006) 'The politics and policy of energy system transformation – explaining the German diffusion of renewable energy technology', *Energy Policy*, vol 34, no 3, pp256–276.

Jacques, M. (2012) *When China Rules the World: The End of the Western World and the Birth of a New Global Order*, Penguin, London.

Jamison, A. (2001) *The Making of Green Knowledge: Environmental Politics and Cultural Transformation*, Cambridge University Press, Cambridge.

Jamison, A. (2012) 'Agri-food and social movements', *Science as Culture*, vol 21, no 4, pp587–591.

Jasanoff, S. (1990) *The Fifth Branch: Science Advisers as Policymakers*, Harvard University Press, Cambridge, MA.

Jasanoff, S. (2005) *Designs on Nature*, Princeton University Press, Princeton, NJ.

Jasanoff, S. and Martello, M. L. (2004) *Earthly Politics: Local and Global in Environmental Governance*, MIT Press, Cambridge, MA.

Jessop, B. (1990) *State Theory: Putting the Capitalist State in its Place*, Polity Press, Cambridge.

JMPR (Joint Meeting on Pesticide Residues) (n.d.) Reports of the Joint (FAO WHO) Meeting on Pesticide Residues, www.who.int/foodsafety/chem/jmpr/publications/en/ and http://apps.who.int/pesticide-residues-jmpr-database, accessed 11 June 2014.

Jordan, A. and Adger, N. (eds) (2009) *Governing Sustainability*, Cambridge University Press, Cambridge.

Just Transition Alliance (JTA) (2011) About the Just Transition Alliance, www.jtalliance.org/docs/aboutjta.html, accessed 16 June 2014.

Kanchan, K. A. (2013) 'Power utilities oppose hike in wind tariff price', www.downtoearth.org.in/content/power-utilities-oppose-hike-wind-tariff-price, accessed 25 February 2014.

Kern, F. (2013) 'Energy transitions and deliberate transition management: Implementing the Green Economy', *Okologisches Wirtschaften* (3.2013), pp20–22.

Kern, F. and Smith, A. (2008) 'Restructuring energy systems for sustainability? Energy transition policy in the Netherlands', *Energy Policy*, vol 36, no 11, pp4093–4103.

Knopf, B., Kowarsch, M., Flachsland, C. and Edenhofe, O. (2012) 'The 2°C target reconsidered', in O. Edenhofer, J. Wallacher, H. Lotze-Campen, M. Reder, B. Knopf and J. Muller (eds) *Climate Change, Justice and Sustainability: Linking Climate and Development Policy*, Springer, Dordrecht, pp121–138.

Kovel, J. (2002) *The Enemy of Nature: The End of Capitalism or The End of the World*, Zed Books, London.

Krackhardt, D. (1990) 'Assessing the political landscape: Structure, cognition, and power in organizations', *Administrative Science Quarterly*, vol 35, no 2, pp342–369.

Kwak, J. (2013) 'Cultural capture and the financial crisis', in D. Carpenter and D. Moss (eds) *Preventing Regulatory Capture: Special Interest Influence, and How to Limit It*, Cambridge University Press, Cambridge, pp71–98.

La Porta, R., Lopez-de-Silanes, F., Shleifer, A., Vishny, R. (1998) 'Law and finance', *Journal of Political Economy*, vol 106, no 6, pp1113–1155.

Laetz, C.A., Tracy, D. H., Collier, K., Hebert, V., Stark, J. D. and Scholz, N.L. (2009) 'The synergistic toxicity of pesticide mixtures: Implications for risk assessment and the conservation of endangered pacific salmon', *Environmental Health Perspectives*, vol 117, no 3, pp348–353.

Laird, F. and Stefes, C. (2009) 'The diverging paths of German and United States policies for renewable energy: Sources of difference', *Energy Policy*, vol 37, no 7, pp2619–2629.

Lampton, D. (2014) 'How China is ruled: Why it's getting harder for Beijing to govern', *Foreign Affairs*, vol 93, pp74–84.

Landberg, R. (2012) 'China to make regional adjustments for solar power incentives', *Bloomberg News*, 19 December, www.bloomberg.com/news/2012–12–19/china-to-make-regional-adjustments-for-solar-power-incentives.html, accessed 24 January 2013.

Latin, H. A. (2012) *Climate Change Policy Failures*, World Scientific Publishing, Singapore.

Latour, B. (2005) *Reassembling the Social: An Introduction to Actor-Network Theory*, Oxford University Press, Oxford.

Lauber, V. and Mez, L. (2006) 'Renewable electricity policy in Germany, 1974 to 2005', *Bulletin of Science, Technology & Society*, vol 26, no 5, pp105–120.

Lazonick, W. and Mazzucato, M. (2013) 'The risk-reward nexus in the innovation-inequality relationship: Who takes the risks? Who gets the rewards?', *Industrial and Corporate Change*, M. Mazzucato (ed.), special issue, vol 22, no 4, pp1093–1128.

Leach, M. (2013) 'Democracy in the Anthropocene? Science and sustainable development goals at the UN', www.huffingtonpost.co.uk/../../Melissa-Leach/democracy-in-the-anthropocene_b_2966341.html, accessed 3 June 2014.

Leach, M. and Mearns, R. (1996) *The Lie of the Land: Challenging Received Wisdom on the African Environment*, James Currey, Oxford.

Leach, M. and Scoones, I. (2005) 'Science and citizenship in a global context', in M. Leach, I. Scoones and B. Wynne (eds) *Science and Citizens: Globalisation and the Challenge of Engagement*, Zed Press, London, pp15–38.

Leach, M. and Scoones, I. (2006) *The Slow Race: Making Technology Work for the Poor*, London, Demos.

Leach, M. and Scoones, I. (2007) *Mobilising Citizens: Social Movements and the Politics of Knowledge*, IDS Working Paper 276, Institute of Development Studies, Brighton.

Leach, M. and Scoones, I. (2013) 'Carbon forestry in West Africa: The politics of models, measures and verification processes', *Global Environmental Change*, vol 23, no 5, pp957–967.

Leach, M. and Scoones, I. (forthcoming, 2015) *Carbon Conflicts and Forest Landscapes in Africa*, Routledge/Earthscan, London.

Leach, M., Scoones, I. and Wynne, B. (eds) (2005) *Science and Citizens: Globalization and the Challenge of Engagement*, Zed Press, London.

Leach, M., Scoones, I. and Stirling, A. (2010) *Dynamic Sustainabilities*, Earthscan, London.

Leach, M., Raworth, K. and Rockström, J. (2013) 'Between social and planetary boundaries: Navigating pathways in the safe and just space for humanity', *World Social Science Report*, ISSC and UNESCO, Paris, pp84–89.

Leach, M., Rockström, J., Raskin, P., Scoones, I., Stirling, A. C., Smith, A., Thompson, J., Millstone, E., Ely, A., Arond, E., Folke, C. and Olsson, P. (2012) 'Transforming innovation for sustainability', *Ecology and Society*, vol 17, no 2, p11.

Leftwich, A. (2009) *Bringing Agency Back In: Politics and Human Agency in Building Institutions and States*, synthesis and overview report of phase one of the leaders, elites and coalitions research programme, Research Paper 06, Department of Politics, University of York, York.

Leggett, J. (1996) *Climate Change and the Financial Sector*, Gerling Akademie Verlag, Munich.

Leggett, J. (2014) *The Energy of Nations: Risk Blindness and the Road to Renaissance*, Earthscan, London.

Leggewie, C. and Messner, D. (2012a) 'The low-carbon transformation: A social science perspective', *Journal of Renewable and Sustainable Energy*, vol 4, no 4.

Leggewie, C. and Messner, D. (2012b) 'Chronicle of a disaster foretold: How climate change is communicated – and why global warming must not exceed two degrees', in O. Edenhofer, J. Wallacher, H. Lotze-Campen, M. Reder, B. Knopf and J. Muller (eds) *Climate Change, Justice and Sustainability: Linking Climate and Development Policy*, Springer, Dordrecht.

Leib, E. J. and He, B. (eds) (2006) *The Search for Deliberative Democracy in China*, Palgrave Macmillan, New York.

Lema, A. and Ruby, K. (2007) 'Between fragmented authoritarianism and policy coordination: Creating a Chinese market for wind', *Energy Policy*, vol 35, no 7, pp3879–3890.

Lema, R., Berger, A. and Schmitz, H. (2013) 'China's impact on the global wind power industry', *Journal of Current Chinese Affairs*, vol 42, no 1, pp37–69.

Lenton, T. M. (2013) 'Environmental tipping points', *Annual Review of Environment and Resources*, vol 38, pp1–29.

Letty, B., Shezi, Z. and Mudhara, M. (2012) *An Exploration of Agricultural Grassroots Innovation in South Africa and Implications for Innovation Indicator Development*, UNU-MERIT Working Paper 2012–023, UNU-MERIT, Maastricht.

Levidow, L. (2014) 'What green economy? Diverse agendas, their tensions and potential futures', IKD Working Paper, no 73, www.open.ac.uk/ikd/publications/working-papers/, accessed 15 July 2014.

Levidow, L. and Carr, S. (2007) 'GM crops on trial: Technological development as a real-world experiment', *Futures*, vol 39, no 4, pp408–431.

Lewis, J. (2007) 'Technology acquisition and innovation in the developing world: Wind turbine development in China and India', *Studies in Comparative International Development*, vol 32, nos 3–4, pp208–232.

Lewis, J. (2011) 'Building a national wind turbine industry: Experiences from China, India and South Korea', *International Journal of Technology and Globalisation*, vol 5, pp281–305.

Lewis, M. (2014) *Flash Boys: Cracking the Money-Code*, W. W. Norton & Company, New York.

Li, C. (1997) 'Confucian value and democratic value', *The Journal of Value Inquiry*, vol 31, pp183–193.

Li, J. (2010) 'Decarbonising power generation in China: Is the answer blowing in the wind?' *Renewable and Sustainable Energy Reviews*, vol 14, no 4, pp1154–1171.

Lim, B. and Rabinovitch, S. (2010) 'China mulls $1.5 trillion strategic industries boost: Sources', *Reuters*, 3 December, www.reuters.com/article/2010/12/03/us-china-economy-investment- idUSTRE6B16U920101203, accessed 24 June 2014.

Lipietz, A. (2013) 'Fears and hopes: The crisis of the liberal productivist model and its green alternative', *Capital and Class*, vol 37, no 1, pp127–141.

Liu, C. (2011) 'China uses feed-in tariff to build domestic solar market', *New York Times*, 14 September, www.nytimes.com/cwire/2011/09/14/14climatewire-china-uses-feed-in-tariff-to-build-domestic-25559.html?pagewanted=all, accessed 24 June 2014.

Liu, Y. (2012) 'China increases target for wind power capacity to 1,000 GW by 2050', Renewableenergyworld.com, 5 January, www.renewableenergyworld.com/rea/news/article/2012/01/china-increases-target-for-wind-power-capacity-to-1000-gw-by-2050, accessed 24 June 2014.

Lockwood, M., Kuzemko, C., Mitchell, C. and Hoggett, R. (2013) *Theorising Governance and Innovation in Sustainable Energy Transitions*, IGov Working Paper 1304, Energy Policy Group, University of Exeter.

Lomborg, B. (2013) 'Don't hold your breath', *The European*, 7 November, www.the european-magazine.com/bjorn-lomborg/7590-the-failure-of-climate-talks, accessed 20 June 2014.

Loorbach, D. (2007) *Transition Management: New Mode of Governance for Sustainable Development*, International Books, Utrecht.

Louw, A. (2013) *Development Banks: Breaking the $100 bn-a-year Barrier*, Bloomberg, New Energy Finance, London.

Lövbrand, E., Stripple, J. and Wiman, B. (2009) 'Earth system governmentality', *Global Environmental Change*, vol 19, no 1, pp7–13.

Luetkenhorst, W. and Pegels, A. (2014) *Stable Policies: Turbulent Markets, Germany's Green Industrial Policies: The Costs and Benefits of Promoting Solar PV and Wind Energy*, Research Report, International Institute for Sustainable Development.

Lyon, T. P. and Maxwell, J. W. (2011) 'Greenwash: Corporate environmental disclosure under threat of audit', *Journal of Economics & Management Strategy*, vol 20, no 1, pp3–41.

Ma, H., Oxley, L., Gibson, J. and Li, W. (2010) 'A survey of China's renewable energy economy', *Renewable and Sustainable Energy Reviews*, vol 14, no 1, pp438–445.

McAdam, D., Tarrow, S. and Tilly, C. (2001) *Dynamics of Contention*, Cambridge University Press, Cambridge.

McAdam, D., Tarrow, S. and Tilly, C. (2003) 'Dynamics of contention', *Social Movement Studies*, vol 2, no 1, 9, pp9–102.

McAfee, K. (2012) 'The contradictory logic of global ecosystem-services markets', *Development and Change*, vol 43, no 1, pp 105–131.

MacGregor, S. (2006) *Beyond Mothering Earth: Ecological Citizenship and the Politics of Care*, UBC Press, Vancouver.

MacKensie, D. (2013) 'How to make banks less fragile', draft version for *London Review of Books*, www.sps.ed.ac.uk/__data/assets/pdf_file/0006/129939/Banks16.pdf, accessed 6 July 2014.

MacKenzie, D., Beunza, D., Millo, Y. and Pardo-Guerra, J. P. (2012) 'Drilling through the Allegheny mountains: Liquidity, materiality and high-frequency trading', *Journal of Cultural Economy*, vol 5, no 3, pp279–296.

Madrigal, A. (2011) *Powering the Dream: The History and Promise of Green Technology*, Da Capo Press, Cambridge, MA.

MAFF (Ministry of Agriculture, Fisheries and Food) (1990) *Ministers Further Announcement on Saccharin*, Ministry of Agriculture, Fisheries and Food, Document Reference ADF 1029, Annex D, p12.

Magalhães, P., Aragão, A., Moreno Pires, S., Oliveira, N. and Jacobs, S. (2013) 'Planetary boundaries: The keystone for a new object of law', Condominium contribution to the Planetary Boundaries Initiative Symposium, London.

Majone, G. (1996) 'Regulation and its modes', in G. Majone (ed.) *Regulating Europe*, Routledge, London, pp9–27.

Malesky, E. (2008) 'Straight ahead on red: How foreign direct investment empowers subnational leaders', *Journal of Politics*, vol 70, no 1, pp1–23.

Malthus, T. R. (1798) *An Essay on the Principle of Population: Or, a View of its Past and Present Effects on Human Happiness*, John Murray, London.

Mapes, J. and Wolch, J. (2011) '"Living green": The promise and pitfalls of new sustainable communities', *Journal of Urban Design*, vol 16, no 1, pp105–126.

Martin, A. (2013) 'Global environmental in/justice, in practice: Introduction', *The Geographical Journal*, vol 179, no 2, pp98–104.

Martin, A., McGuire, S. and Sullivan, S. (2013) 'Global environmental justice and biodiversity conservation', *The Geographical Journal*, vol 179, no 2, pp122–131.

Martínez Novo, R. (2012) 'Controversias en torn al "bein vivir" de los kichwas canelos: una aproximación conceptual', *Quadrens de Ciències socials*, no 22, Universitat de València, València.

Martínez-Alier, J. (2002) *The Environmentalism of the Poor: A Study of Ecological Conflicts and Valuation*, Edward Elgar, Cheltenham.

Martinot, E. (2010) 'Renewable power for China: Past, present and future', *Frontiers of Energy and Power Engineering in China*, vol 4, no 3, pp287–294.

Marx, K. (1974 [1867]) *Capital*, Lawrence & Wishart, London.

Marx, K. and Engels, F. (1998 [1848]) *The Communist Manifesto*, Verso, London.

Mathews, J. A. and Tan, H. (2011) 'Progress toward a circular economy in China', *Journal of Industrial Ecology*, vol 15, no 3, pp435–457.

Mathews, J. A., Tang, Y. and Tan, H. (2011) 'China's move to a Circular Economy as a development strategy', *Asian Business & Management*, vol 10, no 4, pp463–484.

Maxfield, S. (1991) 'Bankers' alliances and economic policy patterns: Evidence from Mexico and Brazil', *Comparative Political Studies*, vol 23, no 4, pp419–458.

Mazzucato, M. (2011) *The Entrepreneurial State*, Demos, London.

Mazzucato, M. (2013a) 'Financing innovation: Creative destruction vs. destructive creation', *Industrial and Corporate Change*, vol 22, no 4, pp851–867.

Mazzucato, M. (2013b) *The Entrepreneurial State: Debunking Public vs. Private Sector Myths*, Anthem Press, London.

Mazzucato, M. and Penna, C. (forthcoming, 2014) 'Keynes and Minsky meet Schumpeter & Polanyi: The rise of mission-oriented state investment banks', Block, F. (ed.), special issue, *Politics & Society*.

Meadowcroft, J. (2011) 'Engaging with the politics of sustainability transitions', *Environmental Innovation and Societal Transitions*, vol 1, no 1, pp70–75.

Meadows, D. H., Meadows, D., Randers, J., and Behrens III, W. W. (1972) *The Limits to Growth: A Report for the Club of Rome's Project on the Predicament of Mankind*, Universe Books, New York.

Millstone, E. (1997) *Lead and Health*, Earthscan, London.

Millstone, E. (2007) 'Can food safety policy-making be both scientifically and democratically legitimated? If so, how?', *Journal of Agricultural and Environmental Ethics*, vol 20, pp483–508.

Millstone, E., van Zwanenberg, P., Levidow, L., Spök, A., Hirakawa, H. and Matsuo, M. (2008) *Risk-assessment Policies: Differences Across Jurisdictions*, Institute for Prospective Technological Studies, Seville, Spain, EUR Number: 23259 EN, http://ipts.jrc.ec.europa.eu/publications/pub.cfm?id=1562, accessed 11 June 2014.

Minsky, H. (1992) 'The financial instability hypothesis', Working Paper no 74, The Jermome Levy Institute of Economics at Bards College, Annandale-on-Hudson, NY.

Mintzberg, H. and Waters, J. A. (2009) 'Of strategies, deliberate and emergent', *Strategic Management Journal*, vol 6, no 3, pp257–272.

Miranda, I., Lopez, M. and Couto Soares, M. C. (2011) 'Social technology network: Paths for sustainability', *Innovation and Development*, vol 1, no 1, pp151–152.

Mitchell, C. and Connor, P. (2004) 'Renewable energy policy in the UK 1990–2003', *Energy Policy*, vol 32, no 17, pp1935–1947.

Mitchell, C., Bauknecht, D. and Connor, P. (2006) 'Effectiveness through risk reduction: A comparison of the renewable obligation in England and Wales and the feed-in system in Germany', *Energy Policy*, vol 34, no 3, pp297–305.

Mitchell, T. (2011) *Carbon Democracy: Political Power in the Age of Oil*, Verso, London.

Mittelman, J. H. (1998) 'Globalisation and environmental resistance politics', *Third World Quarterly*, vol 19, no 5, pp847–872.

MIX (Microfinance Information Exchange) (2009) 'MicroBanking Bulletin', *Issue 19*, December, Microfinance Information Exchange.

Moore, J. (2009) 'Ecology and the accumulation of capital: A brief environmental history of neo-liberalism', paper for the workshop Food, Energy, Environment: Crisis of the Modern World-System, Binghamton University, 9–10 October.

Morales, A. (2014) 'Vestas regains wind turbine market share lead in navigant study', *Bloomberg News*, 26 March, www.bloomberg.com/news/2014–03–26/vestas-regains-wind-turbine-market-share-lead-in-navigant-study.html, accessed 24 June 2014.

Morgan, G., Campbell, J., Crouch, C., Pedersen, O. K. and Whitley, R. (2010) *Oxford Handbook of Comparative Institutional Analysis*, Oxford University Press, Oxford.

Morgan, M. G. and Ricke, K. (2009) *Cooling the Earth through Solar Radiation Management: The Need for Research and an Approach to its Governance*, International Risk Governance Council (IRGC), Geneva.

Mouffe, C. (1999) 'Deliberative democracy or agonistic pluralism', *Social Research*, vol 66, no 3, pp745–758.

Nabuurs, G. J., Masera, O., Andrasko, K., Benitez-Ponce, P., Boer, R., Dutschke, M., Elsiddig, E., Ford-Robertson, J., Frumhoff, P., Karjalainen, T., Krankina, O., Kurz, W. A., Matsumoto, M., Oyhantcabal, W., Ravindranath, N. H., Sanz Sanchez, M. J.

and Zhang, X. (2007) 'Forestry', in B. Metz, O. R. Davidson, P. R. Bosch, R. Dave and L. A. Meyer (eds) *Climate Change 2007: Mitigation. Contribution of Working Group III to the Fourth Assessment Report of the Intergovernmental Panel on Climate Change*, Cambridge University Press, Cambridge.

NEF (New Economics Foundation) (2010) *The Great Transition: A Tale of How it Turned Out Right*, New Economics Foundation, London.

Nelkin, D. (1984) *Controversy: The Politics of Technical Decisions*, Sage, Beverly Hills, CA.

Neumeyer, E. (2010) *Weak versus Strong Sustainability*, Edward Elgar, London.

Newell, P. (2005) 'Race, class and the global politics of environmental inequality', *Global Environmental Politics*, vol 5, no 3, pp70–94.

Newell, P. (2008) 'Civil society, corporate accountability and the politics of climate change', *Global Environmental Politics*, vol 8, no 3, pp124–155.

Newell, P. (2010) 'Democratising biotechnology? Deliberation, participation and social regulation in a neo-liberal world', *Review of International Studies*, vol 36, pp471–491.

Newell, P. (2012) *Globalization and the Environment: Capitalism, Ecology and Power*, Polity, Cambridge.

Newell, P. and Paterson, M. (1998) 'Climate for business: Global warming, the State and capital', *Review of International Political Economy*, vol 5, no 4, pp679–704.

Newell, P. and Paterson, M. (2010) *Climate Capitalism: Global Warming and the Transformation of the Global Economy*, Cambridge University Press, Cambridge.

Newell, P. and Paterson, M. (2011) 'Climate capitalism', in E. Altvater and A. Brunnengräber (eds) *After Cancun: Climate Governance or Climate Conflicts*, VS Verlag, Berlin, pp23–45.

Newell, P. and Bumpus, A. (2012) 'The global political ecology of the CDM', *Global Environmental Politics*, vol 12, no 4, pp49–68.

Newell, P. and Mulvaney, D. (2013) 'The political economy of the just transition', *The Geographical Journal*, vol 197, no 2, pp132–140.

Newell, P., Boykoff, M. and Boyd, E. (eds) (2012) *The 'New' Carbon Economy: Constitution, Governance and Contestation*, Wiley Blackwell, Oxford.

Newton, P. (1998) 'A manual for planetary management', *Nature*, vol 400, no 674, p399.

Nill, J., Kemp, R. (2009) 'Evolutionary approaches for sustainable innovation policies. From niche to paradigm?', *Research Policy*, vol 38, no 4, pp668–680.

Noddings, N. (2002) *Starting at Home: Caring and Social Policy*, University California Press, Berkeley, CA.

Nordhaus, T., Schellenberger, M. and Blomqvist, L. (2012) *The Planetary Boundaries Hypothesis: A Review of the Evidence*, Breakthrough Institute, http://thebreakthrough.org/blog/Planetary%20Boundaries%20web.pdf, accessed 2 June 2014.

NRDC (National Resources Defence Council) (2013) *The Story of Silent Spring*, www.nrdc.org/health/pesticides/hcarson.asp, accessed 11 June 2014.

NSB (National Science Board) (2012) 'Science and engineering indicators 2012', *National Science Foundation*, www.nsf.gov/statistics/seind12/start.htm, accessed 24 June 2014.

Nuttall, W. J. (2005) *Nuclear Renaisance: Technologies and Policies for the Future of Nuclear Power*, Institute of Physics, Bristol.

Obach, B. (2004) *Labor and the Environmental Movement: The Quest for Common Ground*, MIT Press, Cambridge, MA.

O'Connor, M. (ed.) (1994) *Is Capitalism Sustainable? Political Economy and the Politics of Ecology*, Guilford Press, New York.

O'Connor, M. (1998) *Natural Causes: Essays in Ecological Marxism*, Guildford Press, London.

OECD (Organisation for Economic Co-operation and Development) (2010) *Cities and Climate Change*, Organisation for Economic Co-operation and Development, Paris.

OECD (2011) *Towards Green Growth*, Organisation for Economic Co-operation and Development, Paris.

OECD (2012) *Innovation and Inclusive Development: Conference Discussion Report*, Cape Town, South Africa, 21 November, Organisation for Economic Cooperation and Development, Paris.

OECD (2013) *Effective Carbon Prices*, Organisation for Economic Co-operation and Development, Paris.

OGFJ (Oil and Gas Financial Journal) (2011) 'Germany's KfW bank invests US$130 billion in renewable energy', *Oil & Gas Financial Journal,* 14 October, www.ogfj.com/articles/2011/10/germany-s-kfw-bank.html, accessed 24 June 2014.

Oreskes, N. (2004) 'The scientific consensus on climate change', *Science*, vol 306, no 5702, p1686.

Oreskes, N. (2005) 'Anti-realism in government', *Science*, vol 310, no 5745, p56.

Oreskes, N. and Conway, E. M. (2010) *Merchants of Doubt: How a Handful of Scientists Obscured the Truth on Issues from Tobacco Smoke to Global Warming*, Bloomsbury Press, New York.

Osterhammel, J. (2014) *The Transformation of the World: A Global History of the Nineteenth Century*, Princeton University Press, Princeton, NJ.

Paarlberg, R. (2009) *Starved for Science: How Biotechnology is Being Kept out of Africa*, Harvard University Press, Cambridge, MA.

Pagano, M. and Volpin, P. (2001) 'The political economy of finance', *Oxford Review of Economic Policy*, vol 17, no 4, pp502–519.

Pagliari, S. (2012) *Making Good Financial Regulation: Towards a Policy Response to Regulatory Capture*, International Centre for Financial Regulation, London.

Pagliari, S. and Young, K. (2012) 'Who mobilizes? An analysis of stakeholder responses to financial regulatory policy consultations', in S. Pagliari (ed.) *Making Good Financial Regulation: Towards a Policy Response to Regulatory Capture*, International Centre for Financial Regulation, London, pp85–98.

Panitch, L. and Gindin, S. (2012) *The Making of Global Capitalism*, Verso, London.

Paredis, E. (2013) *A Winding Road: Transition Management, Policy Change and the Search for Sustainable Development*', doctoral dissertation, Universiteit Gent.

Parhelion and Standard & Poor's (2010) *Can Capital Markets Bridge the Climate Change Financing Gap?*, www.parhelion.co.uk/pdf/Parhelion_Climate_Financing_Risk_Mapping_Report_2010.pdf, accessed 24 June 2014.

Parry, R., Hood, C. and James, O. (1997) 'Reinventing the treasury: Economic rationalism or an econocrat's fallacy of control?', *Public Administration*, vol 75, no 3, pp395–415.

Patashnik, E. M. and Zelizer, J. E. (2009) 'When policy does not remake politics: The limits of policy feedback', paper presented at the Annual Meeting of the American Political Science Association, Toronto, Canada.

Paterson, M. (2001) 'Risky business: Insurance companies in global warming politics', *Global Environmental Politics*, vol 1, no 3, pp18–42.

Paterson, M. (2007) *Automobile Politics: Ecology and Cultural Political Economy*, Cambridge University Press, Cambridge.

Patton, D. (2012) 'Further huge boost to solar target "not on China's agenda"', *Recharge News*, 12 September, www.rechargenews.com/news/policy_market/article1298370.ece, accessed 24 June 2014.

Pearce, D. W. and Warford, J. J. (1993) *World without End: Economics, Environment, and Sustainable Development*, World Bank Publications, Washington, DC.

Pearson, P. and Foxon, T. (2012) 'A low carbon industrial revolution? Insights and challenges from past technological and economic transformations', *Energy Policy*, vol 50, pp117–127.

Peck, J. (2013) 'Disembedding Polanyi: Exploring Polanyian economic geographies', *Environment and Planning A*, vol 45, pp1536 – 1544.

Peiffer, C. (2012) *Reform Coalitions: Patterns and Hypotheses from a Survey of the Literature* (Concept Paper 03), retrieved from Developmental Leadership Program, www.dlprog. org, accessed 25 June 2014.

Pellizzoni, L. (2004) 'Responsibility and environmental governance', *Environmental Politics*, vol 13, no 3, pp541–565.

Peltzman, S. (1976) 'Towards a more general theory of regulation', *Journal of Law and Economics*, vol 19, no 2, pp211–248.

Perez, C. (2002) *Technological Revolutions and Financial Capital: The Dynamics of Bubbles and Golden Ages*, Edward Elgar, Cheltenham.

Perez, C. (2013) 'Unleashing a golden age after the financial collapse: Drawing lessons from history', *Environmental Innovation and Societal Transitions*, vol 6, pp9– 23.

Perlin, J. (1999) *From Space to Earth: The Story of Solar Electricity*, Aatec Publications, Ann Arbor, MI.

Peterson, G. (2013) 'Human development in a "good" Anthropocene', Symposium on 'Our future in the Anthropocene', *The Royal Swedish Academy of Sciences*, 27 November.

Pfeffer, J. (1992) 'Understanding power in organizations', in J. Pfeffer, *Managing with Power: Politics and Influence in Organizations*, Harvard Business School Press, Boston, MA, pp337–347.

Pielke, R. (2013) 'Planetary boundaries as power grab', 4 April, http://rogerpielkejr. blogspot.co.uk/2013/04/planetary-boundries-as-power-grab.html?m=1, accessed 3 June 2014.

Pierson, P. (1993) 'When effect becomes cause: Policy feedback and political change', *World Politics*, vol 45, no 4, pp595–628.

Pierson, P. (2000) 'Increasing returns, path dependence and the study of politics', *American Political Science Review*, vol 94, no 2, pp251–267.

Piketty, T. (2014) *Capital in the Twenty-First Century*, Harvard University Press, Cambridge, MA.

Polanyi, K. (1980 [1944]) *The Great Transformation: The Political and Economic Origins of our Time*, Beacon Press, Boston, MA.

Pollitt, M. (2010) *UK renewable Energy Policy since Privatisation*, Working Paper 1002, Electricity Policy Research Group, University of Cambridge, Cambridge.

Pollock, C. (ed.) (2013) *Feeding the Future: Innovation Requirements for Primary Food Production in the UK to 2030*, http://feedingthefutureblog.files.wordpress.com/2012/11/feedingthe future2013-web.pdf, accessed 11 June 2014.

Ponting, C. (2007) *A New History of the World: The Environment and the Collapse of Great Civilisations*, Vintage, London.

Popkin, S. L. (1970) 'Pacification: Politics and the village', *Asian Survey*, vol 10, no 8, pp662–671.

Porritt, J. (2011) '"The greenest government ever": One year on', *Friends of the Earth*, foe.co.uk/resource/reports/greenest_gvt_ever.pdf, accessed 24 June 2014.

Power, M. (2000) 'The Audit Society: Second thoughts', *International Journal of Accounting*, vol 119, pp111–119.

Prasad, M. and Munch, S. (2012) 'State-level renewable electricity policies and reductions in carbon emissions', *Energy Policy*, vol 45, pp237–242.

Proctor, P. N. (1995) *Cancer Wars: How Politics Shapes What We Know and Don't Know about Cancer*, Basic Books, New York.

Prudham, S. (2013) 'Men and things: Karl Polanyi, primitive accumulation, and their relevance to a radical green political economy', *Environment and Planning A*, vol 45, pp1569–1587.

PwC (Pricewaterhouse Coopers) (2010) *100% Renewable Electricity: A Roadmap to 2050 for Europe and North Africa*, PricewaterhouseCoopers, London.

Qian, Y. (2003) 'How reform worked in China', in D. Rodrik (ed.) *In Search of Prosperity: Analytic Narratives on Economic Growth*, Princeton University Press, Princeton, NJ and Oxford, pp297–333.

Rajan, R. G. and Zingales, L. (2003) 'The great reversals: The politics of financial development in the twentieth century', *Journal of Financial Economics*, vol 69, pp5–50.

Randalls, S. (2010) 'History of the 2°C climate target', *Wiley Interdisciplinary Reviews: Climate Change*, vol 1, no 4, pp.598–605.

Raven, R., Kern, F., Verhees, B. and Smith, A. (2014) 'Niche construction and empowerment through socio-political work of sustainable technology advocates. A meta-analysis of six cases', mimeo, School of Innovation Sciences, Eindhoven University and SPRU, University of Sussex.

Raworth, K. (2012) 'A safe and just space for humanity: Can we live within the doughnut?', *Oxfam Discussion Paper*, Oxfam, Oxford.

Redclift, M. (2005) 'Sustainable development (1987–2005): An oxymoron comes of age', *Sustainable Development*, vol 13, no 4, pp212–227.

Reuters (2012) 'Germany's KfW to lend 100 bln euros for switch to renewables', *Reuters*, 8 August, http://in.reuters.com/article/2012/08/08/germany-energy-kfw-idINL6E8 J8DJI20120808, accessed 24 June 2014.

Ridgwell, A., Freeman, C. and Lampitt, R. (2012) 'Geoengineering: Taking control of our planet's climate', in *Science Sees Further*, The Royal Society, London, pp22–23.

Rist, G. (2011) *The History of Development: From Western Origins to Global Faith*, 3rd edn, Zed Books, London.

Robbins, P. and Watts, M. (2011) *Global Political Ecology*, Routledge, London.

Robinson, W. (2004) *A Theory of Global Capitalism*, Johns Hopkins University, Baltimore, MD and London.

Rockström, J. (2010) 'Let the environment guide our development', TED, www.ted.com/talks/johan_rockstrom_let_the_environment_guide_our_development.html, accessed 19 February 2014.

Rockström, J. (2012) 'Planetary boundaries: Addressing some key misconceptions', www.stockholmresilience.org/21/research/research-news/7-2-2012-addressing-some-key-misconceptions.html, accessed 20 January 2014.

Rockström, J. (2013) 'Planetary boundaries and resilience', symposium on 'Our future in the Anthropocene', *The Royal Swedish Academy of Sciences*, 27 November.

Rockström, J., Steffen, W., Noone, K., Persson, Å., Chapin, III, F. S., Lambin, E. F., Lenton, T. M., Scheffer, M., Folke, C., Schellnhuber, H. J., Nykvist, B., de Wit, C. A., Hughes, T., van der Leeuw, S., Rodhe, H., Sörlin, S., Snyder, P. K., Costanza, R., Svedin, U., Falkenmark, M., Karlberg, L., Corell, R. W., Fabry, V. J., Hansen, J., Walker, B., Liverman, D., Richardson, K., Crutzen, P. and Foley, J. A. (2009) 'A safe operating space for humanity', *Nature*, vol 461, pp472–475.

Roe, M. J. (2003) *Political Determinants of Corporate Governance*, Oxford University Press, Oxford.

Rosset, P. (2003) 'Food sovereignty: Global rallying cry of farmer movements', *Food First Backgrounder*, vol 9, no 4, pp1–4.

Rotmans, J., Kemp, R., Asselt, M. V. (2001) 'More evolution than revolution: Transition policy in public management', *Foresight*, vol 3, no 1, pp1–17.

Rowell, A. (1996) *Green Backlash: Global Subversion of the Environmental Movement*, Routledge, London.

Ruddiman, W. F. (2005) *Plows, Plagues and Petroleum: How Humans Took Control of Climate*, Princeton University Press, Princeton, NJ.

Ruegg, R. and Thomas, P. (2011) 'Linkages from DOE's solar photovoltaic R&D to commercial renewable power from solar energy', United States Department of Energy, Office of Energy Efficiency and Renewable Energy, April, www1.eere.energy.gov/analysis/pdfs/solar_rd_linkages_report7.18.11.pdf, accessed 24 June 2014.

Rupert, M. (1995) *Producing Hegemony: The Politics of Mass Production and American Global Power*, Cambridge University Press, Cambridge.

Rutkowski, R. (2013) 'The price of power: The new Chinese leadership begins rebalancing with resource prices', *China Economic Watch*, Peterson Institute for International Economics, http://blogs.piie.com/china/?p=2913, accessed 12 February 2014.

Sachs, W. (ed.) (1993) *Global Ecology: A New Arena of Political Conflict*, Zed Books, London.

Sachs, W. (2007) 'Global challenges: Climate chaos and the future of development', *IDS Bulletin*, vol 38, no 2, pp36–39.

Sawin, J. (2004) *National Policy Instruments: Policy Lessons for the Advancement and Diffusion of Renewable Energy Technologies around the World*, Thematic Background paper, International Conference for Renewable Energies, Bonn http://wofuco.inet.de/fileadmin/user_upload/Miguel/Sawin__2004__National_policy_instruments.pdf, accessed 1 July 2014.

Scarse, I. and Smith, A. (2009) 'The non-politics of managing low carbon socio-technical transitions', *Environmental Politics*, vol 18, no 5, pp707–726.

Schmidt, V. (2002) *The Futures of European Capitalism*, Oxford University Press, Oxford.

Schmitz, H. (forthcoming, 2014) 'How does China's rise affect the green transformation?', *Journal of Technology and Globalisation*.

Schmitz, H., Johnson, O. and Alternburg, T. (2013) *Rent Management: The Heart of Green Industrial Policy*, Working Paper 418, Institute of Development Studies, Brighton.

Schneider, B. (2009) 'Hierarchical market economies and varieties of capitalism in Latin America', *Journal of Latin American Studies*, vol 41, no 3, pp553–575.

Schot, J. and Geels, F. W. (2008) 'Strategic niche management and sustainable innovation journeys: Theory, findings, research agenda, and policy', *Technology Analysis & Strategic Management*, vol 20, no 5, pp537–554.

Schumpeter, J. (1975) [1942] *Capitalism, Socialism and Democracy*, Harper, New York.

Schurman, R. (2004) 'Fighting "Frankenfoods": Industry opportunity structures and the efficacy of the anti-biotech movement in Western Europe', *Social Problems*, vol 51, no 2, pp243–268.

Scoones, I. (2007) 'Sustainability', *Development in Practice*, vol 17, pp589–596.

Scoones, I. (2008) 'Mobilizing against GM crops in India, South Africa and Brazil', *Journal of Agrarian Change*, vol 8, no 2–3, pp315–344.

Scoones, I. (2009) 'The politics of global assessments: The case of the International Assessment of Agricultural Knowledge, Science and Technology for Development (IAASTD)', *The Journal of Peasant Studies*, vol 36, no 3, pp547–571.

Scott, J. C. (1998) *Seeing Like a State: How Certain Schemes to Improve the Human Condition Have Failed*, Yale University Press, New Haven, CT.

Scott, J. C. (2008) *Weapons of the Weak: Everyday Forms of Peasant Resistance*, Yale University Press, New Haven, CT.

Scott-Cato, M. and Hillier, J. (2010) 'How could we study climate-related social innovation? Applying Deleuzean philosophy to transition towns', *Environmental Politics*, vol 19, no 6, pp869–887.

SDSN (Sustainable Development Network Solutions) (2014) *Sustainable Development Solutions Network*, http://unsdsn.org/, accessed 20 January 2014.

Selwyn, B. and Miyamura, S. (2013) 'Class struggle or embedded markets? Marx, Polanyi and the meanings and possibilities of social transformation', *New Political Economy*, www.tandfonline.com/doi/abs/10.1080/13563467.2013.844117#preview, accessed 16 June 2014.

Sen, A. (2005) *The Argumentative Indian: Writings on Indian history, Culture and Identity*, Farrar, Straus and Giroux, New York.

Sessions, G. (ed.) (1995) *Deep Ecology for the 21st Century*, Readings on the Philosophy and Practice of the New Environmentalism, Shambhala, Boston, MA and London.

Seyfang, G. and Smith, A. (2007) 'Grassroots innovations for sustainable development: Towards a new research and policy agenda', *Environmental Politics*, vol 16, no 4, pp584–603.

Seyfang, G. and Haxeltine, A. (2012) 'Growing grassroots innovations: Exploring the role of community-based initiatives in governing sustainable energy transitions', *Environment and Planning C-Government and Policy*, vol 30, no 3, pp381–400.

Shapiro, R. (1996) *Monsanto Environmental Review 1996*, cited by K. Bruno www.corp watch.org/article.php?id=4088, accessed 11 June 2014, and in *The Ecologist*, vol 28, no 5, September/October 1998.

Sharma, A., Srivastava, J., Kar, S. K. and Kumar, A. (2012) 'Wind energy status in India: A short review', *Renewable and Sustainable Energy Reviews*, vol 16, pp1157–1164.

Shaw, C. (2010) 'Is the dangerous limits discourse dangerously limited?', blog contribution at Earthscan: *Blogging for a Sustainable Future.*

Shepherd, J., Caldeira, K., Cox, P., Haigh, J., Keith, D., Launder, B., Mace, G., MacKerron, G., Pyle, J., Rayner, S., Redgwell, C. and Watson, A. (ed.) (2009) *Geoengineering the Climate: Science, Governance and Uncertainty*, The Royal Society, London.

Shrimali, G. (2014) 'Wind energy auctions in India' Bharti Institute of Public Policy, http://blogs.isb.edu/bhartiinstitute/2014/01/13/wind-energy-auctions-in-india/, accessed 12 February 2014.

Shrimali, G. and Tirumalachetty, S. (2013) 'Renewable energy certificate markets in India – a review', *Renewable and Sustainable Energy Reviews*, vol 26, pp702–716.

Sikor, T. (ed.) (2013) *The Justices and Injustices of Ecosystem Services*, Routledge, London.

Sikor, T. and Newell, P. (2014) 'Globalizing environmental justice?', *Geoforum*, vol 54, pp151–157.

Simmons, B., Dobbin, F. and Garrett, G. (2008) 'Introduction: The diffusion of liberalization', in B. Simmons, F. Dobbin, and G. Garrett (eds) *The Global Diffusion of Markets and Democracy*, Cambridge University Press, Cambridge.

Skocpol, T. (1979) *States and Social Revolutions: A Comparative Analysis of France, Russia and China*, Cambridge University Press, Cambridge.

Slote, M. (2007) *The Ethics of Care and Empathy*, Routledge, Oxford.

Slusarska, D. (2013) *Energiewende made in China*, Background Briefing, Friends of Europe, Brussels.

Smith, A. (2005) 'The alternative technology movement: An analysis of its framing and negotiation of technology development', *Human Ecology Review Special Issue on Nature, Science and Social Movements*, vol 12, no 2, pp106–119.

Smith, A. and Raven, R. (2012) 'What is protective space? Reconsidering niches in transitions to sustainability', *Research Policy*, vol 41, no 6, pp1025–1036.

Smith, A., and Seyfang, G. (2013) 'Constructing grassroots innovations for sustainability', *Global Environmental Change*, vol 23, no 5, pp827–829.

Smith, A., Stirling, A. and Berkhout, F. (2005) 'The governance of sustainable socio-technical transitions', *Research Policy*, vol 34, no 10, pp1491–1510.

Smith, A., Voß, J. P. and Grin, J. (2010) 'Innovation studies and sustainability transitions: The allure of the multi-level perspective and its challenges', *Research Policy*, vol 39, no 4, pp435–448.

Smith, A., Fressoli, M. and Thomas, H. (2013) 'Grassroots innovation movements: Challenges and contributions', *Journal of Cleaner Production*, vol 63, pp1–11.

Smith, J. and Jehlička, P. (2013) 'Quiet sustainability: Fertile lessons from Europe's productive gardeners', *Journal of Rural Studies*, vol 32, pp148–157.

Smith Stegen, K. and Seel, M. (2013) 'The winds of change: How wind firms assess Germany's energy transition', *Energy Policy*, vol 61, pp1481–1489.

Sperling, D. and Gordon, D. (2009) *Two Billion Cars: Driving Toward Sustainability*, Oxford University Press, Oxford, New York.

Spratt, S. (2012) 'Environmental taxation and development: A scoping Study', *International Centre for Tax and Development Working Paper*, no 2, ICTD, Brighton.

Spratt, S. and Griffith-Jones, S., with contributions from Ocampo, J. A. (2013) *Mobilising Private Investment for Inclusive Green Growth*, BMZ, German Federal Ministry for Economic Cooperation and Development.

Stahel, W. R. (2010) *The Performance Economy*, Palgrave Macmillan, London.

Star, S. L. and Griesemer, J. R. (1989) 'Institutional ecology, 'translations' and boundary objects: Amateurs and professionals in Berkeley's Museum of Vertebrate Zoology, 1907–39', *Social Studies of Science*, vol 19, no 3, pp387–420.

Steffen, A. (2009) 'Bright green, light green, dark green, gray: The new environmental spectrum'. *Worldchanging*, 27 February, www.worldchanging.com/archives/009499.html, accessed 21 April 2014

Steffen, W., Crutzen, P. J. and McNeill, J. R. (2007) 'The Anthropocene: Are humans now overwhelming the great forces of nature?', *Ambio*, vol 36, no 8, 614–621.

Steffen, W., Sanderson, A., Tyson, P. D., Jäger, J., Matson, P. A., Moore III, B., Oldfield, F., Richardson, K., Schellnhuber, H. J., Turner II, B. L., and Wasson, R. J. (2004) *Global Change and the Earth System: A Planet Under Pressure*, Springer, Berlin.

Steffen, W., Persson, Å., Deutsch, L., Zalasiewicz, J., Williams, M., Richardson, K., Crumley, C., Crutzen, P., Folke, C., Gordon, L., Molina, M., Ramanathan, V., Rockström, J., Scheffer, M., Schellnhuber, H. J. and Svedin, U. (2011) 'The Anthropocene: From global change to planetary stewardship', *Ambio*, vol 40, no 7, pp739–761.

STEPS (Social, Technological and Environmenal Pathways to Sustainability) (2010) *Innovation, Sustainability, Development: A New Manifesto*, STEPS Centre, Brighton, *http://steps-centre.org/anewmanifesto/*, accessed 12 July 2014.

Stern, N. (2006) *The Stern Review: The Economics of Climate Change*, HM Treasury, London.

Stern, N. (2007) *The Economics of Climate Change: The Stern Review*, Cambridge University Press, Cambridge and New York.

Stern, N. (2014) 'Climate change is here now and it could lead to global conflict', *The Guardian*, 14 February, www.theguardian.com/environment/2014/feb/13/storms-floods-climate-change-upon-us-lord-stern, accessed 16 June 2014.

Stern, N. and Rydge, J. (2012) 'The new energy-industrial revolution and an international agreement on climate change', *Economics of Energy and Environmental Policy*, vol 1, pp1–19.

Steves, F. and Teytelboym, A. (2013) *Political Economy of Climate Change*, Working Paper 13–02, Smith School of Enterprise and the Environment, University of Oxford.

Stigler, G. (1971) 'The theory of economic regulation', *The Bell Journal of Economics and Management Science*, vol 2, no 1, pp3–21.

Stilgoe, J., Irwin, A. and Jones, K. (2006) *The Received Wisdom: Opening Up Expert Advice*, Demos, London.

Stirling, A. (1998) 'Risk at a turning point?', *Journal of Risk Research*, vol 1, no 2, pp97–109.

Stirling, A. (2011) 'Pluralising progress: From integrative transitions to transformative diversity', *Environmental Innovation and Societal Transitions*, vol 1, no 1, pp82–88.

Stirling, A. (2014a) *Emancipating Transformations: From Controlling 'the Transition' to Culturing Plural Radical Progress*, STEPS Working Paper 64, STEPS Centre, Brighton.

Stirling, A. (2014b) 'From sustainability to transformation: Dynamics and diversity in reflexive governance of vulnerability', in A. Hommels, J. Mesman and W. E. Bijker (eds) *Vulnerability in Technological Cultures: New Directions in Research and Governance*, MIT Press, Cambridge, pp1–61.

Stirling, A. (2014c) 'Transforming power: Social science and the politics of energy choices', *Energy Research and Social Science*, vol 1, pp83–95.

Storper, M. and Walker, R. (1989) *The Capitalist Imperative: Territory, Technology and Industrial Growth*, Blackwell, Cambridge, MA.

Strahan, D. (2009) 'Interview with Lord Oxburgh', www.davidstrahan.com/blog/?p=40, accessed 16 June 2014.

Streeck, W. and Thelen, K. (2005) 'Institutional change in advanced political economies', in W. Streeck and K. Thelen (eds) *Beyond Continuity: Institutional Change in Advanced Political Economies*, Oxford University Press, Oxford, pp1–39.

Sullivan, S. (2013) 'Banking nature? The spectacular financialisation of environmental conservation', *Antipode*, vol 45, no 1, pp198–217.

Swilling, M. and Annecke, E. (2012) *Just Transitions: Explorations of Sustainability in an Unfair World*, UCT Press, Cape Town, South Africa.

Swyngedouw, E. (2010) 'Apocalypse forever? Post-political populism and the spectre of climate change', *Theory, Culture and Society*, vol 27, no 2–3, pp213–232.

Szarka, J. (2006) 'Wind power, policy learning and paradigm change', *Energy Policy*, vol 34, no 17, pp3041–3048.

Szerszynski, B. (1997) 'Voluntary associations and the sustainable society', *The Political Quarterly*, vol 68, B, pp148–159.

Tarrow, S. (1998) *Power in Movement: Social Movements and Contentious Politics*, 4th edn, Cambridge Studies in Comparative Studies, Cambridge.

Tarrow, S. (2005) *The New Transnational Activism*, Cambridge University Press, Cambridge.

Taylor, H. and Nölke, A. (2008) 'Regulatory governance and the rise of non-triad multinational companies: A modified "varieties of capitalism" perspective on Indian multinationals', paper prepared for the ECPR Standing Group on Regulatory Governance Conference '(Re)Regulation in the Wake of Neoliberalism: Consequences of Three Decades of Privatization and Market Liberalization,' Utrecht, 5–7 June, http://regulation.upf.edu/utrecht-08-papers/htaylor.pdf, accessed 14 February 2014.

TEEB (The Economics of Ecosystems and Biodiversity) (2014) 'Making nature's values visible', www.teebweb.org/wp-content/uploads/2012/10/TEEB-brochure.pdf, accessed 4 July 2014.

Tellam, I. (ed.) (2000) *Fuel for Change: World Bank Energy Policy – Rhetoric and Reality*, Zed Books, London.

Thatcher, M. (1999) 'Statement No 401 to the BSE Inquiry', in N. Phillips, J. Bridgeman and M. Ferguson-Smith (2000) *The BSE Inquiry Report: Evidence and supporting papers of the Inquiry into the emergence and identification of Bovine Spongiform Encephalopathy (BSE) and variant Creutzfeldt-Jakob Disease (vCJD) and the action taken in response to it up to 20 March 1996*, The Stationery Office, London.

Thornton, P. H., Ocasio, W. and Thornton, P. H. (1999) 'Institutional logics and the historical contingency of power in organizations: Executive succession in the higher education publishing industry, 1958–1990', *American Journal of Sociology*, vol 105, no 3, pp801–843.

Thorpe, A. (2012) *Architecture and Design versus Consumerism: How Design Activism Confronts Growth*, Earthscan, Abingdon, Oxford.

Tilly, C. (1978) *From Mobilization to Revolution*, Addison-Wesley, Reading, MA.

Toke, D. (2013) 'Climate change and the nuclear securitisation of UK energy policy', *Environmental Politics*, vol 22, no 4, pp553–570.

Toke, D. and Lauber, V. (2007) 'Anglo-Saxon and German approaches to neoliberalism and environmental policy: The case of financing renewable energy', *Geoforum*, vol 38, no 4, pp677–687.

Tol, R. S. J. (2007) 'Europe's long_term climate target: A critical evaluation', *Energy Policy*, vol 35, pp424–432.

Trainer, T. (1996) *Towards a Sustainable Economy: The Need for Fundamental Change*, Jon Carpenter, Oxford.

UN (United Nations) (2012) *The Future We Want*, UN, Geneva, www.uncsd2012.org/content/documents/727The%20Future%20We%20Want%2019%20June%201230pm.pdf, accessed 2 July 2012.

UN (2013) *Statement on Planetary Boundaries*, United Nations, Bonn.

United Nations Environment Programme (UNEP) (1992) Agenda 21, www.unep.org/Documents.Multilingual/Default.asp?documentid=52, accessed 14 February 2014.

UNEP (2011) *Towards a Green Economy: Pathways to Sustainable Development and Poverty Eradication*, United Nations Environment Programme, Nairobi, www.unep.org/green economy, accessed 12 July 2014.

United Nations Framework Convention on Climate Change (UNFCC) (1992) *United Nations Framework Convention on Climate Change*, https://unfccc.int/files/essential_background/background_publications_htmlpdf/application/pdf/conveng.pdf, accessed 4 May 2014.

Unmüßig, B., Sachs, W. and Fatheuer, T. (2012) 'Critique of the green ecology: Toward social and environmental equity', *Ecology Series*, No. 22. Heinrich Böll Stiftung, Berlin.

Unruh, G. C. (2000) 'Understanding carbon lock-in', *Energy Policy*, vol 28, no 12, pp817–830.

US Congress (1966) *Public Law*, 89–487.

US Congress (1976) *Government in the Sunshine Act*, Public Law, 94–409.

United States Environmental Protection Agency (US EPA) (undated) 'Step 2 – dose-response assessment', www.epa.gov/risk_assessment/dose-response.htm, accessed 11 June 2014.

US FDA (United States Food and Drug Administration) (2013) *Code of Federal Regulations*, revised 1 April 2013, title 21, vol 3, 21CFR180.37, www.accessdata.fda.gov/scripts/cdrh/cfdocs/cfcfr/cfrsearch.cfm?fr=180.37, accessed 11 June 2014.

US NAS (United States National Academy of Sciences) (1978) *Saccharin: A Technical Assessment of Risks and Benefits: Part 1*, National Academy of Sciences, Committee for a Study of Saccharin and Food Safety Policy, Washington, DC.

US NAS and RSL (Royal Society of London) (2014) *Climate Change: Evidence and Causes*, 27 February, US National Academy of Sciences and Royal Society of London, http://royalsociety.org/policy/projects/climate-evidence-causes/, accessed 11 June 2014.

USA (2004) *European Communities – Measures Affecting the Approval and Marketing of Biotech Products (WT/DS291, 292, and 293)*, First Submission of the United States to the World Trade Organization's Dispute Panel, April 21, www.worldtradelaw.net/reports/wtopanelsfull/ec-biotech%28panel%29%28full%29.pdf, accessed 11 June 2014.

USDOT (United States Department of Transportation) (2009) *Cash for Clunkers Wraps up with Nearly 700,000 Car Sales and Increased Fuel Efficiency*, US Government report, DOT 133–09, www.nhtsa.gov/staticfiles/administration/pdf/CARS_stats_DOT13309.pdf, accessed 24 June 2014.

Utting, P. (forthcoming, 2015) *Social and Solidarity Economy: Beyond the Fringe?* Zed Books, London.

van der Pijl, K. (1998) *Transnational Classes and International Relations*, Routledge, London.

van der Sluijs, J., van Eijndhoven, J., Shackley, S. and Wynne, B. (1998) 'Anchoring devices in science for policy: The case of consensus around the climate sensitivity', *Social Studies of Science*, vol 28, no 2, pp291–323.

van Zwanenberg, P. and Millstone, E. (2000) 'Beyond sceptical relativism: Evaluating the social constructions of expert risk assessments', *Science, Technology & Human Values*, vol 25, no 3, pp259–282.

van Zwanenberg, P. and Millstone, E. (2005) *BSE: Risk, Science and Governance*, Oxford University Press, Oxford.

Verbong, G. and Loorbach, D. (eds) (2012) *Governing the Energy Transition*, Routledge, London.

Vincent, J. R. (2000) 'Green accounting: From theory to practice', *Environment and Development Economics*, vol 5, no 1, pp13–24.

Vitousek, P. M., Mooney, H. A., Lubchenco, J. and Melillo, J. M. (1997) 'Human domination of earth's ecosystems', *Science*, vol 277, no 5325, pp494–499.

Vogler. J. and Jordan, A. (2003) 'Governance and the environment', in F. Berkhout, M. Leach and I. Scoones (eds) *Negotiating Environmental Change: New Perspectives from Social Science* Edward Elgar, Cheltenham, pp137–158.

Wackernagel, M. and Rees, W. E. (2013) *Our Ecological Footprint: Reducing Human Impact on the Earth* (no 9), New Society Publishers, Gabrioloa Island, BC, Canada.

Wall, D. (2010) *The No-Nonsense Guide to Green Politics*, New Internationalist Publications, Oxford.

Wang, Z., Qin, H. and Lewis, J. I. (2012) 'China's wind power industry: Policy support, technological achievements and emerging challenges', *Energy Policy*, vol 51, pp80–88.

Wanner, T. (2014) 'The new "passive revolution" of the green economy and growth discourse: Maintaining the 'Sustainable Development' of Neoliberal Capitalism', *New Political Economy*, DOI: 0.1080/13563467.2013.866081, www.tandfonline.com/doi/abs/10.1080/13563467.2013.866081, accessed 12 July 2014.

Ward, B. and Dubos, R. (1972) *Only One Earth: The Care and Maintenance of a Small Planet*, W. Norton & Co., New York.

German Advisory Council on Global Change (WGBU) (2011) *World in Transition: A Social Contract for Sustainability*, German Advisory Council on Global Change, Berlin.

Weaver, R. K. (2010) 'Paths and forks or chutes and ladders: Negative feedbacks and policy regime change', *Journal of Public Policy*, vol 30, no 2, pp137–162.

White, R. and Stirling, A. (2013) 'Sustaining trajectories towards sustainability: Dynamics and diversity in UK communal growing activities', *Global Environmental Change*, vol 23, no 5, pp838–846.

World Health Organization (WHO) (1993) *Toxicological Evaluation of Certain Food Additives and Contaminants*, WHO Food Additives Series 32, World Health Organization, Geneva, pp105 – 133.

Wichterich, C. (2012) 'The future we want: A feminist perspective', *Ecology Series*, vol 21, Heinrich Böll Stiftung, Berlin.

Wilkinson, R. amd Pickett, K. (2010) *The Spirit Level: Why Equality is Better for Everyone*, Penguin Books, London.

Winters, J. A. (1994) 'Power and the control of capital', *World Politics*, vol 46, no 3, pp419–452.

Wodicka, V. O. (1984) 'Risk assessment and safety evaluation', in J. V. Rodericks and R. G. Tardiff (eds) *Assessment and Management of Chemical Risks*, American Chemical Society, Washington, DC.

Wood, E. M. (2002) *The Origin of Capitalism: A Longer View*, Verso, London.

World Bank (2003) *World Development Report: Dynamic Development in a Sustainable World: Transformation in the Quality of Life, Growth, and Institutions*, Oxford University Press, New York.

World Bank (2012) *Inclusive Green Growth: The Pathway to Sustainable Development*, World Bank, Washington, DC.

World Bank (2014) 'Landscape approaches in sustainable development' http://web. worldbank.org/WBSITE/EXTERNAL/TOPICS/EXTARD/0,,contentMDK:23219902~pagePK:148956~piPK:216618~theSitePK:336682,00.html, accessed 21 April 2014.

World Council of Credit Unions (2013) Statistical Report 2012, www.woccu.org/ publications/statreport, accessed 18 July 2014.

World Resources Institute (WRI) (2008) *Correcting the World's Greatest Market Failure: Climate Change and Multilateral Development Banks*, WRI, Washington, DC, www.wri.org/ publication/correcting-the-worlds-greatest-market-failure, accessed 16 June 2014.

Wynne, B. (1992) 'Uncertainty and environmental learning: Reconceiving science and policy in the preventive paradigm', *Global Environmental Change*, vol 2, pp111–27.

Yuan, X. and Zuo, J. (2011a) 'Pricing and affordability of renewable energy in China – A study of Shandong Province' *Renewable Energy*, vol 36, no 3, pp1111–1117.

Yuan, X. and Zuo, J. (2011b) 'Transition to low carbon energy policies in China – from the Five-Year Plan perspective', *Energy Policy*, vol 39, no 6, pp3855–3859.

Zenghelis, D. (2012) *A Strategy for Restoring Confidence and Economic Growth Through Green Investment and Innovation*, Policy Brief, Grantham Research Institute on Climate Change and the Environment, London School of Economics, London.

Zhang, S., Andrews-Speed, P. and Zhao, X. (2013) 'Political and institutional analysis of the successes and failures of China's wind power policy', *Energy Policy*, vol 56, pp331–340.

Zhang, S., Andrews-Speed, P. and Ji, M. (2014) 'The erratic path of the low-carbon transition in China: Evolution of solar PV policy', *Energy Policy*, vol 67, pp903–912.

Zimov, A. S. A. Chuprynin, V. I., Oreshko, A. P., Chapin III, F. S., Reynolds, J. F. and Chapin M. C. (2011) 'Steppe-tundra transition: A herbivore-driven biome shift at the end of the Pleistocene', *The American Naturalist*, vol 146, no 5, pp765–794.

INDEX